P9-DMF-181

When Aging Parents Can't Live Alone

When Aging Parents Can't Live Alone

A Practical Family Guide

ELLEN F. RUBENSON, M.S.W.

NEW HANOVER COUNTY
PUBLIC LIBRARY
201 CHESTNUT STREET
WILMINGTON, N. C. 28401

LOWELL HOUSE

LOS ANGELES

NTC/Contemporary Publishing Group

Library of Congress Cataloging-in-Publication Data
Rubenson, Ellen F.
    When aging parents can't live alone : a practical family guide / Ellen F. Rubenson.
        p. cm.
    Includes bibliographical references and index.
    ISBN: 0-7373-0370-4 (pbk.)
        1. Aging parents—Care—Decision making. 2. Aging parents—Housing—Decision
    making. 3. Adult children—Handbooks, manuals, etc. I. Title
    HQ1063.6.R83 2000
    306.874—dc21   00-023248

Published by Lowell House
A division of NTC/Contemporary Publishing Group, Inc.
4255 West Touhy Avenue, Lincolnwood, Illinois 60646-1975 U.S.A.

Text design by Kate Mueller.

Copyright © 2000 by Ellen F. Rubenson.

All rights reserved. No part of this work may be reproduced, stored in a retrieval system, or
transmitted in any form or by any means electronic, mechanical, photocopying, recording, or
otherwise, without the prior permission of NTC/Contemporary Publishing Group, Inc.
Printed in the United States of America

International Standard Book Number: 0-7373-0320-4

00 01 02 03 04 RRD 18 17 16 15 14 13 12 11 10 9 8 7 6 5 4 3 2 1

To my grandmother
Edna Skigen Hirschhaut

✻ Contents

❧ Acknowledgments

I would like to thank my family and friends, the staff at Providence Medford Medical Center, and the many social services agencies, health-care organizations, and individuals who provided help and support to me during the writing of this book. Special acknowledgments to:

My husband, Dan, for his patience and encouragement

My children, Maddy and Zac, for giving me the time to work without interruption

My parents, Sylvia and Robert Frank and Marge and Joe Rubenson, for never doubting for a moment that I would write this book

Barb Hansen for the long hikes and conversation

Rich Vanderwyst for his practical thoughts

Polly Beach for morning coffee, talk, and encouragement

Dennis Powers for his encouragement, enthusiasm, humor, and support

Bruce Robinson for his comments and editing

Dick and Linda Riegelman for their long-distance support

Kathie Rubenson, Rebecca Reid, and other friends for sharing their personal experiences

James Brown for his friendship and editing expertise

Marion Karpinski for showing me that anything is possible

Bill Gholson for his empathy and humor

Bud Sperry, my first editor, for seeing the potential

L. Hudson Perigo, my second editor, for helping me complete the book in a timely manner

❧ Introduction

After receiving many calls from baby-boomer friends with aging parents, I became aware of the need for a book that helps families decide if placement in an alternative living situation is the best choice for an elder family member. I reviewed numerous books on aging and caregiving and found housing information secondary to other topics, such as aging, medical, or nursing aspects of caregiving. In addition, knowing how to take this information and combine it with available social services, such as home health care, durable medical equipment, and other direct-services programs, was rarely addressed.

I was also aware of the increasing demand by families in the United States for elder-care alternatives. Perhaps due to work schedules, time, finances, or emotional or medical concerns, many families did not seem capable, prepared, or willing to assume the great task of providing a home and daily caregiving to elder family members. Or they opened their homes to their elder family member and were quickly overwhelmed by the changes in their lifestyles, family relationships, the time involved in providing care, and the additional financial burdens. Although a continuum of care existed, families did not seem to know how to evaluate their elder's needs and find the proper home and care for them.

In the past, social workers have worked hand in hand with families, helping them reach decisions regarding appropriate living situations. This included looking at each individual elder in a holistic way. By providing necessary information along with professional guidance, a family could reach a realistic decision that encompassed emotional well-being, physical health-care needs, housing issues, safety, family support, and personal finances. But with the rise in managed care and changes in hospital financing, health-care professionals no longer have time to provide this guidance, and families are increasingly left on their own.

In my fifteen years as a medical case manager and social worker in hospitals and skilled nursing facilities, providing direct assistance and services to elders and their families, I recognized that recent changes in Medicare and managed care have significantly decreased the number of hours I now spend offering information to elders and their families. *When Aging Parents Can't Live Alone: A Practical Family Guide* was written to fill this "information gap" and help elders and their families make the choice to change from independent living to living in an alternative home environment a thoughtful and informed decision.

In an age of Medicare, managed care, and health maintenance organizations (HMOs), it has become increasingly difficult for the average person and family to stay abreast of the numerous changes in Medicare health programs. As the federal government amends the current Medicare regulations governing hospitals, nursing facilities, and home health-care agencies, it becomes increasingly difficult for our elderly to receive medical care in a timely manner and to obtain home health-care services or skilled nursing care following a hospitalization or illness. Many people find it difficult to get an appointment to see their primary-care physician the day they need medical service. This in turn increases the use of emergency room care for nonemergency medical needs.

In addition, eligibility requirements for low-income assistance programs are tighter, leaving a greater number of our nation's elderly in the "gray" area: They have too much income and too many assets to be eligible for assistance, yet not enough income or assets to cover the cost of health-care deductibles, hospital bills, adequate housing, and vital prescription medications.

Medicare HMO programs were created to reduce the cost of health care and increase the number of benefits to our nation's elderly. In reality, these programs often have significant limitations for the average person. They may restrict which physicians a person can see, or require pre-authorizations for referrals to specialists or tests ordered by the physician. If they determine that the treatments, tests, or specialists are not medically necessary, insurers may deny the referral for services. These decisions may actually be based on the service's financial cost rather than an individual's medical need. Some HMOs may exclude vital services such as unlimited drug benefits (not covered under government Medicare). In addition, some may use stricter guidelines for what constitutes emergency care, the need for rehabilitation, or skilled nursing care services.

When Aging Parents Can't Live Alone was written to help families anticipate all the factors that may affect the care of an aging family member. By guiding the family step-by-step through the complicated maze of alternatives to living at home, aging programs, and services, this book provides practical, down-to-earth information as it examines physical and mental health; emotional concerns; personal finances; insurance coverage and benefits; safety in the home; varying costs of in-home services and live-in care facilities; accessibility to family and friends; and helpful community and government services. It empowers families by helping them think ahead about all the aspects of providing a safe and loving home environment for their aging family member.

Aging Is a Fact of Life!

This stage of life can be a time of joy and freedom or a turbulent and worrisome period for elders and their families. Some people age gracefully, maintaining both intelligence and physical stamina. Others gradually—or sometimes suddenly—lose the ability to think clearly or perform life's simplest tasks. As a concerned family member, you need to anticipate changes in your elder's ability to manage independently in his own home. You must make decisions that respect your elder family member's wishes, as well as help her prepare for declines in her physical or mental health and changes in her living situation.

Your family can approach the process of aging in two ways: by feeling powerless or by feeling empowered. Those who choose to be powerless will take life as it comes and be unprepared for the changes that occur during this advanced period. Empowerment will enable your family to prepare your elder family member's future by recognizing and accepting those changes that naturally occur during aging.

What You Should Know About Aging

Recognize and accept the aging process. Ignoring the physical and mental changes that are occurring in your elder family members will not alter the reality. Your elder family member may become less physically active and develop some physical health problems. He may experience a decrease in his normal thought process. Supervision and assistance either from family, community, state, or federal agencies and programs may be needed. He may not be able to continue living independently in his own home and may require some type of alternative housing or long-term care.

Recognize the warning signs. These signs are indicators of obvious or subtle changes occurring in your elder family member. Sometimes families choose to rationalize or ignore these warning signs not because they don't care, but because they hope these physical or mental changes—so common in the elderly—will pass. Some common warning signs include significant changes in your elder's usual routine:

- unexplained or erratic behavior and increased forgetfulness or confusion
- taking an incorrect or unscheduled dose of medication
- unexplained bruising, possibly the result of loss of balance or falls
- moldy food in the refrigerator accompanied by an unexplained loss of appetite or weight

Adapt to change. It is important to be able to adjust to the changes in your loved one's physical capabilities and mental health. This will help you and your elder family member meet the demands of new and different responsibilities and, if needed, adjust to a new home environment.

Prepare for the future. When the unexpected occurs and difficult decisions must be made quickly, it is imperative for your family to have all the information necessary to make reasonable and informed decisions. These decisions will affect the future of someone close to you.

Familiarize yourself with the resources available to seniors. Consider all the material your family may need to make an informed decision. It should include the following information:

- *You should maintain a record of personal information* about your elder family member, including his confidential requests.
- *You should know your elder's health-insurance policy numbers, coverage, and benefits,* including information on private supplemental and long-term care policies, HMOs, Medicare, Medicaid, and veteran's benefits.
- *You should know your elder's personal financial resources* in order to help pay for needed services and to determine eligibility for community and government-assistance programs.
- *You should maintain a listing of local community, state, and federal agencies* that provide direct services to the elderly. In *When Aging Parents Can't Live Alone,* you will find information on national agencies, detailing what services are offered and when indicated, how to apply for services, their cost, whom to contact, helpful hints, and available publications. Toll-free (800 or 888) numbers and Internet websites are used extensively. Resources in this book include the state area agencies on aging,

senior and disabled services and social services agencies, health-care programs such as the American Cancer Society, home health-care agencies, and many more. These programs are presented in general terms to help you understand how to determine eligibility and apply for specific services and benefits.

- You should gather information on care facilities. This information contains a wide range of elder residences, including standard and continuing-care retirement communities; assisted living facilities; adult-care homes; intermediate and skilled nursing care facilities; and hospice care. Rehabilitation centers and hospitals are discussed because families often need to make prompt decisions regarding care after a hospitalization, serious illness, or accident.

Use the resource information effectively and efficiently. By knowing which questions to ask when you approach community agencies, you will be able to determine quickly which programs are appropriate for your elder family member.

Use the glossary, appendices, and index at the back of this book. The glossary contains simple, easy-to-understand definitions of terms and phrases used in the book. The index can be used as a directory and guide to help you pinpoint specific sections and information in the book.

Leave preconceived notions, ideas, or plans behind. To use this book effectively, place your opinions, views, beliefs, and expectations somewhere else—maybe in a jar with the lid tightly closed, in a box in the hall closet, or in the refrigerator freezer. Why? Because some families think they know what is best for an elder family member based on their own personal preferences. These preconceived ideas can interfere with how you evaluate your elder's care needs and her ability to live independently in her home or in an alternative living situation.

Work together toward a common goal. If your loved one is capable of understanding and participating in discussions, encourage her participation. After all, she still has the wisdom of many active and productive years. Although there may be differences in background, ideas, tastes, and politics, remember that finding a solution that will make your elder family member happy, comfortable, and safe is your primary goal. If your elder family member is unable to take an active role in the decision making, try to keep her informed in a low-key manner. Let her know some kind of change may soon happen. Prepare her, but don't overwhelm her. Supply her with simplified information that she can understand. *Don't* overdose her with details.

Getting Started

The goal of *When Aging Parents Can't Live Alone* is to provide your family with practical information to help you examine all the factors that may influence decisions regarding the care of your elder family member. It will help you think ahead about all the aspects of providing a safe and loving home environment.

You will consider physical and mental health; emotional concerns; personal finances; insurance coverage and benefits; safety in the home; varying costs of services; alternatives to living at home; and accessibility and support from family, friends, and helpful community and government agencies. Before you begin to call or visit care facilities and community agencies, you will know your elder's current living situation. You will also know the general physical and mental condition of your elder family member and whether he is able to independently care for himself and understand and actively participate in discussions and decision making.

As you evaluate alternatives to living at home or in-home services, you will know which residences and services are appropriate for your elder's specific situation. You will also have all the necessary information, including financial resources and insurance benefits, to contact and make a competent and thorough referral to social service agencies and federal or state assistance programs.

Begin by reading chapter 1, "There's No Place Like Home: Independent Living." This chapter focuses on the customary—and often preferred—independent living situation for an elder person. This chapter poses a series of questions about your elder family member. As you answer them, you will begin to individualize this book to meet your elder's specific set of circumstances. The goal is to encourage you to think about how your elder's life is changing and to reflect comfortably on whether a significant change in her present living situation is necessary.

Primarily, the narrative in *When Aging Parents Can't Live Alone* uses two universal elders, John and Marcy, to represent everybody's parent, grandparent, uncle, aunt, relative, or significant other. The gender used in each chapter will vary depending on the character being used. Other anecdotes are used to illustrate different life situations.

Using a series of brief questionnaires and checklists, this book will lead you step-by-step through the decision-making process, helping you decide what needs to be done and how to set it in motion. By going to the heart of the action-oriented topics, *When Aging Parents Can't Live Alone* will enable you to react quickly and decisively when you must, secure in the knowledge that no major factors have been overlooked and that all the pertinent resources have been explored.

The summary guide will help you keep track of your responses to questions. Key words or phrases will help you summarize the main ideas in sections of the book. These key words and phrases will be used later to help you make decisions and move to the appropriate sections of the book.

Have a pen or pencil and a pad of paper handy to take notes and mark questions. This guide will stimulate discussion and raise new issues. It will suggest questions to ask your elder family member, his physician, or resident managers in other home settings. It will also direct you to appropriate agencies and hidden community resources. At times, you will be asked to complete work sheets, which are designed to help you gather the necessary information when your elder requires additional help, supervision, or placement in a care facility. Finally, *When Aging Parents Can't Live Alone* will enable your family to address common, everyday issues and be prepared for the unexpected health and aging concerns when they occur.

Chapter 1

There's No Place Like Home: Independent Living

———————— ❧ ————————

Home is the house in which a person lives, especially the place where a person has lived with her spouse and raised a family. A home represents the individual's personality—family photographs, a well-worn, favorite chair, bookshelves filled with the writings of preferred authors, porcelain teacups and bowls displayed in beveled-glass china cabinets. It is likely filled with happy and sad memories.

Given a choice, most people would choose to live at home alone or with a spouse, to live at home with assistance, or to live with their families. Some would choose to live in a retirement community, an assisted living community, an adult-care home, or a nursing facility. Others might find that their health-care needs, finances, or insurance benefits determine where they can live. In this chapter, your family will explore independent living with or without assistance and decide if it is the safest and best choice for your elder family member.

Two Elders Living Independently

The word *independent* means a person does not rely on others for support or assistance to perform activities of daily living (ADLs). In other words, your elder is able to get up in the morning, take a shower or bath, brush his teeth and hair, shave, dress, properly take daily medications, prepare meals, shop for groceries, clean the house, keep schedules, and get to appointments in a timely manner. He can competently handle financial matters on his own or delegate them to a trusted family member, friend, or attorney. Physical-health problems should not interfere with these daily activities, although at times they may create a temporary need for assistance. He should be alert and oriented, with minimal problems of memory or forgetfulness. He should be able to make decisions on his own behalf and use reasonable judgment.

The phrase "living at home with assistance" implies that independent living has become more difficult due to increasing personal-care needs or changes in physical or mental health. If your elder is living alone under such circumstances, these changes may place him at risk for injury. It may be necessary to arrange for in-home services to help him with tasks that have become more difficult to perform.

Your family may also have two aging parents living together, determined to care for each other despite the physical and mental hardships it imposes on each. Both may be healthy, one elder may be in good health and caring for the other, or they may both have significant health problems.

If both are healthy and able to make good decisions on their own behalf, it is important to honor their choices and judgment regarding where and how they choose to live.

If your healthy elder parent is caring for her ailing spouse or companion, as long as the living situation does not place either of them at risk for injury, they should be supported by your family. Sometimes a community service provider such as a home health-care agency can offer added support, monitoring, and assistance.

If both elder family members are in poor health and the home situation places them at risk of harm, your family should provide as much support in the home as possible. Although your family may prefer to move one or both of them to a supervised setting, many elders will strongly resist a move of any kind. If it is possible to honor this need for continued autonomy, your family should increase its support, with the help of private and community agencies. If the elders refuse additional in-home support from agencies, speak with family and friends about arranging an organized network of support, splitting the care between several people.

There is usually a "right" time to move elder family members from their homes to a supervised setting. Sometimes it occurs during a crisis: An elder family member enters the hospital and requires extended medical care, or an injury such as a fall occurs. This time of crisis often changes the way your elder may feel about continuing to care for her loved one. Although she may wish to continue, she may also develop a more realistic understanding of the situation. Speaking with a medical social worker or case manager may provide your family with realistic options.

Carefully review your elder's needs and determine if caring for a spouse is a reasonable plan. With help and support, it may be possible. Without help and support from family, a friend, or a hired caregiver, this decision may not be the best choice. The healthy spouse may wear herself out by providing continuous twenty-four-hour care-giving, resulting in caregiver burnout and adverse changes in her own health.

Living Alone, Independently

It is fairly common to find an elder parent or relative living alone independently, fol-lowing the death of a beloved spouse. Some elders can handle the transition from shar-ing their lives, making decisions, and undertaking daily activities and chores with someone else to doing these alone or with some family support. Others may not be able to function adequately without daily support and guidance from family, friends, and community agencies. For example, your parent may feel ill at ease being home alone, or he may be overwhelmed by the number of responsibilities he can no longer share with his spouse.

For some healthy and active elders, it may be easy to participate in social gather-ings, clean their homes and cook independently, and maintain a well-balanced daily routine.

For elders who have relied heavily on their spouses to handle the finances or per-form the cooking, cleaning, and social planning, life without a spouse may be depress-ing, stressful, lonely, and difficult. These elders may find that they need someone to help them maintain their independence, or they may find that another setting, such as assisted living, is more conducive to their personal needs.

❧ At Home with John, an Elder Parent

For ten years, John, a seventy-eight-year-old widower, lived alone in his own home. His closest family member was his son, George. Other fam-ily lived in another state. George and his family visited his father twice a week. During their visits, George's wife prepared meals for him to freeze, while he helped with simple home repairs.

In response to a job promotion, George and his family moved to a town 150 miles away. George asked his father if he would like to move with his family. After some thought, John declined, stating that he was reluctant to leave his own home. He also did not want to deal with the constant noise of small children, or to feel he was in the way and a burden to his son's family.

John continued to live independently in his own home. He took care of all his personal-care needs, such as bathing, grooming, and dressing. He prepared his own simple meals, did his own laundry, and kept a fairly clean house. His weekly medication was arranged in a pillbox he filled every Sunday. He alone handled his financial matters, although he granted his son a general durable power of attorney for handling his finances "just in case" something should happen. John made all his decisions, displaying good judgment and understanding.

Remaining active was important to John. He went on daily walks, occasionally using a cane for balance. Weekly activities included playing golf with his friends and attending church on Sundays. He also enjoyed reading, watching sports on television, and working on woodwork projects. Except for occasional loss of balance, he remained in good physical health.

After moving, George called twice a week to check on his father. During one call, John informed his son that, due to the long walk, grocery shopping had become increasingly difficult. John also informed him that he had contacted the local grocery store and requested home delivery. For a small charge, the store brought John's groceries to his home, unpacked the bags, and placed the food in his cabinets. George felt relieved; his father had solved a problem independently and wisely.

Several months later, John forgot that he had already taken his medication and inadvertently doubled his daily dose. He was found by a neighbor wandering in his backyard disoriented and confused. The neighbor called George and alerted him to the situation.

When George arrived several hours later, he found his father slightly confused. He could not remember how he had spent his morning. He was worried and upset. He informed his son that he was experiencing difficulty with meal preparation and sometimes forgot to turn off the stove's burners. During his weekly golf game, his partners had remarked on how many times he lost his golf ball. Although his physical health was good, he had been experiencing balance problems, resulting in two falls. Since he had not injured himself, John decided not to inform anyone. He "did not want his family or friends to worry."

Although his father had managed on his own with no assistance from family or community agencies, George felt it was time to consider making some changes in his father's living situation. He recognized how important his father's independence was to him. As they discussed his living situation, George found that John was able to respond with understanding and coherence. His father was aware of the safety risk when he was alone, but he was reluctant to move from his home. Together they prepared a list of activities he needed help with, including meal preparation, grocery shopping, and some personal-care needs. George also examined the house for safety hazards, removing throw rugs, movable furniture, and general clutter.

In the evening, however, George noticed that his father became increasingly confused. He expressed concern to him about his safety at home, especially during the evening hours. George made an appointment with his father's physician to evaluate his balance problems, medication, and ensuing confusion and forgetfulness.

John's shift from being fully independent to requiring some assistance and supervision in his home occurs over a short period of time. Consider his living situation: Should he remain in his home, alone or with assistance, or should alternatives to living at home be considered? What changes make it more difficult for John to remain in his home?

1. His family moved, leaving him without family support.

2. Walking became more difficult due to balance problems, resulting in several falls at home.

3. Grocery shopping and meal preparation became more difficult.

4. John became more forgetful, confused, and disoriented at night.

5. He took an incorrect dose of medication, due to his forgetfulness.

If only one or two changes had occurred, John could probably continue to live independently, with some assistance from the community. But when all these changes were added up, a significant shift in his capacity to function safely in his home became evident.

JUST THE FACTS:
A PERSONAL QUESTIONNAIRE

This questionnaire is designed to help you think about your elder's living situation and guide you through the crucial areas of importance. In this chapter, you will answer basic questions about your elder family member, his physical and mental health, safety in his home, and activities of daily living, which will personalize this guide for him.

As you progress through *When Aging Parents Can't Live Alone*, narrowing the choices for reasonable alternatives to home, you will be directed to detailed information about potential residences, community programs, and in-home services. Don't worry if all your questions are not answered immediately. More detailed and specific information will be provided in later chapters.

Is Independent Living the Best Choice for Your Elder Family Member?

Answer the following questions as accurately as you can. Check the correct key words or key phrases at the end of each section.

Mental Health: What's Your Elder Thinking?

1. Does your elder have difficulty easily and accurately remembering recent activities?
2. Does your elder have difficulty easily and accurately remembering familiar dates, such as his birth date?
3. Does your elder show signs of forgetfulness?
4. Does your elder have difficulty recognizing family and friends?
5. Does your elder have difficulty easily and accurately remembering activities from the past?
6. Does your elder have difficulty remembering the correct dosage and times for taking his medication?
7. Does your elder have difficulty following directions easily and accurately?
8. Does your elder seem more confused or disoriented?

9. Does your elder seem more confused at night?

10. Do you feel your elder has difficulty understanding information presented to him and making reasonable decisions on his own behalf?

11. Would your elder have difficulty calling for help if he needed assistance?

12. Does your elder seem sad, quiet, withdrawn, or low on energy?

13. Does he sleep more than usual, especially during the day?

If you answered "yes" to most of these questions, your elder family member may need some supervision in his home.

If you answered "no" to most of these questions, your elder should be able to make decisions on his own behalf.

Please check the appropriate key words or key phrases. My elder family member is:

____ disoriented	____ oriented
____ confused	____ alert
____ forgetful or has memory problems	____ able to understand information and make his own decisions

---

Review: Mental Health

If your elder family member is disoriented, or has some memory loss or forgetfulness, staying alone in his home is an unsafe situation. It places him at great risk of wandering from home and becoming lost, having an accident, leaving the oven burners on, or injuring himself and being unable to summon help. If your elder is confused or forgetful and unable to call for help if he falls or injures himself, he should not be left alone.

Sometimes the elderly are temporarily confused and disoriented following a hospitalization or illness. This may be a result of new surroundings, the trauma of hospitalization or surgery, or a change in medication. Or it may represent the beginning stages of a progressive disease such as Alzheimer's or a developing physical-health problem. If this is a new condition, or if the problem persists, consult with his primary-care physician.

Taking incorrect amounts of medication is common following a hospitalization or illness, because medication schedules often change. A registered nurse from a home health-care agency can help set up an easy- to-remember schedule and/or medication box for your elder family member.

If your elder appears less confused during the day and increasingly confused in the evening, he could have sundowner's syndrome. This means he may become more confused after the sun has set. Arranging nighttime supervision will help decrease the chances that he will have an accident and injure himself.

If your elder seems unhappy, lethargic, and distant, he may have symptoms of depression. This common problem in the elderly can interfere with performing the basic activities of life, decrease socialization and communication, and, ultimately, affect his physical and mental health. There are many causes of depression, such as a reaction to medication. If the depression persists, consult his primary-care physician or the doctor responsible for coordinating his medical care with other physicians, hospitals, and health-care agencies.

If your elder can understand information and make reasonable decisions on his own behalf, try to respect his wishes as long as they do not place him at risk of injury.

If your elder does not understand information and is not using good judgment, still try to keep him informed of any decisions that may affect his life. Talk with him in simple, easy-to-understand language. Consider talking with his physician about possible causes, as well as with an attorney regarding the need for a durable power of attorney or guardianship.

If your elder is alert and able to call for help if he falls or injures himself, you may want to obtain a Lifeline service. You may remember the commercials: An elderly person is lying on the floor of her home. She pushes a button around her neck or on her wrist and says, "Help me. I've fallen and I can't get up," and instantly summons emergency help. This service is available in most areas for a small monthly fee.

If your elder is alert and aware of his surroundings, able to understand and make decisions on his own behalf, and uses reasonable judgment, independent living at home could be a viable option for him.

Physical Health: How Is Your Elder's Physical Health?

Determining your elder's state of health is necessary, because in-home services or alternatives to home are often influenced by a person's ability to care for himself. A change or crisis in an elderly person's physical health is often the determining factor in the decision to choose an appropriate alternative to living at home.

Physical Health

13. Does your elder have difficulty with his vision, or has he experienced a recent change or loss of vision?
14. Does your elder wear prescription glasses?
15. Has your elder had difficulty hearing or had a recent change or loss of hearing?
16. Does your elder wear a hearing aid?
17. Does your elder have a history of significant drug or alcohol use?
18. Do you feel your elder is in good general health?
19. Does your elder have any health problems that need to be watched closely?
20. Does your elder need to give himself any injections?
21. Does your elder have difficulty controlling his bladder or bowels?
22. Has your elder had a recent illness, hospitalization, outpatient surgery, or an accident?

If you answered "yes" to most of these questions, your elder may need some supervision and assistance.

If you answered "no" to most of these questions, your elder should be able to live independently in his home or with limited in-home assistance.

Please check the appropriate key words or key phrases. My elder family member has:

_____ health concerns	_____ no health concerns
_____ vision problems	_____ no vision problems
_____ hearing problems	_____ no hearing problems

Review: Physical Health

To continue living independently, your elder should maintain good and reasonable health. Although temporary health problems can necessitate accepting in-home services, such as homemaking assistance, for a short period of time, these services can be discontinued as soon as your elder is able to safely provide his own care in his home.

Temporary assistance in the home is acceptable if your elder can return to independent living. If the temporary assistance becomes more or less full-time or permanent, your elder may need to consider living with his family or in a facility that can provide the care and supervision he needs. The financial cost of full-time help in the home can be expensive.

If your elder needs daily assistance, consider how many hours each day he needs it. Sometimes a caregiver or person who helps with personal care can be hired to work a split shift. This means the caregiver can help get your elder out of bed in the morning and prepare breakfast and lunch and return in the evening to help him get ready for bedtime.

If your elder has difficulty with his vision, consult his primary-care physician or an eye specialist. If he has limited vision or is blind, it is important to keep him in familiar surroundings for as long as possible. Seeing Eye dogs, special telephone equipment, and other services for the blind should also be explored. Elderly people may not always be up front about the difficulties they are having with their vision. They may fear they will lose their driver's licenses or be unable to manage in their current homes. They may worry about the financial cost of an eye exam and eyeglasses. This is not covered under Medicare except for glasses required after cataract surgery. Medicaid may provide some benefits. Check your elder's private-insurance coverage for benefits.

If your elder has difficulty hearing, consult his primary-care physician or a hearing specialist. If he has a hearing aide, its effectiveness may need to be reevaluated. You may want to obtain an amplified telephone system, apply to the Dogs for the Deaf program, and alert neighbors and other people providing him with care or supervision. Elderly people may not realize they do not hear as well as they used to.

Look for cues, such as extreme loudness or softness in volume when your elder is speaking or your elder turns up the volume on the television or radio. You may need to repeat what you are saying to your elder, because he is unable to follow conversations. Or your elder may repeatedly use words or phrases like "What," "Huh," "What did you say?," or "You never told me that." Your elder may also stop answering the doorbell or telephone because he cannot hear it.

If your elder does not respond or hear you, try eliminating any background or loud noises. Gently touch your elder's shoulder to gain his attention. Look directly at him when you speak, and speak loudly and slowly.

If your elder has a significant history of alcohol and/or drug abuse, he may develop physical illnesses, such as liver disease, or exhibit changes in his behavior or a deterioration in his thought process, including disorientation, forgetfulness, and memory loss. These changes may result in verbal or physical abuse and family problems. Seeking help through his physician or a drug and alcohol program or counselor is recommended.

If your elder is diabetic able to self-administer insulin injections, it should not be necessary to obtain assistance. For basic questions, your elder can contact his primary-care physician. A visit from a home health-care nurse for instruction on giving injections can be ordered by the physician if your elder is homebound.

If your elder has frequent problems with bladder or bowel control, there are easy solutions. Adult diapers purchased at any drugstore or pharmacy can provide protection for urinary and/or bowel incontinence. Sometimes a physician will prescribe medication or exercises, or recommend inserting a urinary catheter, which allows the urine to flow into a bag strapped to the leg. The catheter can easily be maintained at home with minimal visits from a home health-care nurse. Consulting with his primary-care physician and/or obtaining a referral for home health-care nurses to teach catheter care is recommended.

If your elder has recently been in a hospital or had an injury, accident, or outpatient surgery, he may benefit from temporary home health-care services, outpatient therapies or care, or therapy in a nursing facility. Medical questions and problems can be directed to his primary-care physician, who can evaluate his physical and mental health and make treatment recommendations. Sometimes a change in medication or sessions with a physical or occupational therapist can make a difference. The physician can also request or make a referral to a home health-care agency for skilled nursing care in the home.

Following a hospitalization or accident, while your elder recovers, different options for care are available depending on the duration and type of medical care required. For long-term medical care, nursing facilities can provide several levels of care. For terminal care, inpatient and outpatient hospice programs through a home health-care agency or hospital may be available. Rehabilitation centers may provide extended restorative programs for long- or short-term disabilities. It may be necessary to review insurance benefits and financial resources if you decide to consider long-term care for your elder family member.

Home Safety

23. Does your elder have any difficulties with his balance?

24. Is your elder in any danger of falling?

25. Has your elder fallen at home?

26. Does your elder have difficulty getting out of bed, out of a chair, or standing up from the toilet?

27. Is it difficult for your elder to take a shower or bath by himself?

28. Is it difficult for your elder to get up at night by himself to use the bathroom?

If you answered "yes" to any of these questions, your elder may need some supervision.

If you answered "no" to these questions, your elder may not need supervision.

Please check the appropriate key words or key phrases. My elder family member is:

_____ safe in his home   _____ unsafe in his home

Make personal safety a priority when you are evaluating your elder's ability to remain in his home.

If your elder is experiencing any difficulty walking, carefully explore whether he has fallen at home. Often, an elder person won't inform his family about falls, because he fears he will lose his independence, or he may downplay any falls he has had. Sometimes durable medical equipment, such as a bedside commode, raised toilet seat, or grab bars, can significantly help.

If your elder is experiencing some loss of balance or is having difficulty moving from a chair to standing position, or from a bed to a chair, the danger of falling is real. A night-light in the bathroom or bedroom, removing loose throw rugs, and placing handrails in critical locations can help decrease the risk of a fall or injury. Handrails on staircases can help your elder maintain his balance and provide additional stability when he climbs up or down the stairs. Carpeted steps are less slippery than bare wood steps.

Often, a walker or cane is recommended for safety and balance. Physicians and physical therapists can assist your elder by evaluating his strengths and weaknesses. They can help him order the appropriate walking device. With a doctor's order, a physical therapist can visit his home, perform a safety evaluation, and make recommendations for safety equipment.

Getting out of bed at night to use the bathroom can be dangerous for your elder if he has balance problems or difficulty getting up by himself. Providing him with assistance is the best choice.

If your elder has difficulty getting up from the toilet, durable medical equipment and supplies, such as raised toilet seats and grab bars, can be purchased or rented through a medical-supply company.

When taking a shower or bath, shower stools and support bars in the bathroom area can reduce the risk of injury. A removable showerhead with an extension arm may also be helpful. Or, if getting into the bath or tub area places your elder at risk of falling or injury, consider giving him a bed bath.

If your elder's bedroom is upstairs, he can rent, purchase, or obtain a free loan for the necessary medical equipment to set up an easily accessible downstairs living area. A doctor's order and prescription are required to order durable medical equipment for his home.

Activities of Daily Living (ADLs)

ADLs are the routine activities of everyday living, such as eating, dressing, grooming, bathing, toileting, personal care, and medication management.

29. Does your elder need assistance in the morning with bathing, dressing, and personal hygiene?

30. Does your elder need assistance in the evening when he prepares for bed?

31. Does your elder need assistance with meal preparation?

32. Does your elder need assistance with grocery shopping?

33. Does your elder need assistance cleaning his home?

34. Does your elder need assistance setting up a medication box or administering his medications properly?

35. Is it difficult for your elder to safely use a car as his main method of transportation?

If you answered "yes" to most of these questions, your elder family member may need some supervision and assistance in his home. Consider an alternative to living at home.

If you answered "no" to most of these questions, he should be able to remain in his own home without significant help.

Please check the appropriate key words or key phrases. My elder family member:

_____ does not need supervision and assistance

_____ needs supervision and assistance

Review: Activities of Daily Living

If your elder moves slowly, but can bathe and dress himself and prepare his own meals without difficulty, try to support his efforts at remaining independent. Senior and disabled services or a state area agency on aging program may be able to assist him with homemaking services if he meets their eligibility requirements.

If your elder requires daily assistance with personal care, dressing, bathing, shopping, or meal preparation, independent living may not be the best choice for him. By remaining alone without support and assistance, your elder places himself at risk of injury. Consider getting him help in his home, or explore other alternatives to living at home.

If your elder needs assistance with grocery shopping, contact the local grocery store regarding delivery services. Meals-on-wheels may also be available to provide one meal a day, Monday through Friday, delivered right to his home. Some local taxi services have coupon books with discount rates for seniors. Wheelchair vans may also be available through seniors programs and taxi services to help with transportation to supermarkets.

If your elder needs help or supervision taking his medication, a home health-care nurse can help him set up an easy-to-use medication box and schedule.

If your elder has a car and driver's license, evaluate his current driving skills. Does he get lost or forget where he is driving? Does he drive at a reasonable speed? Is he attentive? Does he have any physical problems, such as difficulty with vision or hearing, that could interfere with safe driving? To your elder, driving a car may represent freedom and independence. Withdrawing his driver's license in response to unsafe driving conditions can discourage him and make him feel helpless, frustrated, and angry. Without his car, he may become more dependent on others for transportation to shopping and medical appointments. However, if he presents a danger to others and himself while driving, taking away his license may be necessary. Contact the Department of Motor Vehicles (DMV) or his primary-care physician for information.

You have briefly looked at your elder's physical and mental health, safety in the home and on the road, and his activities of daily living to help you determine the type of care, assistance, and supervision your elder family member may need. Check the key words and key phrases that best describe your elder.

SUMMARY: KEY WORDS AND KEY PHRASES

Column 1	Column 2
____ good health	____ health problems
____ alert	____ confused
____ oriented	____ disoriented
____ no memory problems	____ forgetful
____ understands and makes decisions	____ unable to make decisions
____ safe	____ not safe
____ no assistance or supervision needed	____ needs assistance and supervision
Total _____	**Total** _____

If most of the phrases checked are in column 1, your elder should be able to remain safely in his home even if he needs some in-home help. Or he may choose to live in a retirement community if his income and/or assets allow.

If most of the phrases checked are in column 2, your elder will benefit from assistance and supportive services in his home. Or he may need to consider living with family or other alternatives to living at home.

Using the Getting to Know Your Elder Work Sheet

Making important decisions that affect a family member's living situation is a difficult task. Decisions regarding placement or in-home services must often be made quickly, facilities must be evaluated efficiently, and information about community resources must be reviewed effectively. Blending information from brochures, recommendations from family, friends, physicians, and other professionals with impressions from visiting residential facilities or contact with community agencies is essential if you're to make a thoughtful decision.

Every call your family makes to a social service agency or potential home alternative requires specific information about your elder family member. Each call leads to an acceptable or an unacceptable alternative to living at home or community service.

It is difficult to know what questions to ask. It is difficult to understand the technical language used by social service and health professionals. One facility may describe itself as a retirement home, another a full-service or continuing-care retirement community.

Are these facilities appropriate for your elder? How are they different? How do you eliminate the inappropriate ones? How do you know if a facility provides the appropriate level of care and necessary services required by your elder family member?

The Getting to Know Your Elder work sheet is commonly referred to as a contact sheet or referral form. It is designed to help the family gather the essential information needed to complete applications, contact community and government agencies, arrange in-home services, and visit care facilities. This information will present a clear picture of your elder family member. By keeping it with you, you will be able to discuss his situation and answer specific questions about his medical care, finances, insurance coverage, and legal issues.

If you do not have all the data you need, such as financial resources, to complete a section, estimate the figures as accurately as you can.

The personal-information section asks for basic facts about your elder family member. Carefully consider the emergency contact—this person can be a spouse, relative, friend, or neighbor and should be easily accessible and have a caring relationship with your elder.

Look at his insurance cards and check for exclusions or preexisting medical conditions *not* covered by the insurance policies. Check the Medicare card for both Parts A and B. Make a copy of all your elder's insurance cards, since care facilities and agencies often request a copy.

Financial income is considered high if it exceeds $4,000 per month, moderate if it is between $2,000 and $4,000 per month, low-moderate if it is $900 to $2,000 per month, and low if it is less than $900 per month.

Financial assets, which include stocks, bonds, CDs, and bank accounts, are considered high if they exceed $35,000, moderate if they are $15,000 to $35,000, low-moderate if they are $5,000 to $15,000, and low if they are less than $5,000.

The legal information will help your family designate a reliable and competent family member to manage likely financial, insurance, medical, or legal issues that can arise. The designated family member will be responsible for leading family discussions, delegating tasks to family members, coordinating services, and, if needed, signing facilities admission papers.

The medical section will give your family a clear understanding of basic medical issues. Many agencies request information, such as diagnosis, types of medications, and recent hospitalizations, as they review a request or application for assistance or admission to a care facility. This information can be obtained from the primary-care physician or hospital with a release of information signed by your elder family member.

GETTING TO KNOW YOUR ELDER WORK SHEET

Provide the following information as accurately as you can.

Date _____

Personal Information for (fill in name) _____

Social Security # _____ - _____ - _____ **Age** _____ **Birth date** _____

Height _____ **Weight** _____

Marital Status: Single _____ **Married** _____ **Divorced** _____ **Widowed** _____

Current address _____

City _____ **State** _____ **Zip code** _____

Telephone # _____

Name of spouse or nearest relative _____

Relationship _____

Spouse's Social Security # _____ - _____ - _____ **Age** _____ **Birth date** _____

Telephone Emergency Contact #1 or nearest relative _____

Telephone Emergency Contact #2 _____

INSURANCE INFORMATION

Look at the red-white-and-blue Medicare card to verify your elder family member's participation in Medicare Parts A and B. Also, note the policy number and any exclusions on all insurance cards. Private-insurance policies should be reviewed for basic benefits, such as home health care, durable medical equipment, skilled nursing facility, hospice, and prescription coverage. Note the expiration or renewal date on all policies.

Medicare # _____ **Part A** _____ **Part B** _____

Medicaid # _____

Private insurance: Name of company _____

Policy# _____

Catastrophic insurance: Name of company _____

Policy# _____

Long-term-care insurance: Name of company _____

Policy# _____

Veterans benefits _____

Non-service-connected _____ **Service-connected** _____

No health insurance

If your elder does not have health insurance, contact your nearest senior and disabled services office to help you determine if your elder is eligible for medical benefits through the state or federal government.

FINANCIAL RESOURCES: INCOME

Total monthly income _____ **Name of bank** _____

Checking account balance _____ **Savings account balance** _____

Under Medicaid regulations, each person is allowed $2,000 in a savings account.

Sources/Amounts of Income

Wages: Monthly _____ **Weekly** _____ **Hourly** _____ **Employer** _____

Unemployment compensation _____

Social Security benefits _____

Supplemental Security Income (SSI) _____

Social Security Disability Income (SSDI) _____

Veterans benefits _____

Pension benefits _____

General assistance _____

Food stamps _____

FINANCIAL RESOURCES: ASSETS

Value of stocks, bonds, CDs, rental property, or investments _____

Other assets (type and total value) _____

GETTING TO KNOW YOUR ELDER continued

Other assets (type and total value) _____

Owns home _____   **Does not own home** _____
Owning a home does not necessarily affect eligibility for financial assistance from state or federal programs. However, under the current Medicaid program, the state may place a lien on property after both husband and wife are deceased.

Outstanding debts (such as medical bills, credit cards). Please list source and amount.
_____

_____

Burial funds: Yes, I have set aside burial funds _____
No, I have not set aside burial funds _____
Under the current Medicaid program, each person over age sixty-five can set aside $1,500 and designate it as a burial fund or money to be used for funeral-related expenses.

LEGAL INFORMATION

Name of responsible family member _____   **Telephone #** _____

Name of person with Durable Power of Attorney _____
          with Guardianship _____
          with Conservatorship _____

Name and telephone of Family Attorney _____

I have: Power of attorney for health care_____   **Living will** _____
     POLST (Physician Orders for Life-Sustaining Treatment) _____
     General durable power of attorney _____   **Advanced directives** _____
     Other _____

MEDICAL INFORMATION

Name of primary-care physician _____   **Telephone #** _____

Other physicians: Name _____   **Telephone #** _____
          Name _____   **Telephone #** _____
          Name _____   **Telephone #** _____

List any medical conditions for which you are being treated.

_____

_____

List any allergies you have. _____

List any medications you are currently using. Include the dosages, the number of times per day they are taken, and special instructions. For example, Amoxil, 250mg/3x/day with meal.

_____

_____

_____

_____

_____

_____

_____

Please complete this section only if you are currently or have recently been in a hospital, skilled nursing facility, rehabilitation center, or hospice unit.

Name and address of facility _____

_____ **Room #** _____

Contact person _____ **Telephone #** _____

Date of admission _____ **Date of discharge** _____

Admitting diagnosis _____ **Secondary diagnosis** _____

Attending physician _____ **Telephone #** _____

Payment Source:

Medicare _____ **Medicaid** _____ **Private insurance** _____

Private pay _____ **Worker's compensation** _____ **Veteran** _____

No insurance or funds available _____ **Other** _____

Services Received:

Physical therapy _____ **Occupational therapy** _____ **Speech therapy** _____

Skilled nursing care _____ **Dietary services** _____ **Other** _____

GETTING TO KNOW YOUR ELDER continued

Current Services Needed:

Physical therapy _____ Occupational therapy _____ Speech therapy _____

Skilled nursing care _____ Dietary services _____ Other _____

EVALUATION

Do you feel living at home independently is the best choice for your elder?

If your answer is "yes," turn to chapter 3, "Getting Help in Your Home." If your family and elder decide he can live at home independently or with assistance, your family will need to contact some of the social service agencies in his area to set up supportive services in his home.

If your answer is "no" or you are undecided, do you feel living with your family is an option for your elder family member?

If your answer is "yes," turn to chapter 2, "Living with Your Family."

If your answer is "no," turn to chapter 4, "Living in a Retirement Community." Or, if your elder has recently been in the hospital, review chapter 7, "Understanding Hospital Acute Care."

Chapter 2

Living with Your Family

——————— ❦ ———————

The voice of reason
is the voice of silence
is the voice of authority
is the voice of severity
is the voice of compromise
is the voice of reason
is the voice of love
is the voice of family.

—*Author unknown*

Fact: Five million Americans spend part of the day caring for ailing or dependent parents.

Fact: 12 to 15 percent of the workforce provides elder care.

Fact: Approximately 2 to 6 percent of the workforce care for elders who live more than an hour away.

Fact: From 1982 to 1992, the number of people sixty-five and older who moved from one state to another increased by 65 percent.

In chapter 1, you were introduced to John, an independent and self-reliant widower living without assistance or supervision in his own home. As John's physical and mental health gradually diminished, he became partially dependent on his family and community for help in his home. Questionnaires in chapter 1 helped you to examine his health, activities of daily living, financial resources, insurance benefits, and home safety issues. Now John has reached a turning point—he must decide, with his family, whether to move into their home or to consider another living arrangement, such as a retirement community, assisted living facility, adult foster-care home, or nursing care facility.

John Considers Living with His Family

John lived alone in his home, receiving assistance from family, friends, neighbors, and community agencies. Meals-on-wheels brought him a hot lunch five times during the week. For a small fee, his local grocery store delivered additional food and supplies. Through the state area agency on aging, John located a woman to help with homemaking chores and meal preparation. In addition to visits from his friends and community agencies, his son George called every other day and visited twice a month.

With his son's help and assistance from a home health-care agency, John reorganized his daily medication by using a medication box. A preset timer helped him to keep track of when to take his medication, which helped eliminate his periodic confusion regarding when to take his pills each day. At his physician's recommendation, John began using his cane for stability and balance while walking around his home. John and his son were pleased that with supportive and helpful community services, John maintained a relatively safe home environment.

During one of his visits, George decided to spend a night in his father's home. At 2 A.M. he was awakened by a thud—it was the sound of his father falling to the floor. Instead of placing his shoes in the closet or under the bed, John had left them in the center of the room. He had also forgotten to turn on his night-light before going to bed. Due to the darkness, his poor vision, and the clutter in the room, he had tripped over his shoes.

As George helped him get up, he noted that his father seemed confused and disoriented. He did not remember that he had wanted to use the bathroom and, as a result, wet his bed. He also seemed surprised to see his son at his home in the middle of the night.

The next morning, George realized that his father had only a poor recollection of falling or wetting his bed. He discussed his safety concerns with him and, after speaking with his wife, George offered to have his father move in with his family.

The story of John raises several important points:

1. John was safely living alone while receiving in-home assistance with grocery shopping, meals, homemaking chores, and basic health care.
2. Due to gradual and recent changes in his physical and mental capabilities, living alone in his home is no longer the safest home environment for him. It places him at risk and increases the likelihood of his sustaining a serious injury in his home.
3. Minimal clutter in his room, poor vision, and loss of balance contributed to his fall.
4. During nighttime, his confusion, disorientation, and forgetfulness increased.
5. Incontinence or loss of bladder control may have been a result of his confusion.

Although prior to his son's visit John appeared to be doing well in his home, he may have been experiencing difficulty and had been hiding it from his family. With additional supervision, especially in the evening, he could remain in his home. However, the cost of increasing supervision in the home may be greater than what John or his family could realistically afford. Living with his family or in a retirement community, assisted living facility, or nursing care center become options for careful review.

As you read this chapter, you will be asked whether you feel living with family is the best choice for your elder family member. If you do not feel it is the correct choice, you will be directed to other alternatives to independent living. If you decide you would like to have your elder move in with your family, you will be directed to chapter 3, "Getting Help in the Home," which contains information about local and national resources.

This chapter assumes that independent living is no longer a viable option for your elder. Because living with family is not the answer for everyone, it is approached as another option to living at home. It is necessary to explore your family's feelings, the level of support needed, and more tangible factors: personal-care needs, financial resources, insurance benefits, work schedules, and home safety and layout. These factors will play an instrumental role in helping you decide the best living situation for your elder.

Important Issues to Discuss

Open discussions and daily communication are essential in any family. By presenting concerns, asking questions, and stating opinions up front, you will lay a foundation that will help you learn about each other.

Your elder's daily routine, including any matters that are important to him. Many elder parents and relatives are accustomed to "doing things a certain way." A regular routine may play an important role in how quickly your elder adjusts to a new home. It may help him adapt to the new surroundings and to the recent changes in his life.

Your elder may have expectations, concerns, desires, and worries that he has not expressed to your family. By talking about them, he will encourage communication with your family.

Family expectations and concerns. Your family members may assume they can anticipate your elder's needs without discussing them with him. It is important to hear what issues are important to him, because poor communication can cause misunderstandings and be more difficult to solve when addressed later. Emotional and hands-on support from other family members are essential to a smooth and successful transition from living independently to living with family.

It is necessary for your family to think about your elder's physical-care needs and the amount of care and supervision your elder family member needs to safely live in your home. Personal care and activities of daily living include helping him with dressing, shaving, brushing his teeth and hair, bathing, and personal hygiene. Laundry services, meal preparation, and some supervision may be necessary to assist him with walking and eating and to prevent wandering.

Your elder may also have specific physical-care needs that require some nursing care or teaching and education for family members. If he has many personal-care needs, it may be difficult to provide proper care for him in your home. If his personal-care needs are minimal, it may be reasonable to have him live with your family. Supportive care in your home may be provided by community agencies, such as home health-care and state-funded aging programs.

Discuss financial matters openly and directly with your elder. Additional bills and household expenses incurred by having another family member in the home can create tension within the nuclear family. Decide what your elder's financial responsibilities will be. Will he pay part of the weekly grocery or utility bills? Will he contribute to the payment of rent or mortgage? A checklist at the end of this chapter will help your family determine how to manage shared household expenses.

If your elder has few financial resources, there are fewer alternatives to living at home or with family. If his financial resources are moderate to high, retirement communities, assisted living facilities, and nursing homes can be viable options.

Define realistic living arrangements with your elder before he moves in with your family. Privacy may be important to him, as well as to your family. It provides him with some independence and the feeling of autonomy. Will your elder have his own room? Will he share a room with a child? Will he have close and easy access to the bathroom? Will he share kitchen facilities and general living space?

Safety features and changes in the layout of your home may be needed to accommodate your elder. You may have to install basic safety devices in the bathroom and kitchen and on stairways. Furniture may need to be rearranged to open passageways, while bedrooms may need to be switched to give him easier access to the bathroom.

Your elder should have responsibilities in your home. Think about easy and helpful chores that your elder can do while living in your home, for example, dusting, washing or drying dishes, or getting the mail. By ensuring that he is actively involved in household chores, he may feel that he is less of a burden and more of a contributing member of the family.

Talking with Your Elder

> The best of life is conversation, and the greatest success is confidence, or perfect understanding between two people.
> —*Ralph Waldo Emerson (1803–1882)*

It may be difficult for your elder to make the decision to move from her own home and familiar surroundings. She may not understand your family's concerns for her physical and emotional well-being, or she may feel that her problems are being exaggerated. Your family may recognize the subtle changes associated with the aging process before she does. As a result, when helpful suggestions are made concerning her home situation, your elder may downplay or deny any problems. She may direct her anger at your family because she feels they're interfering in her life.

❦ The Story of Mary C.

After falling at home and breaking her ankle, Mary C., age seventy-five, was told by her physician to use crutches for several weeks. Because she was unable to easily and safely climb the stairs in her home without assistance, her family suggested she live with them during her recuperation. In her son's home, Mary would be far from her friends and the seniors center where she socialized. In addition, she feared that agreeing to live with her family would be the first step toward losing her independence. Her family discussed her concerns with her, reemphasizing the temporary nature of the living arrangement and their desire to have her back in her home as soon as possible. They suggested they could drive her to the seniors center when she wished to go there.

Mary was proud of her ability to care for herself and to exercise daily either by walking or by peddling her stationary bike. She felt that moving in with her family, even temporarily, might mean she would lose her independence. Yet, she recognized her need for assistance. She discussed with her family other options, such as home health care, hiring a caregiver, or having a grandchild live with her while she recovered.

Sometimes a family can openly discuss their concerns with their elder family member. Other times, their elder may adamantly refuse to consider any options to her current living situation. This can be frustrating and upsetting to the family. However, forcing a competent elder to move against her will can cause significant disruptions in the family and great distress to the elder family member.

Sometimes it is best to compromise and to leave your elder family member in her home but to also voice your concerns, arrange some supportive in-home services, and any necessary supervision. Although even this level of interference may be met with resistance, it can help prevent a serious injury in a less-than-safe home environment.

Sometimes a crisis, such as a fall or an illness, forces a change in the home situation. When this occurs, it is important to be prepared, to understand your options, and to be familiar with information on community and government agencies, financial resources, and insurance benefits.

If your elder decides to move in with your family, she is moving from an area of familiarity to a new, unfamiliar setting. Even as she boxes her belongings, she may question whether she is making the right decision.

It is important for your elder to understand that moving in with her family does not need to be a permanent situation. If living with family does not seem the best choice for her or your family, you can decide to change the living arrangements.

Your Elder's Feelings About Moving in with Your Family

Your elder may have strong feelings about moving from his home into his family's home. He may feel he is a burden. Your elder may worry about "all the trouble" he is causing. Reassure him by letting him know your family wants him to live with them.

Your elder may feel depressed about moving from his home. Depression may present itself as a physical symptom, for example, a decrease in appetite, stomach discomfort, sleeping problems, loss of energy or fatigue, difficulty concentrating, or a loss of interest in his usual activities. If depression persists or jeopardizes your elder's physical or mental health, contact his primary-care physician.

He may also feel isolated from his friends and familiar surroundings. Moving to a new living situation means leaving behind close friends and familiar places. Readjusting and feeling comfortable in his new surroundings and home may take time and understanding from your family. Getting involved in social activities at a seniors center or performing volunteer work can help ease the feelings of loneliness and isolation.

He may feel embarrassed for needing assistance from his family. Your elder has lived independently for many years. It may not be easy for him to ask for help when he needs it. Help him set realistic expectations, goals, and tasks.

He may feel frustrated and helpless because of his inability to care for himself. The shift from independence to partial dependence may be a difficult transition for your elder. Accepting assistance from family for activities he has performed most of his life may make him feel unproductive or useless. He may seem more impatient with himself and others. Although this frustration may seem to be directed at individuals, it may be this new situation that is eliciting this emotional response.

He may harbor a fear of the unknown, which is common for many of our elder family members. The future may seem uncertain, and mortality may seem closer. Reassure your elder that he is loved and an integral part of your family.

Your elder may feel a loss of control because of increasing age and care needs. He no longer has the ability to manage his own affairs or to control the physical or mental changes associated with the aging process.

He may feel a loss of independence and freedom as an individual. When your elder moves in with your family, his daily activities and care needs become interdependent on other family members.

Your elder family member, like many elders, may fear poverty. He may worry about selling his home, moving costs, medical expenses, future expenses, finances, and daily costs of living. Remember, many of our aging parents lived through the Depression.

It is important for you to discuss these real concerns with your elder. With reassurance from your family, he may be able to view his move with more positive feelings. He may feel appreciative and relieved to have a family that cares about him. He may feel hopeful for the future.

Your Feelings About Living with Your Elder

It is normal for caring family members and caregivers to experience a wide range of feelings about the decision to provide an elder family member with a home. Some of these feelings can be negative; others will be positive. It is important for your family to recognize these feelings and openly discuss them with family, friends, clergy, the primary-care physician, or a professional therapist.

As you read over the following, think about your negative feelings. It is common for a family to feel responsibility or obligation to provide a home for their elder family member. Your family may also feel some guilt for not wanting their elder to live with them. Or you may experience resentment toward other family members for not helping or offering their homes or support. Resentment toward your elder for disrupting or changing the normal routine in your household may also surface. Additional feelings may include concerns regarding the lack of family privacy and the additional financial burden.

Some caregivers and family members may have positive feelings about your elder moving in. Communicating and understanding your elder's feelings will help him feel more comfortable in his new home. Your family may feel useful for helping their elder in his time of need and be appreciative of their elder for choosing to live with them. By being generous and welcoming your elder family member into your home, your family may feel satisfaction for improving his quality of life. Your elder's role as grandfather to your children may also strengthen family relationships.

Think about how you feel about your elder moving in with your family.

Expressing these positive feelings will help your elder feel welcomed. He will feel that he retains some control over his living situation and other parts of his life, making the transition from independent living to partial dependence smoother and less stressful.

Thinking About Your Relationship

Before deciding whether living with you is the best choice for your elder, you should consider your family's feelings.

❦ The Story of Harold and Kathy

Harold and Kathy and their children visited his elderly mother every weekend for ten years. Even though they often wanted to do other things, they felt a strong obligation to visit her. Harold's mother lived in a small apartment only thirty minutes away by car. Although there were many seniors in the apartment building, his mother preferred to play cards and Scrabble™ with a select group of women. When his mother became ill and was no longer able to maintain her apartment, Harold and Kathy considered having her live with them. However, they were also concerned about taking her from her few friends, which might increase her isolation and make her dependent on them twenty-four hours a day. The obligatory weekly visits combined with his mother's demanding personality had created family problems in the past, so both were concerned about how Harold's mother would fit in with their family, work schedules, and other daily family activities.

Think about your usual weekend or one-week visit with your elder and imagine how it would be to live with her.

1. What is the longest period of time your family has visited or lived with your elder?

2. Do you feel obligated to spend time visiting with your elder?

3. Do you feel happy and relaxed during the visit, and leave with good feelings?

4. Do you feel relieved when the visit is over?

5. Do you feel anxious or worried before or after the visit?

6. Does your elder have habits, such as smoking or drinking, that you would rather not have in your home?

7. Will it be difficult for your family to balance work schedules, family time, caring for children and pets, and providing personal care for your elder?

8. Does your family lack the energy to handle the extra household chores and responsibilities?

9. Who will provide most of the daily care and supervision?
   Name of individual(s) #1 _____
   Name of individual(s) #2 _____

It is important to reflect on your elder's personal characteristics. This will help you determine if your family is compatible with her. Think about experiences and conversations you have had with her. Think about how she responds to suggestions, criticism, or praise and whether she prefers solitude or social situations.

---

*Think about how easy or difficult it will be
to balance caring for your family and elder.*

*Think about how much your family enjoys
spending time with your elder family member.*

Use the following checklist to help you think about her personal qualities.

YOUR ELDER'S PERSONAL QUALITIES

Please check the closest response. My elder family member is:

Column 1

_____ active

_____ candid

_____ content

_____ cooperative

_____ easy to talk to

_____ encouraging

_____ friendly

_____ generous

_____ good-natured

_____ happy

_____ independent

_____ kind

_____ self-motivated

_____ social

_____ flexible

Total _____

Column 2

_____ lazy

_____ manipulative

_____ dissatisfied

_____ demanding

_____ difficult to talk to

_____ controlling

_____ disagreeable

_____ selfish

_____ temperamental

_____ sad

_____ dependent

_____ discouraging

_____ mean

_____ antisocial

_____ stubborn

Total _____

If most of the lines checked are in column 1, your elder should be easy to live with in your home.

If most of the lines checked are in column 2, your elder may be difficult to live with in your home.

ELDER-CARE AND ASSISTANCE CHECKLIST

Financial activities

___ organizing and paying bills

___ handling basic banking activities

Homemaking activities

___ laundry

___ housecleaning

Meal preparation

___ assistance with meal preparation

___ assistance with eating

___ meals-on-wheels needed

___ special diet needed

Mobility

___ walks without assistance

___ uses walker or cane

___ no balance problems

___ balance problems

___ uses furniture to maintain balance

___ uses wheelchair

___ bedridden

___ needs medical equipment and supplies

Nursing care

___ blood pressure check

___ dressing changes

___ injections

___ medication management

___ other_____

Personal care

___ bathing

___ brushing hair and teeth

___ dressing

___ incontinence care

___ personal hygiene

___ other_____

Supervision

___ daytime

___ nighttime

___ twenty-four hours per day

Transportation

___ to medical appointments

___ to social activities

___ other _____

EVALUATION

After reviewing your elder's feelings and personal qualities, her care needs, and your family's feelings, please answer the following questions.

Do you still feel living with your family is the best choice for your elder?

If your answer is "yes" or you are undecided, continue reading this chapter.

If your answer is "no," and financial resources are moderate to high, turn to chapter 4, "Living in a Retirement Community," or chapter 5, "Living in an Assisted Living Facility."

If your answer is "no," and financial resources are limited, turn to chapter 5, "Living in an Assisted Living Facility," or chapter 6, "Living in an Adult-Care Home."

If you are continuing to read this chapter, you may feel that living with family is the best choice for your elder. Or you may be undecided about what living situation is best for her. By evaluating communication and support from other family members, potential financial costs, work schedules, and preparing your home, you can decide how the changes in your day-to-day life might affect your family.

Family Support: Nearby and Long-Distance

Many elders have a family member living nearby; they may also have family living in other cities or states. When one member of the family accepts the responsibility of caring for an elder family member, this does not mean other family members no longer have any responsibility toward him. In fact, they may find that in addition to providing support to

Think about the needs of your elder family member.

the elder, they may also need to provide emotional and financial support and respite care or break time for the family members assuming the primary caregiver role.

Family support, even from a distance, can make a significant difference in the family relationship. Even if the actual time spent helping the caregiving family and elder is limited, it is the effort and the desire to stay in touch that will provide them with the understanding that they have not been abandoned by other family members.

🦋 The Story of Louise

After her divorce, Louise decided to ask her aging parents to live with her family to help with her household expenses. Although she had always had a good relationship with them, she had not lived with them in more than thirty years. When her elderly parents accepted her offer, Louise felt both relieved and anxious. During the first few months, Louise was able to balance her career and family needs. Her parents were independent; her mother helped with meal preparation, and her father worked on easy home projects. After living together for three months, her mother became ill and passed away. Her father's health also began to decline; his memory began to fail and his driving ability made him dangerous to himself and others on the road. When Louise tried to discuss her concerns with her father, he became belligerent. The situation continued to grow more difficult, with Louise repeatedly receiving calls at work from her father demanding more attention. She found herself feeling constantly worried and being distracted at work. She was short-tempered with her family. Louise approached her two brothers for help or respite time with their father. Both brothers explained they were too busy to have their father stay with them. They suggested she find him an apartment or place him in a retirement or assisted living facility. When Louise advised them of the cost, they told her it was her responsibility, because their father was living with her.

Talking with Your Family

Speak frankly and directly with other family members about your feelings and concerns regarding your elder moving in with your family. Hiding your true feelings can lead to resentment toward your elder or other family members.

Try not to alienate family members who are not offering your elder a home with their family. They may feel guilty because they can't provide an adequate living situation, direct care, or financial assistance. Let them know you may need some help in the future and hope they will be able to provide some support at that time.

It is important to include close and long-distance family members when major decisions regarding care are being made. This will allow them to feel they are contributing family members and that their suggestions and recommendations are important to you. If long-distance family members initially seem uninterested in participating or becoming involved with your elder's care, try to leave a comfortable way for them to become active family members in the future.

Long-distance family may find it more difficult to feel involved in decisions being made by family in another city or state. Offering financial assistance, maintaining telephone contact several times a week, or flying or driving to offer short-term support to family caring for the elder are three ways to feel involved in an elder's care.

Keep close and long-distance family members updated. Inform them about your elder's physical and emotional health, general capabilities, financial concerns, community support, and alternative housing options.

Family relationships may be strengthened by your elder's declining health and dependence on other family members. Siblings and other family members who have chosen different paths in life may find they bond or join forces to work on a plan for providing care and support to your elder and each other. Although relationships may be repeatedly tested—especially during times of crisis—by maintaining common goals and expectations, your family should be able to provide the emotional, physical, or financial support needed to help each other and alleviate the situation.

Don't be afraid to ask other family members if they can work with you and support your efforts to provide a home for your elder. Ask other family members if you can contact them in times of crisis, illness, or personal need.

Long-distance family may also remain just that: distant, remote, and detached from the daily routine of caring for your elder family member in your home. They may choose to remain uninvolved with your situation and concerns. They may distance themselves from you because they are uncomfortable, feel guilty, or have no interest in providing personal care or other assistance. Recognize these feelings, and accept them. A time may come in the future when these family members will feel able to offer some form of help.

Think about your conversations with family members regarding emotional, respite, and financial support.

Encourage them to remain in contact with you and to let you know when they can help in any way, large or small.

If your family remains adamant about not providing care, financial assistance, emotional support, or respite care, try to accept these feelings. Your role as caregiver will be easier if you do not have unrealistic expectations of other family members. Such expectations can lead to family feuding and estrangement.

Talking About Finances

It is important for your elder's family to understand and have a clear picture of his financial situation. If your elder is competent and able to manage his own financial affairs, he should be encouraged to continue making his own decisions. If he requires some assistance with keeping track of his finances, he should be encouraged to speak with an attorney about a durable general power of attorney, guardianship, or conservatorship, depending on his level of competence. If your elder is not able to make decisions on his own behalf, a family member should speak with an attorney about the best way to help him manage his affairs.

Discuss up front your elder's financial picture. Like many elders, he may have a real fear of poverty or losing control over his personal finances. Without a "nest egg" or savings, he may feel he has also lost the ability to manage his own affairs or to make choices regarding his living situation.

Your elder's finances may represent the difference between moving to a retirement community rather than to an adult-care home or hiring a caregiver rather than being placed in a nursing facility. Without his money, your elder may feel he is also without choices. Try to reassure him. Let him know his money will only be used for his needs, to pay his bills, and to help with previously agreed upon household expenses.

Your elder may be suspicious over family motives for "wanting financial information." He may unfairly perceive family as "trying to get my money" for their own personal use. As a result, he may be reluctant to discuss financial matters with you or may become secretive about his income and investments.

Financial matters may interfere with family relationships, especially when they are not clearly defined. One family member may feel he is assuming a greater financial burden than another. Or due to his involvement, he may feel that he is entitled to a greater portion of your elder's estate than are other family members. If financial issues become an area of disagreement between family members, contact an attorney to help establish financial guidelines and, if necessary, to complete legal documents that clearly define the role of family members in relation to your elder's financial affairs.

It is customary for your elder to contribute a portion of his monthly income to room, board, and general living expenses if he decides to live with your family. If he is selling his home or has a reasonable pension and/or Social Security benefits, this contribution should be within his budget. Be sure to clearly define his financial contribution to the household before he moves in with your family. This will help eliminate potential financial disputes.

Potential Costs for In-Home Care

The cost of services and programs for the elderly vary state to state; generally, they cost more in urban areas than in rural areas. Basic potential costs associated with moving your elder into your home can include:

adult day-care centers	moving costs
clothing	respite care
food and sundries	telephone calls
health care	transportation
home improvements	utility costs
in-home assistance	

By planning ahead and anticipating these costs, you can manage the financial aspects of shared and additional expenses. The Shared Household Expenses work sheet on the following page will help you organize these expenses and decide how to divide them.

Preparing Your Home for Your Elder Family Member

Every nuclear family has a unique relationship with other family groupings. Every family interacts in different ways with people outside its extended family. Every family has its own special way of doing daily household tasks, scheduling appointments, shopping for groceries, preparing meals, and paying bills.

When a new person, your elder, for instance, begins living with your family, the familiar routine may change in subtle or more dramatic ways. Your elder may prefer or require a diet different from the one you usually cook. Or grocery shopping may be more difficult if someone needs to stay with him. You may need to wait until another family member is available or call on a neighbor for assistance. You may need to rearrange your social activities around his need for care and supervision.

SHARING HOUSEHOLD EXPENSES WORK SHEET

For information on your elder family member's finances, please refer to Getting to Know Your Elder work sheet on page 18 in chapter 1, "There's No Place Like Home: Independent Living."

GENERAL MONTHLY COSTS	FAMILY PAYS	ELDER FAMILY MEMBER PAYS
rent or mortgage		
utilities		
gas		
electric		
water		
garbage		
telephone		
MEDICAL EXPENSES		
medical care		
medication		
medical equipment and supplies		
home health care		
OTHER EXPENSES		
insurance premiums		
credit cards		
food		
transportation		
moving expenses		
home modifications		
adult day care		
respite care		
other _____		

Your elder family member relinquishes some of his autonomy or independence when he moves in with your family. He may not be able to plan his day without considering the plans and work schedules of other family members. He may not be able to see friends unless he can obtain transportation from family members. He may not be able to watch his favorite television show because it is on at the same time as the favorite family television show. The way he spends his day is now closely linked to the daily routines and schedules of his family and/or caregiver.

Work Schedules

Most families have at least one adult working full-time. A second adult may work full-time, part-time, or primarily as a homemaker, taking care of small children or actively participating in volunteer work. When your elder moves in with your family, the customary schedules and routines may need to be adjusted to meet his needs. Consider your work schedules and how they will affect your ability to provide care for him.

Think about your responses and whether work schedules can be arranged to accommodate your elder family member.

❧ The Story of George and Carol

George is a salesman for a large furniture chain. His typical hours are 7:30 A.M. to 5:30 P.M., Monday through Friday. His workweek usually includes thirty hours in the office and twenty hours on the road. Occasionally, he is away from home overnight. His wife, Carol, is employed at a clothing shop twenty hours a week. She has arranged her work schedule around her children's schedule so she can get them ready for school in the morning and be home when they finish their school day.

Balancing her work schedule, her children's school and activities, and John's personal-care needs could quickly become an overwhelming and frustrating schedule for a lengthy period of time. Carol may find that in addition to her children's schedules, she is now responsible for helping John with personal care and meal preparation and in arranging supervision during the day and providing transportation to medical appointments, the pharmacy to pick up his medication, and the seniors center for activities.

WORK SCHEDULE WORK SHEET

1. What are your normal working days and hours?

2. What are your spouse's normal working days and hours?

3. Are your work hours firm?

4. Are your spouse's work hours firm?

5. Is it difficult for you or your spouse to take time off for an emergency?

6. Will it be difficult to arrange for other family members or friends to stay with your elder family member when you take vacation or respite time?

7. Will you need to arrange supervision for your elder when you and your spouse are at work?

8. Will the cost of providing supervision for your elder become a financial burden?

> If you answered "yes" to most of questions 3 through 8, living with family may not be the best choice for your elder.
>
> If you answered "no" to most of questions 3 through 8, it may be easy for your elder to live with your family.

Living Arrangements in Your Home

When your elder moves out of his home to live with nearby family or with family in another city, he leaves behind many memories, familiar surroundings, friends, personal belongings, and some of his independence. It is a period of transition—your elder becomes more dependent on his children or relatives despite his desire to remain independent. As he loses some control over his living situation and daily activities, he needs to reach a balance between his desire to remain independent and his need for care and assistance.

Several types of living situations are available when your elder moves in with your family. Your family home may have an apartment attached, separate living quarters, or a room in the main section of the house. Although a family may choose to remodel their home to accommodate him, many families cannot build an addition or make significant changes.

There are many advantages to having separate living quarters for your elder family member. It may allow him to bring some of his private possessions and furniture with him. Your elder may have his own bathroom and shower. A separate entrance can reinforce your elder's feelings of autonomy, independence, and privacy. The increased privacy will encourage him to invite friends to

Think about whether it would be easy or difficult to accommodate your elder in your family home.

the home. Your elder will also have quieter surroundings. And though your elder lives separately, he will still be close to family, making it easy to provide any needed supervision and assistance. However, if a significant amount of supervision and assistance is needed, it may be more difficult to provide constant supervision, especially in the evening. Separate quarters may be an unsafe home environment for your elder.

Or your elder may live in the main section of the house, sharing the kitchen, bathroom, and living areas. The advantages of this living arrangement include convenience to household areas and greater proximity to family in case of an emergency. This makes supervision for safety and assistance with care by family easier. There is also greater companionship between your elder and family members.

The disadvantages of this living arrangement include less privacy and autonomy for your elder and family. Shared facilities, including use of the kitchen, bathroom, and living area, may be less available to family members. There may be noise and distractions from other family members instead of quiet.

Safety in Your Home

The layout of your home can help you determine which living situation is best for your elder and your family. You need to consider his care needs and his ability to move safely around your home. Let's examine the layout and some of the safety features of your home.

Think about the safety features in your home.

Durable Medical Equipment and Supplies

To ensure your elder's safety in your home, it may be necessary to obtain some basic medical equipment and supplies. Known as durable medical equipment (DME), it includes such items as:

air mattresses	bedpans and urinals
commode chairs	respiratory machine
grab bars	shower stools
hospital beds	suction machines
infusion pumps	therapeutic shoes
patients lifts	transfer board
prosthetic devices	walkers, canes, or crutches
portable oxygen systems	wheelchairs
raised toilet seats	

How to Order Medical Equipment

Home medical equipment and supplies should be ordered through a business that specializes in these items or, for small items, your local pharmacy and drugstore. The staff at these stores know which items are covered by insurance and will often handle billing your insurance company. They work closely with doctors; rehabilitation, physical, occupational, and respiratory therapists; home health-care agencies; and medical social workers. Because they are familiar with the medical equipment, they can make recommendations for specific situations and assist with ordering specialized equipment. Most home medical companies will deliver the items to your home and set them up for you. Some may charge a small fee for this service.

To order medical equipment for home use, it is necessary to have personal information about your elder, including his height and weight.Medical information, including recent illnesses, chronic conditions, and a current diagnosis, will also be necessary. A prescription from your elder's primary-care physician will include the name and address of the person requiring the equipment; the diagnosis; a statement explaining why the equipment is needed; the length of time it is needed; and any specific instructions. This information should be faxed or given to the medical-supply company for insurance billing. Insurance information, including the policy and group numbers, must be provided. In addition, prior approval or pre-authorization from the insurance carrier or Medicaid caseworker must be provided to the medical-supply company.

HOME SAFETY WORK SHEET

1. Is your home on one level or is it multilevel? one _____ multilevel _____

2. If it is multilevel, how many stairways and steps are there? _____

3. Is it necessary for your elder to walk up or down stairs to get into your home or to the house's main living area?

4. Does your elder have difficulties with his balance?

5. Is your elder in any danger of falling?

6. Has your elder ever fallen at home?

7. Does your elder have difficulty getting out of bed, out of a chair, or standing up from the toilet?

8. Is it difficult for your elder to take a shower or bath by himself?

9. Is it difficult for your elder to get up at night by himself to use the bathroom?

> If you answered "yes" to most of these questions, your elder will need some supervision for safety.
>
> If you answered "no" to most of these questions, your elder should be safe living in your home.

If your elder family member would benefit from home medical equipment, a family member, physician, or health-care professional, such as a physical, occupational, or respiratory therapist, or a social worker, may initiate a request for it.

Medicare

It is important to work through a reputable medical-supply company that is Medicare-approved and that will also bill Medicaid if needed. Durable medical equipment is covered under Part B of your elder's Medicare policy. After the annual one hundred dollar deductible has been paid, it pays 80 percent of the cost of necessary equipment prescribed by his primary-care physician and approved by Medicare.

Some of the equipment can be rented; other equipment may need to be purchased. Most of the medical-equipment companies will contact the insurance company for pre-authorization or prior approval, bill the company, and deliver medical equipment to your home.

Medicaid

Items covered by Medicaid require pre-authorization or consent from your Medicaid caseworker and a prescription from the primary-care physician. Medicaid coverage varies from state to state and in some cases covers items that are not covered by Medicare or private insurance.

Private-Insurance Managed Care

Private-insurance policies have different benefits and coverage requirements. Some may have no benefits; others may cover the cost of rental or purchase from 50 to 100 percent. Many insurance companies require pre-authorization before they will approve payment of the equipment. The medical-equipment company or health professional ordering the equipment should be able to contact them for authorization. Check the insurance policy under durable medical equipment before ordering any equipment.

Free Medical-Equipment Rental

In some areas, social service organizations, such as the American Cancer Society or Easter Seals, or service clubs, such as the Rotary, Kiwanis, or the Elks, may provide free loaner equipment. These service clubs and some social service agencies may also offer financial assistance for specific cases.

DURABLE MEDICAL EQUIPMENT COSTS

Equipment	Medicare-covered	Medicaid-covered	Private insurance	Rental cost	Purchase cost	Comments
Cane	Yes	Yes	Yes	—	$7–$15	Most insurance pays for only one device to assist with walking. If more than one device is needed, the medical-equipment company usually bills your insurance for the more expensive one.
Quad cane	Yes	Yes	Yes	—	$25–$45	A quad cane can provide additional stability.
Folding front-wheel walker	Yes	Yes	Yes	$20–$35 per month	$100–$125	Covered by insurance as rental or purchase.
Wheelchair	Yes	Yes	Yes	—	$250–$400 for standard 24"–27" chair, including footrests	For specialized wheelchairs, talk with a rehabilitation or physical therapist.
Portable commode chair	No	Yes, will purchase but not rent	May depend on policy	$20–$35 per month plus extra $5–$10 fee for the bucket	$85–$115 with lid and back	If the bathroom is on a different floor or walking is difficult, Medicare may help pay for this item.
Raised toilet seat 4" high	No	Yes	May depend on policy	—	$16–$40 $45–$60 with grab bars attached	May not be recommended for heavy or awkward people.
Grab bars	No	Yes	May depend on policy	—	$10–$35	Cost may vary, depending on the finish.

The Layout of Your Home

Accessible Doorways and Hallways

The doorways should be wide enough for easy access with a walker or wheelchair. A standard doorway is 32 inches wide; corridors are usually 3 feet wide and 6 to 8 feet high. The average turning space required by a wheelchair is 6 feet by 6 feet. A standard wheelchair is 24 to 27 inches wide. Add $1\frac{1}{2}$ inches to each side of the wheelchair to allow for hand, finger, or knuckle clearance. A standard walker is 16 inches wide.

Bedroom

It is important for your elder to have his own room to ensure some privacy for him and for your family. A bedroom on the first floor is preferable, because he may have difficulty walking up and down stairs without supervision. Set up the room with basic furniture and familiar items. Try to have it sparsely furnished, eliminating any clutter that may present a safety hazard. A dresser with pull handles on the drawers is easiest to use. If your elder has difficulty controlling his bladder or bowel, a bed liner or waterproof pad may be placed on the bed. If needed, bed rails can be placed on the bed to ensure safety in the evening.

Place on the wall or dresser a large-print calendar and clock to help him remember the days of the week and time of day. A comfortable, easy-to-get-out-of reclining chair and a television and/or radio can help provide a homelike area in which he can relax. An easily accessible telephone or intercom system should be placed in the room as well.

Bathroom

Your elder family member may need to share the bathroom with your family, but try to give him the bedroom closest to it. Nearby access to the bathroom makes it easier for him to get up in the middle of the night to use the toilet. The bathroom should have simple and inexpensive safety devices, such as grab bars, a raised toilet seat, a nonskid bath mat, and a shower stool. This will help to prevent fatigue and falls in the bathroom. As a safety precaution, you may need to remove throw rugs from the bathroom and kitchen areas to prevent your elder from tripping on the edges and injuring himself. Check the width of the doorway for wheelchair or walker access.

Supervise your elder's first shower to be sure he can safely step into a bathtub or shower, and adjust the water to the correct temperature. One in every ten elderly burn victims is injured from bathing in water that is too hot. If necessary, your family can lower the temperature in the hot-water heater and get an energy-efficient faucet to help regulate the water flow. Placing color indicators on the hot and cold faucets, blue for cold and red for hot, may also be helpful. A handheld shower and a shower stool will help ensure your elder's safety while taking a shower. If taking a shower proves to be too difficult due to fatigue, poor balance, or difficulty getting in and out of the shower, consider giving your elder a sponge bath. Or have him take a shower only under the supervision of one or more people. If nighttime bathroom use presents a risk of falling, consider purchasing or renting a portable commode chair to place next to your elder's bed. Give him a bell so he can ring for assistance.

Kitchen

If your elder can competently use the kitchen facilities, encourage his independence and participation in meal preparation. Be sure he knows how to use the appliances and the stove properly. Sometimes a person with mild confusion forgets to turn appliances off, or uses them incorrectly. Remove throw rugs and, if necessary, stove handles to prevent the stove or oven from being turned on. Childproof (or elderproof) with safety latches cabinets containing medication, poisons, and cleaning solutions. If necessary, use a gate to limit access to the kitchen. Allow him access to the kitchen only with supervision.

Yard

Encourage your elder to go outdoors when the weather is nice. He may be able to help in the garden, do small projects with tools, or enjoy sitting outside and reading a book. Look out for uneven surfaces, tree roots, stones, and yard clutter, which can present a safety hazard.

Other Considerations

Chores

If your elder can take an active and helpful role in the family, have him help with basic chores. Preparing a simple meal, dusting the house, making his bed in the morning, playing with the children, walking the dog, or watering the plants are easy ways for him to feel that he is contributing to the household.

Children

Your elder may love visits from his grandchildren. He may enjoy their enthusiasm, energy, and companionship during their short visits, but living with them can be a different experience. The noise and constant activity of children can be tiring for him and may interfere with his need for quiet and privacy. If he is demanding and requires lots of attention, he may feel his needs should take precedence over the needs of the children. The children in turn may resent him for the lack of attention they receive from their parents. The caregiver or primary family member should explain to your elder and the children that they are both important and will have to share some of their time and attention.

Pets

While many elders enjoy the company of a small dog or cat, some do not care for animals. In addition, pets can present a danger by running under their feet, causing them to fall or lose their balance. Or elders may not care for the animal smell or fur. A pet, however, can also be a companion. Many dogs may be trained to alert an elder family member to visitors, telephone ringing, stove buzzers, and fire.

In this chapter you and your elder family member have examined your positive and negative feelings about him moving into your home. You have visualized visits with him and thought about his personal characteristics and care needs, as well as explored family communication and support. You have considered the main features of the house and how to accommodate both your elder's and your family's need for privacy.

Look at these key phrases about your feelings, and check the appropriate lines.

YOUR FEELINGS TOWARD YOUR ELDER

Column I

_____ positive feelings toward your elder

_____ easy to balance caring for your elder

_____ enjoy time with elder family member

_____ easy to be with

_____ minimal care needed

_____ good family support

_____ no financial concerns

_____ easy to accommodate with work schedules

_____ easy to accommodate in family home

_____ safe in family home without supervision

Total _____

Column 2

_____ negative feelings toward your elder

_____ difficult to balance caring for your elder and family responsibilities

_____ do not enjoy time with elder family member

_____ difficult to be with

_____ moderate to high level of care needed

_____ inadequate family support

_____ some financial concerns

_____ difficult to accommodate with work schedules

_____ difficult to accommodate in family home

_____ not safe in family home without supervision

Total _____

   If most of the lines checked are in column I, your elder should be able live with you. Turn to chapter 3, "Getting Help in Your Home," for information on resources. Turn to chapter I, "Your Guide to Resources," for additional information.

   If most of the lines checked are in column 2, your elder may need to consider other alternatives to living with you. If your elder's income is moderate or high, turn to chapter 4, "Living in a Retirement Community," and chapter 5, "Living in an Assisted Living Facility." If his income is low, turn to chapter 5, "Living in an Assisted Living Facility," and chapter 6, "Living in an Adult-Care home."

Chapter 3

Getting Help in Your Home

—————— ❦ ——————

This chapter is designed to help your family locate and effectively use community and government services and programs available to seniors living in their own homes or living with family. Resources for people living in other settings, such as retirement communities, assisted living facilities, and adult-care homes, will be reviewed in later chapters. Additional resources, such as low-income utility programs and other helpful social service programs, will be addressed in chapter 11, "Your Guide to Resources."

Warning Signs of Caregiver Burnout

Although *When Aging Parents Can't Live Alone* does not focus on caregiving, it is important to be aware of one of the most common and most difficult aspects of living with or providing care to an elder family member: Caregiver burnout, that feeling of being overwhelmed while receiving few thanks and appreciation, is evident in many loving caregivers and family members and, unless addressed, can interfere with one's ability to provide quality care by reducing one's physical stamina and draining emotional energy. If you think members of your family are beginning to experience burnout, watch for the following warning signs, symptoms, and feelings:

I am overwhelmed by all the daily household tasks, my job, and taking care of my family and elder.

My family doesn't look forward to getting up each day the way we used to.

My family has little or no life other than meeting the care needs and requests of our elder family member.

We have no time for fun family activities.

My family is constantly exhausted.

My family has difficulty sleeping uninterrupted through the night.

My family is short-tempered with our elder and each other.

My family feels frustrated and unable to please anyone.

My family feels anxious, stressed, and tense.

My family is unable to think clearly about important family issues.

I worry constantly about my family.

My family is beginning to feel resentful of or annoyed by small matters.

These feelings are experienced by many caring family members and caregivers. It's important for you to recognize such feelings and openly discuss them with family, friends, your physician, or a professional therapist. They may also be warning signs that having your elder live with you is not the best choice for him or for your family. Don't feel personally responsible if the living situation is not working—it takes at least two people, your elder family member and his primary caregiver, working together to make a new living situation run smoothly.

It may be helpful to keep a daily journal to record both your family's feelings about being caregivers and a dated summary of your elder's physical and emotional care. Try to recognize these feelings and physical symptoms in yourself and other family members. Continuing to provide care to your elder when you are tired, frustrated, dulled, and impatient can lead to a health crisis for you, the caregiver, your family, and your elder.

How to Handle Burnout

The Story of Jane

Jane loved her eighty-seven-year-old mother. She found her agreeable, funny, and even helpful with household chores. It was important to Jane that her mother be comfortable and happy in her twilight years. Several years after moving in with Jane and her family, her mother began displaying signs of progressive Alzheimer's disease. Her mother seemed to have difficulty remembering how to return to her home after going for a walk. Sometimes at night she wandered from her bedroom and was unable to find her way back to it. Jane realized she needed to increase her mother's daily supervision to twenty-four hours a day.

With her husband working and her children at school, the task of providing supervision fell to Jane. Along with her family responsibilities, she also felt obligated to care for her mother. Jane found herself physically and emotionally drained by the constant pressures placed on her by her mother's needs and those of her family.

Before long, Jane's health began to suffer from lack of sleep. When routine tasks, such as grocery shopping and banking, required her to leave her mother at home alone, she found herself rushing through them and constantly worrying about her mother. She felt troubled when leaving her alone, fearing, "What if something should happen to her while I am gone?"

It was not easy for her to speak with her family and siblings about getting help from them. She feared they would say, "We told you not to try to care for her on your own," or "Maybe it's time you placed her in a home." As Jane contemplated her options, she decided her own exhaustion was interfering with her caregiving responsibilities. She wanted to do what was best for her mother, yet she felt guilty for not being able to handle everyone's needs. She decided to explore options that would give her a break from the daily caregiving.

When you identify the signs of caregiver burnout, it is important to take time for yourself. Arrange regular breaks during the week to allow you the necessary time to unwind, shop for groceries, have your hair done, or work out at the gym. This time away from caregiving should give you increased energy and renew your enthusiasm for caring for your elder.

For respite or a break in caregiving, you may decide to contact a family member, friend, or community agency. Arrange periods of time during the week when a friend or family member can relieve you, or hire someone to come to your home to stay with your elder for a few hours two or three times a week. Contact your local church, synagogue, or fraternal or volunteer service organizations, such as the Rotary Club, the Elks Lodge, or the Kiwanis, for assistance. Consider enrolling your elder in an adult day-care program several times a week.

Finding Help Through the Yellow Pages

It is important to approach the task of locating in-home services in an organized way. When you look at available services, the Yellow Pages of your local phone book are an invaluable tool. It will be helpful to become familiar with this section of the telephone book. Open your telephone book to "Index—Your Guide to the Yellow Pages," where you will see thousands of listings for businesses and services. For example:

In a colored section in the front of the telephone book, you will probably find city, county, state, and U.S. government offices.

Local community services are located at the front of the phone book. Look under Information and Referral for helpful listings, such as Helpline and Crisis Intervention Services. Look under Health for specific illnesses or agencies. Tel-Med numbers provide simple explanations of health-related issues, legal concerns, and questions about entitlement programs, including Social Security and Medicare. Look under Legal Assistance and Senior Services for additional services.

For specific categories found in the Yellow Pages, look in appendix A of this book.

Finding In-Home Services

When your elder requires services in the home, you will find there is a wide range of help available from community and government agencies. The cost of these services depends on your elder's income, physical needs, and insurance benefits. Listed below are four ways your elder can receive help in the home.

I. Free Services

Free services may be available through community, state, or federal agencies. The availability of free or no-cost services varies, depending on your location. For example, you'll find more agencies in a large city than in a small, rural town. The agencies providing these services have eligibility guidelines or specific requirements for receiving their help. These guidelines may depend on your elder's financial or emergency needs, his income, or his medical condition and care needs.

Some agencies require basic information about your elder before they will provide any assistance. Other agencies offer immediate assistance or have a waiting period between the time of application and the time the service is provided.

For example, the American Cancer Society may assist cancer patients promptly with a free loan for durable medical equipment and help with transportation to medical appointments.

Easter Seals may have your family complete an application to be eligible for a onetime, limited financial-assistance program. There may be a waiting period while the application is processed.

2. Family Members

Help from family members or friends includes any assistance provided by people with whom you have a friendship or family relationship. This help may be free or be a negotiated fee-for-service. It can include part-time supervision or assistance with shopping, meal preparation, personal-care needs, housework and chores, transportation to medical appointments or church, and yard work. Sometimes family members or friends agree to provide assistance for a limited time. However, when the length of time exceeds more than a few weeks, they may feel overwhelmed by the responsibility and may try to limit the help they provide. Your family may want to contact the state agency on aging, which may have a program that pays family members to provide care to an elder or disabled family member.

3. Insurance Benefits

Insurance benefits can help pay for some medical care and other related services. If a person requires skilled nursing care from a home health-care agency or durable medical equipment for home, many managed care and HMO programs as well as insurance policies, including Medicare, Medicaid, and private carriers, provide benefits. Some require pre-authorization or permission from the insurance company before they will provide any services. Some long-term-care policies may have benefits for adult day care or limited help in the home. Due to strict eligibility guidelines, the benefits in each individual policy must be carefully checked.

4. Fees for Service

Fees for service are charges for help from an individual or agency. Some agencies work with your family, billing insurance when possible, or use a sliding scale based on income to determine their fee. Payment for services provided in the home can be expensive.

Hiring In-Home Assistance

The amount of extra help you will need to provide care and supervision for your elder depends upon several factors:

> his level of care or daily medical and personal-care needs
>
> his need for supervision
>
> his awareness of his surroundings
>
> the home's safety features

Fortunately, there are many avenues to explore before you decide to make a major economic investment. Some in-home services are covered by insurance; others may be free through community or government agencies. By being aware of the costs involved, insurance benefits, and the availability of low-cost or free services in the home, you should be able to develop a cost-effective plan.

Other Considerations

Have the applicant come to your home for a trial visit. Observe her appearance and interaction with the person she will be caring for. Clearly define her responsibilities and chores. Remember to discuss benefits before hiring anyone. Decide on a reasonable probation period, usually one to three months. Check your homeowner's policy for any provisions or coverage for a home-care worker. Check with the Social Security office regarding deducting Social Security and Medicare taxes. This is necessary if you pay a home-care worker more than one thousand dollars cash wages per calendar year. Anyone you hire must complete a W-2 form. To contact the Social Security Administration for information, call toll-free 1-800-772-1213.

Levels of Care

Throughout this book you will see the phrase "level of care." This refers to the amount of assistance and medical attention an individual needs. The level of care standards will varies in each of the home settings and alternatives to home. The level of care needed by your elder may also change. He may begin as a level 1 and yet a year later need level 2 or level 3 due to an increase in his care needs.

The Story of Martin L.

When Martin was seventy-six years old, he decided to live in a retirement community. He was an independent and active man who enjoyed socializing with other seniors and walking three miles every day. He was proud of his self-sufficiency and his ability to remain physically active. Pleased with his lifestyle, Martin had a difficult time imagining a different one.

One night, Martin tripped on an uneven piece of curb. After a visit to the hospital emergency room, he returned with a sling over his broken shoulder. Although care and help from staff were available at the retirement community, Martin had never needed them. Now he found he needed help with dressing, bathing, and grooming. He felt frustrated by his inability to care for himself, irritated because of his clumsiness, and vulnerable by his reduced capabilities. In addition, his level of care had changed from a level 1 to a level 2, which increased his monthly payments.

Martin expressed these private feelings to other residents and staff by constantly complaining and asking for attention. Although he did not vent all his unexpressed feelings, he worried about the future.

"Will I be able to care for myself again?"

"How long will I need help?"

"I don't know if I can afford the extra charges for care."

"I don't like having a stranger help me bathe and dress. I'm a very private person."

"Where is my family when I need them?"

Because he needed help with dressing and bathing, Martin felt he had lost control of his life. He realized his injury was a temporary inconvenience, yet he feared he might permanently lose his independence. He had difficulty putting his feelings in perspective while his shoulder healed. Within six weeks, he was again feeling less dependent on others and able to resume his normal lifestyle and activities.

Level I

If your elder needs minimal care or someone to stay with him during the day to provide limited supervision and help with meals, it may be necessary to hire a person to come to his home. This person—a companion, healthy senior, home health aide, or college student—should be responsible, flexible, trustworthy, caring, and have some basic medical knowledge.

Level 2

If your elder requires moderate care or a more significant amount of supervision and assistance with medical care, medication management, bathing, dressing, eating, and toileting, you may prefer to hire someone who has worked as a home health aide or a licensed practical nurse (LPN) or in a medical setting. The cost of hiring a person with some experience ranges from eight to fifteen dollars per hour, depending upon where you live (urban areas tend to be higher than rural areas), the individual's experience, the amount of care needed, and whether you use a private-home health-care agency to find a home-care worker.

Level 3

If your elder requires maximum care or constant help and supervision with more complicated medical care up to twenty-four hours per day, a person with an extensive health-care background may be needed. A home health-care agency can help you find an assistant for twenty-four-hour care, or they may offer to find three people to work different shifts. This can be costly and is not covered by Medicare, Medicaid, and most private-insurance policies unless specific skilled nursing care requirements are met. If you feel your elder may need this level of care, please read chapter 10, "Using Home Health and Hospice Care."

How to Find a Skilled Caregiver

Whenever a family hires a person to provide personal care, it is necessary to use a reputable agency or to get personal references or recommendations. Unless you know someone to hire, it can be a difficult and time-consuming task. It is important to screen carefully the applicant's qualifications and training for work in your home. Fraud, theft, and misrepresentation by a home-care worker can and do occur.

If your elder has specific medical needs, such as dressing changes or insulin injections, it may be possible to train a person to provide this care. Some home health-care agencies will train caregivers in specific nursing tasks, but before hiring a home-care worker, know your elder's physical-care needs. Think about the days and hours when help is needed. Consider what you can afford to pay, and check your insurance policies for benefits and coverage for hiring help in the home.

Forms to Help You Hire Help in Your Home

Forms for Hiring Help in Your Home will help you screen applicants. Keeping Track of Your Resources and the Schedule Guide will help you contact agencies and organize your daily schedules and appointments. These forms may be found in appendix E at the back of this book.

Helpful Agencies and Programs

There are many agencies that can help your family locate home-care workers, adult day-care programs, and community and government services.

State Area Agencies on Aging

The state area agencies on aging (AAA) listed in appendix B of this book provide free assistance to people older than sixty-five. They offer information and referral to social service agencies, homemaker services, transportation, home-delivered meal programs, seniors centers, home health aide services, chore and home repairs, and legal advice. They also offer free assistance in the home to low-income seniors.

A caregiver list of private home health aides, homemakers, and companions may be available. Usually, people on this list are screened for criminal records, although individual interviews are still necessary and strongly recommended.

If you need more information or assistance, ask to speak with a caseworker or screener who is knowledgeable about available services and programs and who may be able to help you screen the individuals on the caregiver list.

Senior and Disabled Services

Senior and Disabled Services (SDS) assists people with limited income who are older than sixty-five or are disabled. It may have a list of available caregivers, some with nursing training. Some states have programs that pay a family member to provide the necessary patient care. Contact the nearest senior and disabled services office to obtain eligibility and income guidelines, which can vary from state to state.

For example, in Oregon ask for Oregon Project Independence (OPI), a program for low-income homebound seniors, which for free or a small fee provides home health aides, homemaker services, assistance with grocery shopping, and meal preparation.

Veteran Affairs Office

Veteran Affairs (VA) services can come directly from the veteran facility or can be contracted by an outside agency. The person receiving services must have had an honorable discharge and a service-connected disability. This means your elder is receiving money for an injury received while in military service.

Some VA facilities can provide supervision in the home with a certified nurse's aide for short periods of time. Pre-authorization from Veteran Affairs is needed. Contact the Social Work or Benefits department of your nearest Department of Veteran Affairs office for information and assistance.

Social Service Agencies

Social service agencies or hospital social work, case-management, or discharge planning departments often receive telephone calls and brochures from individuals or agencies offering medical and in-home services. Although they cannot recommend a person to hire, they can guide you to more reliable people, as well as provide you with lists and information on the more appropriate agencies. For more information on how social workers and case managers can help you, review chapter 7, "Moving Through Hospital Acute Care."

Home Health-Care Agencies

Home health-care agencies are private or nonprofit businesses that provide a wide range of health services in your home. Their staff includes health professionals, including registered and licensed practical nurses; physical, speech, and occupational therapists; medical social workers; and supplementary staff, such as home health aides, certified nurses, and rehabilitation aides. The home health-care agency requires information about your elder's medical history, medications, and personal-care needs. It can contact your elder's primary-care physician's office, medical facilities, and insurance company to obtain pre-authorization and other medical information. More information on how home health-care agencies can help will be presented later in this chapter and in chapter 10.

Ways to Find In-Home Help

Place an advertisement in the classified section of the local newspaper. For example: "Caregiver wanted for elderly man. Must be caring person with some nursing experience. Light housework. Needed from 7 A.M. to 6 P.M., Monday through Friday. Excellent salary and benefits. References required. Call 555-1234 between 6 P.M. and 9 P.M. if interested."

Your local church or synagogue sometimes keeps lists of members who are willing to assist people in their home. They are nondenominational and assist people of different faiths. Most of these individuals are volunteers.

Obtain a recommendation from someone you know and trust and who knows you, your elder, and your present situation. Of course, an interview, screening, and references are still necessary.

Contact a local university or community college that has a nursing program. Nursing faculty often wish to give their students real-world experience. By discussing your elder's medical care with the staff, they may be able to locate an interested nursing student to assist you in your home.

Adult Day-Care Centers

When to Consider Using an Adult Day-Care Center

The primary goal of adult day care is to keep your elder in a homelike environment for as long as possible. These centers, often affiliated with a multipurpose seniors center, hospital, or medical facility, provide programs in a structured setting for aging or disabled people. Although most who attend adult day-care centers require some form of assistance, others may view it as a social setting. You may want to consider an adult day-care center for your elder when he is isolated or alone during the day, or if he is unsafe without supervision. He may also need assistance with basic medical care and activities of daily living. For the elder who prefers socialization and recreational activities, most adult day-care centers provide a wide range of recreational and social programs, one to two meals daily, and transportation assistance to and from the center. In addition, your family or caregivers can receive needed respite from the daily caregiving tasks. Evaluate a potential center by using the following criteria:

Hours
The usual working hours at an adult day-care center are Monday through Friday, from 8 A.M. to 5 P.M. Some centers may have extended, evening, or weekend hours for an additional fee. Contact the adult day-care centers in your area for their hours of service.

Staff
An adult day-care center should have qualified and experienced staffing, including a full-time registered nurse, a licensed practical nurse, or a nurse's aide and easy access to a social worker and therapists. The professional staff should be available to help the family with arranging transportation, getting information, and making referrals to other agencies for necessary in-home support.

Regulation
There are more than three thousand adult day-care centers nationwide, most of which opened from 1986 to 1990. There are no nationwide regulations, with each state being responsible for implementing its own policies, and these vary state to state. Licensure is required in only twenty-five states; certification is required in twenty-four states.

Fees

Daily fees range from about $20 to $150 per day. The higher fees are usually charged to people who require a high level of supervision and medical care. The average fee range is approximately forty dollars per day. These fees vary from state to state; urban areas tend to charge more than rural areas. When compared with the cost of supervision in the home or in a nursing facility, adult day-care fees are reasonable. Some centers also have a sliding scale fee or base their fees on economic need.

The day-care fee can include assistance with the following services: Trained personnel can assist your elder with his activities of daily living, such as bathing, grooming, personal hygiene, dressing, toileting, eating, and medication management or assistance with administering the proper medication at the proper time. Nursing staff can provide nursing care for dressing changes; injections; monitoring blood pressure, pulse, and respirations; diabetic management; and other necessary medical care. Therapeutic activities, such as physical, speech, occupational, and rehabilitation therapies, as well as social activities, may also be available to seniors attending the day-care center. Supervision for people with Alzheimer's disease or general confusion is also provided.

Insurance Coverage and Benefits

Check your elder's insurance policy to determine his coverage. The insurance company may also require a referral or order from your primary-care physician before approving the benefit. Medicare does not pay for adult day-care centers. Medicaid does provide benefits for adult day care in some states. Some newer private-insurance and long-term-care policies may have limited benefits for attending an adult day-care center. Private pay may need to be considered. Some adult day-care centers, however, will also have a sliding or flexible fee to determine the rate based on the individual's finances and care needs.

The Choosing an Adult Day-Care Center checklist found at the end of this chapter will help you evaluate the adult day-care centers you are considering. In addition to completing the checklist, stay for a lunchtime meal, ask permission to watch the therapist, talk with the registered nurse about your loved one's care needs, and speak with the social worker about any concerns.

Also inform your elder's primary-care physician of your decision to enroll your family member in the adult day-care program. Your doctor may have instructions or orders for the staff about his care.

Additional Services and Programs

Companionship

This private-pay or free service is usually provided by a nonprofessional or volunteer and may cost less than hiring a person who has medical training. The cost for hiring a companion ranges from eight to twelve dollars per hour and may have a required minimum number of hours per visit. Companions may be found through a private nursing service, an advertisement in the newspaper, a church or synagogue, or word of mouth from a friend or neighbor. A companion is not covered under the Medicare or Medicaid programs. However, some community organizations may have a volunteer program that provides visitors who won't charge to assist your elder in his home. These volunteers may be elderly, which means they often provide companionship only and not additional homemaking services.

Telephone/Emergency Services

Senior Hot Line

If your elder is home alone during the day and you are not able to consistently call him to ensure his safety, a seniors hot line or telephone service can be convenient. For a small weekly or monthly fee, an agency (or sometimes a church, synagogue, or religious organization or service clubs such as Rotary, Elks, or Kiwanis) will call your elder at home at a specific time every day. If they do not receive an answer, or they determine that your elder is in danger or having a difficult time, they will call his first or second emergency contact. If necessary, they can go to his home. If there is still no response from your elder, the seniors hot line staff will contact emergency services.

Lifeline/MedicAlert

You have probably seen or heard the advertisement. An elderly person falls, and then pushes a waterproof button on a cord around his neck or around his wrist and says, "Help me, I've fallen and I can't get up." This button activates Lifeline by automatically dialing the twenty-four-hour Lifeline response center.

When your elder applies for this service, the agency setting it up obtains a confidential medical history and personal information, including emergency contacts. If he is unable to respond, the trained personnel at the Lifeline center will contact the people on his information sheet or call an ambulance, the fire department, or other emergency personnel.

The fee for Lifeline is about thirty dollars per month. There is usually a set-up fee and a small monthly charge. However, some agencies have a sliding scale or flexible fee for those with limited income. Indigent elders can receive the service at no charge.

For information on this service, contact the nearest senior and disabled services office, state area agency on aging, or hospital social work, case-management, or discharge planning department.

MedicAlert Bracelets

MedicAlert bracelets are helpful to emergency personnel because they provide valuable medical information during a medical emergency. A stainless-steel bracelet can be ordered for thirty-five dollars by calling 1-800-432-5378.

Meal Programs

Meals-on-Wheels/Loaves and Fishes

Meals-on-wheels and Loaves and Fishes programs provide meals free of charge or for a cost. Meals are delivered Monday through Friday during lunchtime. Special-diet lunches, such as diabetic or low-salt diets, can be requested. Information on this service may be obtained from your nearest state area agency on aging.

Seniors Centers

Your elder can travel to a seniors center to receive his meals. These centers are often managed by the community or a medical or a religious organization. In addition to meals, they support a wide range of social activities.

Hospital Cafeterias

Hospital cafeterias sometimes have seniors-discount meal programs. Contact your local hospital to inquire about this program.

Charity Meals

The Salvation Army and other missions may provide free meals to people in need. Social service agencies usually have lists of local free-meal programs for the homeless or low-income seniors.

Local Restaurants

Sometimes local restaurants deliver meals to an elder's home. They may also have a seniors-discount program. Often, elders who find it difficult to prepare their own meals but are still somewhat mobile take most of their meals in a local restaurant. In addition to a meal, they may spend time socializing and receiving supportive services from the restaurant staff.

Grocery Stores

Local grocery stores may have home-delivery services available for a nominal fee. Contact your local food store to inquire about their services.

Hire an Individual

A hired person can come to your elder's home several times a week to assist with his meal preparation. This person or family member can prepare easy-to-cook meals that can be made in advance and frozen. They may also assist with light housekeeping duties.

Transportation

Ambulance Services

Nonemergency ambulance services provide transportation only when a person is medically stable. They do not usually carry emergency equipment or have paramedics available. Some will provide portable oxygen during the transfer. This service may be indicated if your elder needs to recline or lie down during a transfer from the hospital to home or another facility, or from home to a medical appointment. Compared with emergency ambulance transportation, this service is economical. Cost ranges from $35 to $100 per ride, depending on whether the transfer requires a wheelchair or a gurney and the distance traveled.

Emergency ambulance services are used only in emergency situations and can be quickly reached by dialing 911. These ambulance services operate twenty-four hours a day, 365 days a year. Charges include the use of all medical equipment and the ambulance personnel. The all-inclusive base rate is $600 to $700, with an additional mileage charge of $10 per mile. Medicare covers 80 percent, and most private-insurance policies cover only 35 to 60 percent of the total ambulance fee. Please note that Medicare carefully reviews these charges and has been known to deny payment for this service.

Membership in a yearly ambulance service program is available in many communities with a local fire department or ambulance service. For a moderate fee ranging from $40 to $150 per year, the ambulance service bills the elder's insurance company, accepts the insurance payment, and writes off the balance. Contact your local fire department or ambulance service for information.

Taxi Services

Many taxi services provide excellent transportation services at a reasonable price. Wheelchair vans are often available and provide door-to-door service. The average cost of a taxi ride is $1.80 per mile, with a base rate of $2. This means an average taxi ride in the first mile costs $3.80. This rate reflects urban and rural areas. Some taxi companies have taxi script or discount books available for purchase that reduce the cost of each ride. For example, a $20 book with a 20-percent discount costs only $16.

Bus Services

Public bus service is available in many communities. Many cities provide wheelchair lifts in the public bus transportation system. Although this mode of travel is not as convenient for an elderly or disabled person, it is available at reasonable cost. Discount books with significant discounts may be available for seniors and disabled persons. Contact your local transit district for information on seniors-discount programs and schedules.

Free Transportation Services

Seniors centers provide transportation services to people older than sixty-five or who are disabled. They often have wheelchair vans available at no charge or for a small fee. Arrangements must be made in advance, because they can be busy.

The American Cancer Society may provide free transportation for cancer patients to medical appointments, radiation, and chemotherapy treatments. Contact your local ACS for information.

How Social Services and Health-Care Professionals Can Help You

If you are feeling overwhelmed by all the information about programs and services, talking with an experienced medical social worker, case manager, discharge planner, gerontologist, home health-care nurse, or geriatric-care manager can help. They can guide you through the information and help you focus on specific issues and problems. Social services and health-care professionals are trained to recognize potential social and medical problems, be knowledgeable about local and government resources, contact appropriate agencies for services, and provide follow-up to ensure that services are being furnished. They can act as an effective liaison between the family and physician.

Medical social workers, case managers, and discharge planners are employed by hospitals, medical clinics, nursing facilities, and home health-care agencies, or they may have a private practice. Their expertise is health-related issues in a hospital, medical facility or in the home.

The medical social worker helps your elder and family with emotional, social, financial, and environmental issues. They are trained to look at the whole person: where they live, their family dynamics, safety, and health-related, financial, and legal issues. If the family has questions and is unsure about what to do or where to turn, the medical social worker is familiar with community and government resources and should be able to help.

If your elder needs to change his current living situation on a temporary or permanent basis in order to seek medical care, rehabilitation, or supervision and assistance, your family needs to work closely with his doctor and the hospital case manager or social worker. Social workers and case managers can help your elder and family with the issues listed below. If your elder is not a patient in a health-care facility, call the social work department for information, or stop by the office. Medical facilities sometimes provide social work services to families in the community as a community service.

You may be able to hire a private medical or geriatric social worker to assist you. Be sure the professional is familiar with community resources and agencies for the elderly, since many specialize in a specific area. An effective social service professional can evaluate or assess the whole living situation, taking into account:

assessments of your elder's needs

arranging in-home supports and home safety evaluations

counseling services

explaining insurance benefits

financial assistance

application assistance

placement and long-term-care issues

referrals for home health care

referrals to community, state, and federal agencies for services

referrals for durable medical equipment and supplies

transportation assistance

support group information

When your elder and family meet with a case manager or social worker, you should:

write down any questions *before* the meeting

bring a second family member or friend, because volumes of information may be given to you at the meeting

write down pertinent information during the meeting

after the meeting, call the case manager or social worker with any additional questions

Review chapter 7, "Understanding Hospital Acute Care," for more information regarding medical social workers, case managers, and discharge planners.

Social Services and Health-Care Professionals

Geriatric-Care Managers

Geriatric-care managers (GCMs) are a combination social worker, nurse, and financial adviser. They can represent the absentee family—the adult children who live or work in another state and have limited time to travel to manage their parents' or relatives' affairs. Look for a social worker, nurse, gerontologist, counselor, or health professional with an experienced background in health and extensive knowledge of community resources and government programs for the elderly.

By hiring a GCM, your family can feel assured that your elder is receiving daily personal care and has easy access to someone who can help her with routine problems. Consider hiring a GCM when you must travel a considerable distance to supervise or assist your elder. If you work and are unable to get time to provide care to your elder, a GCM can help you make arrangements for personal and medical care. If the amount of time needed to evaluate, contact and arrange supportive care, and remain up-to-date on care needs exceeds the time your family has available, hiring a GCM may free up some of your time.

The GCM's average caseload or number of clients is between ten and thirty. If the GCM is responsible for more than thirty clients, carefully consider how much time she will be able to provide your elder with the care and services he needs.

🦋 The Robinson Family Hires a Geriatric-Care Manager

Most of the Robinson family lives in northern California. However, Grandma Robinson moved to Florida for the warm weather and to be near several close friends. Due to changes in her health, her care and homemaking needs increased, until it became hard for her to live safely in her home.

Despite several trips a year to Florida by her family, they felt it was difficult to handle her problems and financial issues, which seemed to be occurring weekly. They worried about her falling at home and felt guilty they weren't closer to provide help when she needed it. On one of their visits to Florida, they interviewed and hired a geriatric-care manager to assist Grandma Robinson with her daily care needs and financial issues and to monitor her need for changes in her living situation.

The geriatric-care manager talked with Grandma Robinson about her health concerns, fear of living in a nursing home, and her confidential wishes. He also spoke with her family on a regular basis, reassuring them of Grandma's condition and living situation.

When Grandma Robinson eventually needed to move to an assisted living facility, the geriatric-care manager worked closely with her and her long-distance family, ensuring that she had suitable living arrangements and also providing emotional support and counseling during her transition from independent to dependent living.

Hiring a Geriatric-Care Manager

The initial assessment and setup fee for a complete assessment of your elder's home, physical and mental health, economic and legal issues, and examination of insurance resources is $150 to $500. The GCM identifies current and potential problems and provides practical solutions. In addition to the assessment fee, an hourly fee of $20 to $150 may also be charged and billed by the minute, with a five-to-ten-minute minimum. The average cost per family for this service is approximately $85 per month, although families can expect to pay higher rates in large, metropolitan areas and low rates are usually for limited services, such as providing basic personal care. Extra charges can include telephone contacts, transportation, and legal fees.

Certification as a GCM is a recently recommended requirement, with the first certification test having been offered by the National Association of Professional Geriatric-Care Managers (NAPGCM) in 1996. If you decide to hire a GCM or other health-care professional, your family may want to contact the NAPGCM or the National Association of Private Geriatric Care Managers. Questions to Ask a Geriatric-Care Manager at the end of this chapter may also be helpful. Also see the listings for professional organizations in chapter 11, "Your Guide to Resources."

EVALUATION

Based on resources and community programs available to you, answer the following questions:

Do you feel living at home, independently, or living with your family is the best choice for your elder family member?

If your answer is "yes," turn to chapter 10, "Using Home Health and Hospice Care," and review basic home health-care services, and turn to chapter 11, "Your Guide to Resources."

If your answer is "no" or you are undecided, and your financial resources are moderate to high, turn to chapter 4, "Living in a Retirement Community," or to chapter 5, "Living in an Assisted Living Facility."

If your answer is "no" or you are undecided, and financial resources are low, turn to chapter 5, "Living in an Assisted Living Facility," or to chapter 6, "Living in an Adult-Care Home."

ELDER CARE AND ASSISTANCE CHECKLIST

Financial activities

____ organizing and paying bills

____ handling basic banking activities

Homemaking activities

____ laundry

____ housecleaning

Meal preparation

____ assistance with meal preparation

____ assistance with eating

____ meals-on-wheels needed

____ special diet needed

Mobility

____ walks without assistance

____ uses walker or cane

____ no balance problems

____ balance problems

____ uses furniture to maintain balance

____ uses wheelchair

____ bedridden

____ needs medical equipment and
supplies

Nursing care

____ blood pressure check

____ dressing changes

____ injections

____ medication management

____ other _____

Personal care

____ bathing

____ brushing hair and teeth

____ dressing

____ incontinence care

____ personal hygiene

____ other_____

Supervision

____ daytime

____ nighttime

____ twenty-four hours per day

Transportation

____ to medical appointments

____ to social activities

____ other _____

How to Keep Track of Your Services

Keeping Track of Your Services is a helpful form that can be found in appendix E at the back of this book. Use it after you have decided what type of care, supervision, and assistance would be most beneficial to your elder family member. It will help you organize telephone contacts and to keep track of services. Use a separate sheet for each agency you contact, and make extra copies of Keeping Track of Your Services, as needed. Here is an explanation of each category:

Date of contact: This is the date of your first call to an agency for information.

Name of agency: Record the name of the organization you are calling.

Telephone number: Record the telephone number and extension and/or fax number.

Name of contact person: Whom did you talk to at the agency? Record their name, title, and the best time to reach them. If they are working in a specific program, record the name of the program.

Date to call back agency: Ask for a specific time or day for you to recontact the agency. Or ask when you can expect a call or information from the agency. If services are needed immediately, inform the contact person of your urgency. Give them a reasonable amount of time to process your request for assistance. If you have not been contacted, call back within a day or two. Ask for the person you spoke to about services, and ask about the status of your request.

Available services: What services does the agency provide? Can it help with personal care, transportation, meals, homemaking, or skilled nursing care? Record the services the agency provides.

Start date for services: Record the date when the agency can begin providing assistance.

Cost of services: Record the service's hourly, daily, or weekly cost.

Are insurance benefits available? Record yes or no. Note which insurance carrier will provide benefits.

Is a doctor's order or prescription needed? Record yes or no.

Must an application be completed? Record yes or no. Ask the agency to send you the application, or consider saving time by picking it up at the agency office.

Schedule Guide

Find the Schedule Guide in appendix E. Use it to keep track of arrangements you make with individuals and agencies. If more than one agency will provide care or home support, you may find it difficult to remember all the days and times. Record the following information in the Schedule Guide after you have decided on your elder's care plan. Make extra copies of the guide, as needed.

Name of agency: Record the name(s) of the agency(ies) providing assistance.

Name of the person: Record the name(s) of the individual(s) providing help.

Telephone number: Record the telephone number of the agency or individual.

Hours: Record the specific hours the agency or individual will work. Record whether a split shift will be used. A split shift is when an agency or individual work at least two different times during the same day. For example, a companion can visit in the morning to help with getting out of bed, basic personal care, and breakfast preparation. She can return in the evening to assist with the evening meal and bedtime preparation.

Services provided: Record the services provided by the agency or individual. For example, the Schedule Guide could be completed, an example is given below.

SAMPLE SCHEDULE GUIDE

	Names of Agencies	Telephone Numbers of Agencies	Name of People Providing Care	Hours (split shift?)	Services Provided
Mon.	Senior Services	555-III-1234	Carrie, home health aide	7 A.M.–10 A.M. 6 P.M.–10 P.M.	Meal, bathing dressing, light housework
Tues.	same	same	same	same	same
Wed.	Carewise Home Health-Care Agency	555-222-4321	Maureen, RN	10 A.M. visit	Check blood pressure, change dressing
			Tom, physical therapist	12 P.M. visit	Gait training, transfers, and mobility

QUESTIONS TO ASK A
GERIATRIC-CARE MANAGER

1. What are the GCM's professional qualifications, i.e., experience, training, and degrees?

2. Is the GCM certified by the National Association of Professional Geriatric-Care Managers?

3. What is the private GCM's caseload; how many clients does he currently supervise?

4. What is the maximum number of clients the GCM will have at any one time?

5. Is the GCM familiar with local elder care?

6. In addition to the minute or monthly charge, are there any extra or hidden fees?

7. Is the GCM available twenty-four hours a day?
   If not, what are his normal working hours?_____

8. Does he have backup or someone who handles cases when he is unavailable?

9. Are there any services the GCM will not provide?
   If so, which services are not included? _____

10. How often and by what means will the GCM contact family?

11. Does he correspond by
    telephone _____ postal service _____ fax _____ e-mail _____

12. Is the GCM flexible and easy to work with?

13. Does the GCM have a proven track record or references you can contact?
    Reference #1:_____ Telephone #:_____
    I know this person: Professionally ____ Personally ____ Both ____
    Reference #2:_____ Telephone #:_____
    I know this person: Professionally ____ Personally ____ Both ____

14. Does the GCM have any conflicts of interest?

15. Does he receive a fee from clients and nursing homes simultaneously?

16. Does he have a financial interest in a long-term-care (nursing home, adult-care home) facility?

CHOOSING AN ADULT DAY-CARE CENTER

Choose at least two or three adult day-care centers to visit.

1. What is your first impression of the day-care center?

2. Is the day-care center clean? Are there any unpleasant odors?

3. Does it appear safe and uncluttered?

4. Is the day-care center affiliated with a medical facility?

5. Is the day-care center affiliated with a multipurpose seniors center?

6. What is the average number of people attending the day-care center?

7 What is the average age of the people attending the day-care center?

8. What activities are the people attending the day-care center involved in?

art or music therapy	physical therapy
recreational activities	one to two meals per day
counseling and social services	transportation
nursing care	other _____
occupational therapy	

9. Are they closely supervised by staff?

10. What services are offered: assistance with basic personal care

11. Are there specialized services or programs for people with Alzheimer's disease?

12. Does the staff work closely with your elder's physician, or are staff members willing to work with her?

13. Does the staff complete an initial interview or assessment with each person who enters the day-care program?

14. Does the day-care staff follow an individual-care plan for each person?

15. What is the staff-to-client ratio?

16. What are the day-care center's normal working hours?
    The hours are: _____

17. Is it open on weekends?
    The hours are: _____

18. Is it open during the evening?

19. Is it open during the early morning?

20. What are the daily fees?

21. Does the fee include at least one meal per day?

22. Are there any hidden charges?

23. Is the day-care center regulated, licensed, or certified by any state
    agency?

Chapter 4

Living in a Retirement Community

—————— ❧ ——————

In the previous chapters you were introduced to John who, with community and family support, found living at home or with his family while receiving help from community and government agencies his optimal living situation

When we meet Marcy, another universal elder, she is thinking about moving from her home of thirty years into an established retirement community. Although she is content in her home, she is concerned about her future and wonders about her ability to continue to live independently. Many of her friends have successfully moved in with their families or to retirement communities, assisted living facilities, or other types of living situations. Most seniors considering retirement communities share several common attributes:

They are older than sixty-two.

They are in relatively good health.

They are capable of independent living with little or no extra help.

They are financially secure.

Although Marcy meets the four criteria listed above, she is unsure whether living in a retirement community is her best choice.

❧ Marcy Considers Living in a Retirement Community

Marcy, an independent seventy-year-old woman in good health, lived in her own small two-story home for more than thirty years. When shopping, minor home repairs and maintenance, and yard work became increasingly difficult for her, her family offered to have her live in their home. She carefully considered their thoughtful overture, yet declined because she felt living with her family would make her less independent, reduce her privacy, isolate her from her friends and peers, and require her to change her schedules or habits to accommodate her family. She recalled several friends who had moved to retirement communities and seemed satisfied with their living arrangements.

Marcy decided to ask her family to help her. By visiting several retirement communities, they discovered there were different types, each with their own atmospheres, admission requirements, charges, fee schedules, levels of care, and available services and activities.

In this chapter, your family will examine many aspects of retirement living. You will look at the style of living in a retirement community, the types of residents, the features and services, and the available social activities. You will think about your elder's current and future health needs. If your elder decides to live in a retirement community, she must understand the important similarities and differences in the two types of communities, the available levels of health care, and the admission guidelines, including charges and fees.

Two Types of Retirement Communities

A retirement community is an independent, self-sufficient minivillage specifically designed to meet the needs of seniors who no longer work full-time and have leisure time for volunteer work, hobbies, educational seminars, travel, and social activities. They offer a wide variety of housing opportunities—single-family homes, attached townhouses or condominiums, individual cottages, high-rise apartment buildings, assisted living facilities, and health-care centers.

In some retirement communities, a person can easily move from one type of housing to another, depending on his personal- and medical-care needs. In others, people with significant medical- and personal-care needs may have to move to a facility outside the retirement community that can provide them with appropriate care.

There are two basic types of retirement communities: *standard retirement communities* (SRCs) and *continuing-care retirement communities* (CCRCs).

SRCs are residences similar in design to an apartment or condominium complex, for people aged sixty-two years or older who are capable of independent living. They offer some personal-care assistance but are not equipped to handle chronic or serious medical problems. Although they may offer their residents different levels of care, health-care needs should be minimal and preferably temporary.

These retirement communities usually have a monthly maintenance fee, which pays for home maintenance, security, grounds upkeep, linen service, at least one meal a day, activities, and other basic services. They do not have an endowment requirement, long-term leases, or entrance or buy-in fees. (These terms are discussed later in this chapter on page 95.)

CCRCs are usually large complexes or minivillages for people aged sixty-two and older interested in a long-term housing commitment. Admission requirements often include a confidential financial statement, a physical exam by a staff physician, an interview by CCRC staff, and a sizable deposit, endowment, or entrance or buy-in fees. This fee is required in addition to a monthly service or maintenance charge.

The CCRC complex may range from an exclusive gated community complete with golf course, shops, and banking to a rural facility with gardens and walking trails. Many CCRCs are nonprofit and are sponsored by church groups or organizations such as the Episcopal Ministries to the Aging, Inc., Presbyterian Senior Services, the Lutheran Church, or by other nonprofit corporations such as the Cooperative Retirement Services of America (CRSA).

Others are run strictly for profit by corporations such as Marriott. Some of these communities do not have an endowment or entrance or buy-in fee; however, their maintenance or monthly service fee may be substantially higher than those communities with an entrance fee.

Each CCRC has its own requirements for admission. By becoming familiar with the standard requirements, you will be more aware of unusual features, deposits, fees, contracts, and requirements.

Choosing a Retirement Community

Choosing a retirement community is a personal decision. Each elder and her family will see the atmosphere, residences, residents, staff, security systems, activities, and social programs from her own viewpoint. The retirement community that feels right for your elder may not feel right for another. If your elder has friends who are happy and satisfied with their retirement community, certainly this can be a positive sign.

However, it is still necessary to take some time to evaluate fully several facilities in the area before making a decision and signing a contract. Your elder and family will want to think about the following issues:

Certification and accreditation: Is the retirement community approved by a national organization?

Commitment: Is your elder ready to live in a retirement community on a long-term basis, or is she interested only in a short-term commitment until she decides whether retirement living is the right choice?

Closeness to family, friends, shopping, and medical services: Is the retirement community close to friends and family, or will your elder feel isolated from them? Is it convenient for her to go to the grocery or department store or her medical appointments, or will she be dependent on others for transportation?

Atmosphere: Does the retirement community make your elder feel comfortable or does she feel out of place?

Residents: Are the current residents people with whom your elder would like to socialize?

Staff: Is the staff at the retirement community helpful? Is staff available on a twenty-four-hour basis? Are the staff's health-care professionals easily accessible?

Health: Does your elder have physical or mental limitations or problems that may necessitate supportive help or medical treatment in the future?

Levels of care: What medical and supportive care can be provided by the retirement community if your elder has a change in her health or daily-care needs?

Features: Do the physical characteristics of the residences please your elder family member?

Services: Are the services offered by the retirement community ones your elder will use? Is the retirement community adequately staffed to provide all the services it offers?

Activities: Are there activities that would interest your elder?

Admission requirements may be stricter in a continuing-care retirement community than in a standard retirement community. Since living in a retirement community can be expensive, can your elder afford to make a substantial financial commitment to this living arrangement?

Certification/Accreditation

Continuing-care retirement communities experienced a boom in the 1970s and early 1980s. At that time, licensing was not required or enforced by any agency. By 1985, only 175 CCRCs were accredited by the not-for-profit American Association of Homes and Services for the Aging (AAHSA).

The Office on Aging now offers accreditation of CCRCs. To meet these standards, each facility must perform a self-study with its staff, board of directors, and residents. An on-site visit and evaluation by trained continuing-care professionals and a review by a national commission based in Washington, D.C., is needed before accreditation is granted to the facility. Although this is not a recommendation or endorsement, it indicates that certain state requirements are being met. (These requirements may vary from state to state.) Look for a certificate at the retirement community that states: "Accredited by the Continuing Care Accreditation Commission (CCAC) for the American Association for Homes and Services for the Aging." Look for a certificate or statement from the Equal Housing Opportunity stating: "Does not discriminate against any person because of race, color, sex, familial status, disability, or national origin."

Commitment

Moving from a single-family dwelling to a large community for seniors is a decision that requires thoughtfulness. When your elder family member begins to consider the changes she will be making in her life by moving to a retirement community, she may quickly realize that this decision is not an easy one to make. By moving into some retirement communities, your elder is making a commitment or pledge—both financially and to her new surrounding—to live in the retirement community for all or most of her remaining years.

Standard retirement communities more easily allow for people to change their minds and move to a different living situation. Continuing-care retirement communities can require a substantial financial investment that may or may not be refundable or prorated, depending upon the terms of the admissions contract.

If your elder is unsure if a retirement community is the right place for her to live, a short-term commitment that allows alternatives should be considered instead of a long-term commitment.

Location

It is important to consider where the retirement community is located in relation to family, friends, church or synagogue, shopping, and medical care. Some elders are self-sufficient, able to maintain a car and drive themselves to activities and appointments. Others rely on the services provided by the retirement community staff, using the community van or taxi service.

Family and friends are more likely to visit an elder family member located near them. If visiting involves an hour's drive, many people may not want to take the time for a lengthy excursion. Your elder is more likely to receive frequent visits if she lives close to family.

If Sunday church services or Friday night or Saturday morning services in a synagogue are important, check with the community regarding the nearest services. Many retirement communities maintain a chapel on the premises. Others may provide transportation to a local house of worship.

If going to town to shop or attend the theater is important, the closer your elder is to a city, the more available opportunities. Many communities arrange activities outside the retirement community and transport residents to these activities.

Medical care is an important issue. If your elder prefers a specific physician or hospital, consider how far the retirement community is from her physician's office. Many communities provide transportation to medical appointments within a set distance. Some charge a small fee for this service; others provide transportation free of charge. If family needs to assist with getting your elder to appointments, consider the distance you must travel from home to the retirement community to the doctor's office and back.

Atmosphere

When your elder visits a retirement community, he should get a "feel" for its surroundings. Some may have beautiful gardens, new buildings, and a luxurious setting. Accommodations may be private and palatial. Residents may be more formal, "dressing" for meals in the dining area, where they are served by waiters. Other retirement communities may be more homelike, the setting simpler, the residents more relaxed and informal. Accommodations may feel secure but cozy and comfortable.

It is important for your elder to visit these communities with a family member or friend, spend a day walking the grounds, share a meal, and talk with residents and staff. They should not feel they are being harassed or pushed into making a decision. Some communities encourage an elder to spend at least one night sleeping at the residence.

Residents

Residents and atmosphere go hand in hand. Some seek the faster "country club" life, filled with social activities. Others desire a slower lifestyle, preferring comfort. If the people living in the community are not people your elder can relate to, it may not be the right choice for her. The extent to which your elder participates in activities and shares mealtimes with others may be dependent on companionship developed with other residents.

Staff

The staff in the retirement community is an integral part of the atmosphere. If staff members are inaccessible, short-tempered, impatient, and inflexible, your elder may not feel content. However, if they are accessible, considerate, patient, and flexible, your elder may feel comfortable asking questions and requesting services and help when needed.

The staff may consist of nonprofessionals and professionals. Many communities maintain a registered nurse or licensed practical nurse on the premises to help evaluate their residents' medical needs. Nonprofessionals may assist with homemaking activities, limited medical care, meal preparation, security, and transportation. Often, a social worker is available to help residents with transportation and medical, social, or community issues.

Levels of Health Care

While some retirement communities offer different levels of personal care, many want their residents to be as independent as possible. A typical resident is in good physical and mental health and can live independently with little or no assistance, without placing themselves at risk for injury. For those residents who require some help, some retirement communities try to anticipate health changes in their elder residents by offering up to five levels of care:

Level I: Independent Living

Independent living is the ability to live without assistance from others. This means your elder is capable of caring for herself and performing all the activities of daily living, such as personal care, bathing, dressing, medication management, and attending meals in the dining area without placing herself at risk of harm or injury. She may drive a car, attend theater, shop, and vacation with other seniors or with family members.

Level II: Supportive Services

Supportive services or the need for help with basic personal care, such as bathing and dressing, means your elder is capable of independent living with a minimal amount of assistance. She may need occasional help with her care needs.

Level III: Assisted Living

Although your elder may continue to live independently, she requires moderate assistance with her personal care and activities of daily living. Without assistance, she may place herself at risk of harm or injury.

Level IV: Alzheimer's Special Unit

Some retirement communities have specialized units set up to provide care to people with Alzheimer's disease or related disorders. These units provide extra assistance and supervision.

❧ The Story of Grandma Sylvia

Grandma Sylvia at the age of eighty-nine was very pleasant and displayed a good sense of humor. However, due to progressive Alzheimer's disease, she wandered away from the retirement community and became lost. She was moved from level III care, assisted living, to the level IV Alzheimer's unit. Here, staff members worked with her, helping to orient her to the time of month and the hour of the day. Although she appeared to be 100-percent normal in her usual structured setting, whenever she was moved, she became disoriented and confused. One day, her daughter took her out to lunch. As they looked over the menu, her daughter suggested the daily lunch special. Uncertain of the day of the week, Grandma Sylvia smiled and said, "If it isn't Monday, Tuesday, or Wednesday, it must be Thursday, Friday, or Saturday. I think I'll take the Thursday special."

Away from her structured environment and normal routine, Grandma Sylvia's bewilderment increased, although she was unaware of her lapses.

Level V: Temporary or Permanent Nursing Home or Long-Term Care
Your elder may need temporary or permanent nursing home or long-term care due to medical-care needs that arise after an accident, illness, hospitalization, or surgery. Level V is available only in the continuing-care retirement community.

A SRC usually offers levels I, II, III, and, sometimes, level IV. It usually does not have extensive health-care facilities for long-term or skilled nursing care. If your elder needs care in a hospital or nursing facility, she may be placed in a facility located close to, but not on the grounds of, the retirement community, until she is able to resume independent living. Before she can return to living at the retirement home, a visit by retirement community staff may be needed to evaluate her mobility and medical-care needs. The retirement staff may speak with nursing staff, therapists, medical social workers, case managers, and physicians to determine her ability to manage safely in her residence.

Temporary supportive care and assisted living may be arranged prior to your elder's discharge from the hospital or nursing facility. A registered or licensed practical nurse or a home health aide working at the retirement community may be available to assist her for a short period of time. There may be an extra charge for this service.

For more permanent personal and medical care at an SRC, it may be necessary for your elder to consider an alternative living situation, such as an assisted living facility, an intermediate or skilled nursing facility, or an adult-care home. If she is not able to safely resume independent living, the management at the retirement community may request or suggest an alternative living situation that can provide more direct care. Following a hospitalization, a resident may find they need care in a nursing facility that is not associated with their retirement community.

In a CCRC, a health center may be located on the grounds of the retirement community. It may provide twenty-four-hour medical care for residents recovering from an accident, surgery, illness, or hospitalization. For temporary stays in the health center, most CCRCs don't charge an extra fee for care. There may, however, be extra charges for some medical and pharmaceutical supplies and additional meals. For residents who require long-term or permanent care, a medical evaluation by the CCRC physician may be needed. If a higher level of care is needed, the monthly fee may also be adjusted.

Basic Services in a Health Center

Receiving medical care and services on the premises where you live can be convenient for your elder and family. The continuity of care on all levels—from independent and assisted to requiring medical attention and care—can be very comforting to many seniors. Although not all medical treatment would be provided within the CCRC—hospital care and appointments with physicians would be conducted outside the community—most of the follow-up medical care may be provided. These services may include:

twenty-four-hour nursing care	speech therapy
three meals per day	a convenient laboratory
specialized services	use of health-related equipment
physical therapy	home health-care services
occupational therapy	a full-activity program

Services in a Retirement Community

The basic services in most retirement communities are similar, including meals, housekeeping services, security, transportation and parking, interdenominational services, and other on-site services. An easy-to-use checklist at the end of this section will help you keep track of the services offered by each retirement community you visit.

Meals

Some CCRCs provide one daily meal, often in a communal dining area. Others may provide one to three daily meals, usually with a full-course dinner. SRCs may provide up to three daily meals. Dining areas may be set up cafeteria- or buffet-style; others may have waitresses and waiters serve the residents at their tables.

Atmosphere may vary at different retirement communities. One may expect residents to dress up for dinner in appropriate clothes, such as jackets for men and a nice dress or pants for women. Others may adopt a more casual approach to mealtime.

For residents who need assistance at mealtime, a staff member may be available to bring the residents to the dining area in their wheelchairs and may assist them with setting up their trays and cutting food. Ask if the facility prepares special diets and whether meals can be delivered to your elder's residence if she is unable to eat in the dining area. Some communities discourage the use of assistive devices such as walkers and wheelchairs in the dining room. Check the facility's policy on dining room procedures. Check the terms of your contract for any extra fees for additional meals or assistance during mealtimes.

Housekeeping

Most retirement communities provide a weekly housekeeping and linen service. Others have washers and dryers available in common areas for residents' use. Installing a washer and dryer in your elder's unit may also be possible in some communities. Although housekeeping services can be included in the fee at many retirement communities, others may charge a small weekly fee for this service.

Security

Security systems vary at different communities. Some will maintain a twenty-four-hour security guard or responsible staff member and a security system. Security guards may be found at an assigned post or may patrol the grounds of the retirement community. In some facilities, a security guard may accompany a nurse when she calls on residents.

Some facilities are known as gated communities. The "gate" provides residents with extra security. Any person entering or leaving the grounds must pass through a locked gate, usually staffed by a security guard twenty-four hours a day. This helps to prevent unauthorized people from entering the retirement community.

Transportation/Parking Services

A community van may be available for free or for a small fee to assist residents with personal needs such as medical appointments, shopping, and attending church or temple. The van may also be used to transport residents to social community events such as theater. These are usually wheelchair-accessible.

For residents who have their own vehicles, parking in the community may include valet parking, covered parking spaces, and/or illuminated parking. There may be an extra fee for a parking space.

Interdenominational Services

To many elders, maintaining access to a local church or synagogue is important. Attending services may help them manage stressful situations, maintain their faith, and provide them with social activities. While some facilities maintain a chapel on their grounds, others may provide transportation for free or a small fee to local churches or synagogues.

Stores/Club Rooms/Clinics

Retirement communities often operate as independent minivillages, with a multitude of stores, businesses, and social centers located on the community grounds. As your elder and family visit each retirement community, note which services are available in each retirement community.

On-site services may include a convenient bank, post office, grocery store, or pharmacy. In addition, they may have health-care facilities, including a fitness center, beauty salon, or barber shop.

Features in a Typical Retirement Residence

A standard residence may be a studio; one-, two-, or three-bedroom apartment; townhouse or condominium; cottage; or single-family home. Many of the residences may include a complete kitchen area, independent heating and air-conditioning controls, window coverings, cable television, and safety features, such as smoke detectors, safety grab bars in the tub or shower, and a twenty-four-hour emergency call system. Some communities allow or even encourage residents to bring their own furniture to give their apartment a touch of home.

Please check with each facility for their guidelines regarding pets, making physical changes to the residence at the resident's expense, and extra charges, such as utilities, parking fees, and major maintenance or repair work.

Social Activities

Many retirement communities have an extensive selection of activities for their residents. Those listed below were compiled after reviewing many facilities.

arts and crafts	garden plots	movies
bridge groups	golf course	music
ceramics	health center	nature trails
chapel	indoor pool and spa	needlework
current events	language classes	photography
discussion groups	library	recreational activities
exercise room	line dancing	religious services
game room	low-impact aerobics	shuffleboard

sports	tennis courts	woodworking shop
square dancing	theater	yoga classes
swimming	water exercise classes	

Admission Requirements

These are general guidelines used by many retirement communities. However, when you begin to look at facilities, you may find a wide variance in the requirements for admission. For example, your elder must be:

Sixty-two years of age or have a spouse at least sixty-two years of age. There is no maximum age limit provided the other criteria are met.

In good physical and mental health

Capable of independent living

Financially capable of fulfilling the residency agreement or contract with the facility. Some facilities offer a free personal and confidential financial analysis to help your elder determine if she can afford to live in their community.

Insured with a long-term-care health policy either through an insurance company of your choosing or through a health policy offered by the retirement community. (Requirements vary; however, long-term-care or supplemental insurance policies provide essential benefits and medical coverage for seniors.)

Guidelines for Applying to a Continuing-Care Retirement Community

While the order of the many steps in the application process and the deposit requirements may vary in each retirement community, the following guidelines will help you understand the application process:

1. Choose the type of living accommodation you are interested in.

2. Submit an application form with a nonrefundable application processing fee of $150 to $300.

3. Read and sign the residence and care agreement or contract. Some facilities request that the agreement be signed and returned within ten to fifteen days. At this time, half of the entrance fee may be due and payable.

4. Place a deposit on the residence you are interested in. The endowment or entrance or buy-in fee is a down payment in which a prospective resident or couple pledges or guarantees to pay a sizable amount of money to demonstrate their interest and desire to live in the retirement community.

   Entrance fees may be refundable minus a percentage of the fee or may be completely nonrefundable. These fees may range from as low as $25,000 to as high as $200,000.

   The deposit may be 10 percent or more of the entrance fee. If the application is withdrawn, this deposit is usually 80- to 100-percent refundable. Some facilities may apply this deposit toward the entrance fee.

5. The second half of the entrance fee less the previous deposit may be due on or prior to occupancy.

6. An additional application fee or refundable deposit of $1,000 to $2,000 may be required. If the application is withdrawn, this additional deposit is usually refundable.

7. Submit copies of insurance cards (front and back) to the admissions office.

8. An interview with the retirement community staff may be requested.

9. A physical exam by a retirement community physician may be required prior to acceptance. The applicant may receive this exam free of charge or may be financially responsible for its cost. It may also be covered by the individual's health-insurance policy.

10. A confidential financial statement may be required. Some facilities offer a free or low-cost analysis of your financial situation to help you determine if their facility is a viable choice.

11. The occupancy date may be determined by the retirement community.

12. The first monthly maintenance or service charge may be due on the occupancy date.

Types of Refund Contracts

There are several types of refund contracts offered to the potential resident. They provide an opportunity to change your mind and leave the facility and still receive a prorated or portion of the entrance fee. The terms of the refund contracts varied widely in each retirement community we checked.

The standard contracts are twenty-four- to fifty-month declining-refund contracts. For example, if your elder moved into the Forest Hills Continuing Care Retirement Community under a thirty-six-month declining-refund contract, she would be able to leave the center and move somewhere else during that thirty-six-month period of time and receive a portion of her entrance fee. If she stayed for twelve months, she would receive a prorated amount for the twenty-four remaining months. However, if she decided to move after thirty-six months, she would lose her entire entrance fee.

The entrance fee may be refundable in the event of death or withdrawal of application. Depending upon the length of residence, the refund consists of the entrance fee minus 2 to 10 percent per month for each month of occupancy by the resident for a period up to fifty months.

Some retirement communities may pay the refund only when the residence is reoccupied by another resident. This means another person, not necessarily related to your elder, may move into the apartment unit she has vacated either by choice, illness, or death.

With a 70- to 90-percent refundable contract, a portion of the entrance fee may be refundable in event of death or withdrawal of the application upon reoccupancy by another resident.

Legal Issues

When your elder signs a residence and care agreement, she is signing a complex legal document. It is strongly recommended that your elder and family review this contract with an attorney before signing it.

Fees in a Retirement Community

To realistically consider living in any retirement community, your elder must be financially secure. She must be able to pay her monthly service fee, which can range from six hundred to four thousand dollars per month, depending on the size of the residence she chooses. In addition to the monthly service fee, there can be additional charges for assistance with personal care, transportation to shopping and medical appointments, meals, parking, and cable television. Living in independent or standard retirement communities is usually less costly, since they tend to be smaller communities with fewer services and activities on the premises. In addition, some retirement communities may raise the monthly fee after your elder moves in. Your elder may also be responsible for property taxes and other "hidden" fees. The charts on the following pages will offer additional information on the cost of living in a retirement community.

General Rates in an Independent Living or Standard Retirement Community

Generally, the rates at these facilities are paid in full by an individual. However, some of these facilities may accept limited payments based on the individual's ability to pay according to strict income guidelines. Each resident's required level of care is determined by a staff evaluation at the retirement community. Rates vary depending upon the resident's needs. The greater the need for assistance, the higher the monthly fee. For example, if your elder is living independently without any assistance, her monthly rate will be lower than if she requires some help with personal care.

STANDARD OR INDEPENDENT LIVING COMMUNITY RATES

| | Monthly Service Fees* | | |
| | | Personal Care | |
Living Accommodations	**Independent Living**	*Level 1*	*Level 2*
studio (check availability)	$632–$920	$1,495	$1,695
one bedroom	$935–$1595	$1,700	$2,100
one-bedroom deluxe	$1016–$1550	$2,020	$2,420
two bedroom	$1545–$1875	$2,220	$2,420
two-bedroom deluxe	$1745–$1950	$2,500	$2,700
additional person	$250–$400	$745	$945

* These are average rates found in a sample of retirement communities nationwide and will vary in each facility. Monthly service fees may be subject to adjustment with thirty- to ninety-day notice.

General Rates in Continuing-Care Retirement Communities

The rates found in a CCRC are usually higher overall than in an SRC. In addition to the monthly maintenance charge, there is also a substantial down payment or entrance fee. Like the SRC, the fees depend upon the unit's size and the level of care needed by your elder family member.

CONTINUING-CARE COMMUNITY RATES

Living Accommodations	Entrance Fee	Monthly Service Charge	
		Single	*Double*
Apartments			
efficiency	$20,000–$85,000	$1,490	—
studio	$25,000–$102,300	$787–$1,525	$1,200–$1,700
deluxe studio	$54,000–$118,800	$940–$1,620	$1,310–$2,250
one bedroom	$57,350–$181,500	$844–$1,790	$1,450–$2,965
one-bedroom deluxe	$65,000–$196,350	$888–$2,015	$1,550–$3,190
two bedroom	$118,225–$219,450	$2,273–$2,240	$3,121–$3,415
two-bedroom deluxe	$90,100–$189,200	$935–$2,395	$3,242–$3,720
additional person	$306–$850	—	—
Patio Homes/Cottages			
one bedroom	$105,000–$198,000	$1,145–$1,830	$1,515–$3,005
one-bedroom deluxe	$122,000–$226,050	$1,180–$2,040	$1,550–$3,215
two bedroom	$125,600–$240,900	$1,180–$2,255	$1,550–$3,430
two-bedroom deluxe	$132,100–$288,750	$1,255–$2,565	$1,625–$3,740
Supportive Services			
single unit	$70,000	$2,180	—
double unit	$90,000	$2,620	$4,800
Health Center			
comprehensive care	$105,000	$950–$1,600	$1,800–$3,000
assisted living	$80,000	$950–$2,700	$1,300–$2,800

Note: These rates represent a sample of CCRCs surveyed for When Aging Parents Can't Live Alone. *These rates vary, depending on the rate and conditions of each facility's refund policy. Monthly service fees may be subject to adjustment with thirty- to ninety-day notice.*

Health-Care Insurance

As retirement communities comprise residents older than sixty-two, many who are healthy when they enter the community may develop health problems in their later years. For this reason, many retirement communities require their residents to have some form of health insurance. Insurance benefits may help pay for hospital care, skilled nursing care, home health-care services, durable medical equipment, and supplies. Some of these benefits may be applicable to residents who need care in a health-care center on the premises; others may find these benefits helpful in their home or in a community nursing facility after a hospitalization, accident, or injury.

Medicare

The health center should be state-licensed and Medicare-certified, especially if it provides skilled nursing care or a high level of nursing care. Medicare Part A will pay for medical care received in a skilled health-care facility if the resident meets the standard requirements for skilled nursing care. These requirements are explained in chapter 8, "Understanding Nursing Facilities."

Many people look at their insurance policies and think, "I have one hundred days of care in a nursing facility." What they do not understand is that to receive up to one hundred days of medical care, a person must meet the Medicare requirements for skilled nursing care. This means your elder must:

1. spend three consecutive nights as an inpatient in an area hospital.
   Some hospitals will admit a patient as a twenty-three-hour or overnight patient. These hospital days do not count toward meeting the Medicare requirements of a three-night stay. Your elder must be a regular or full inpatient admission to the hospital, not including the day of discharge.

2. require skilled nursing care such as intravenous feedings, tube feedings, physical or rehabilitative therapy, injections, dressing changes, and other specific medical needs on a daily basis.

3. be admitted to the skilled nursing facility within thirty days of discharge from the hospital.

If your elder meets these requirements, Medicare will pay 100 percent for the first 20 days of medical care. If additional medical treatment is needed, Medicare will pay 80 percent for the next 80 days (Days 21 to 100), leaving a daily coinsurance, payable by your elder or a supplemental insurance policy, of $97 per day. If your elder requires more than 100 days of coverage, each CCRC may have different policies regarding payment. Discern the facility's policy or fee for care needed after the 100 Medicare days are used. Medicare does not pay for intermediate or nonskilled care. However, some CCRCs will provide the needed nursing care in the health center.

For elders who must live in the health-care facility on a permanent basis and

receive intermediate or skilled care, some facilities may only charge the standard monthly fee. Others may add an additional fee for the care, on top of the cost of medications and supplies.

Some CCRCs may also consider other care options, such as returning the resident to her home with supportive home health-care services. The home health-care services may come from the health center or from an outside agency.

Supplemental Insurance

Your elder may have a supplemental health-care insurance policy, such as Blue Cross/ Blue Shield, Aetna, AARP, or Travelers Insurance. Many supplemental policies pay the $97 per day coinsurance and/or may have additional days of coverage after the one hundred Medicare days are used up. It is important to read carefully your insurance policies and to understand your benefits.

Many health centers in a retirement community require a resident to maintain a supplemental insurance policy to offset health or related charges that are not covered under Medicare. Retirement community residents who have not paid their Medicare Part B deductible for the year may be charged for physician services until the deductible is met. The deductible for Medicare Part B is still $100 annually.

Some health centers are not Medicare-certified, which means they cannot accept Medicare payment for the medical care your elder receives at their facility. If the health center does not accept payments from Medicare, your elder should have a supplemental insurance policy with benefits for skilled nursing care. She should be prepared to pay an extra charge for nursing care at the health center or to receive medical care outside the retirement community at a nursing facility that does accept Medicare payments.

There may be additional charges for services, supplies, medication, and care your elder receives in the health-care center. Additional fees may also be charged for specialized services and special nursing assignments. A sampling of services and their average daily rates is summarized in the following chart:

PRIVATE-PAY RATES FOR SERVICES IN A HEALTH CENTER

Services	Average Daily Rates*
diabetic care	$5.00/day
hand-feeding charge	$5.00/day
tube-feeding charge	$15.00/day
incontinent care	$ 5.00/day
decubitus care	$10.00/day
transportation to medical appointments	$20.00/hour (minimum charge)
infection isolation	$10.00/day
alarm trigger module	$ 3.00/day
cable television	$9.75/month

Actual rates will vary between facilities.

Medicaid

Medicaid is a state and federal program for people with low income and limited assets. It is operated by the state government within federal guidelines. The health center should be able to accept Medicaid payments for medical care for people who live in a retirement community and who have spent most of their assets and meet the requirements for receiving Medicaid (also known as Medical Assistance or MediCal in California). Under Medicaid guidelines, a person can receive care in an intermediate or skilled nursing facility. They may also receive other rehabilitative services, medical equipment, transportation, and long-term-care services, such as residential and home health care. Most people living in a retirement community health center, however, probably exceed the income limitations to qualify for Medicaid benefits.

Home Health Care

Home health care may be indicated when a resident living in a retirement community has had an accident, injury, or illness or has been hospitalized. Many retirement communities maintain home health staff on the premises or on contract to the facility. With a physician's order, a home health-care agency can send a skilled professional, such as a registered nurse, physical therapist, or speech/language therapist, to her home.

Additional services include visits from an occupational therapist, medical social worker, respiratory therapist, or home health aide. While the home health-care agency provides health care in the home, your elder must be homebound or unable to easily leave her home and must require skilled services.

Caseworkers are generally assigned to people who receive Medicaid. The caseworker can help your elder obtain pre-authorization so she can receive services and assistance from the Medicaid program. If eligible, Medicaid pays 100 percent of the cost for skilled home health-care services.

Medicare Part A (or Part B if your elder does not have Part A) pays 100 percent of the cost of home health care if:

1. there is reasonable medical necessity for medical care at home

2. there are orders and a plan of treatment from the primary-care physician

3. your elder is homebound or confined to her home

4. the home health-care agency is Medicare-certified to provide and bill for services under Medicare

For more information, review chapter 10, "Using Home Health and Hospice Care."

Durable Medical Equipment and Supplies

Medicare Part B pays the full cost of some medical supplies and 80 percent of the cost for approved durable medical equipment (DME), such as hospital beds, wheelchairs, walkers, and home oxygen after the $100 annual deductible. Medicaid also pays for medical equipment and supplies. It may be necessary to obtain pre-authorization from a caseworker at the nearest Medicaid or senior and disabled services office.

Some supplemental insurance policies pay the 20 percent or the portion of the charge that Medicare does not cover. For additional information, review the section on durable medical equipment and supplies in chapter 2, "Living with Your Family." To easily compare the similarities and differences between standard and continuing-care retirement communities, please review this chart.

SIMILARITIES AND DIFFERENCES BETWEEN STANDARD AND CONTINUING-CARE RETIREMENT COMMUNITIES

Standard Features and Requirements in a Retirement Community	Standard Retirement Community	Continuing-Care Retirement Community
Age requirement: Must be sixty-two years of age	Yes	Yes
Health requirement: Must be in good physical and mental health	Yes	Yes
Financial requirement: Must be financially secure	Yes	Yes
Monthly service fee	Yes	Yes
Requires large deposit or endowment or entrance or buy-in fee	No	Yes
Commitment to living in a retirement community	Can be short-term or long-term	More likely to be long-term due to financial investment
Has different levels of care	Yes, includes independent living, supportive care, and minimal assisted living	Yes, includes independent living, supportive care, and assisted living and health care
Residential units	More like condolike units or apartments	Large complex similar to minivillage, with separate family homes, apartments, or condolike units
Location	Rural or city	Rural or city
Requires physical exam by community physician	Not usually required	More likely to be required
Requires long-term-care health policy	Recommended but usually not required	May be required
Services such as meals, linens, security, transportation	Yes, may include hidden or extra charges	Yes, may include hidden or extra charges; may also include clubhouse, medical clinic, and stores
Activities such as interdenominational services, excursions, social programs	Yes	Yes, may offer more extensive activities

EVALUATION

Do you feel living in a retirement community is the best choice for your elder family member?

If your answer is "yes," review chapter II, "Your Guide to Resources," and use the evaluation form below to evaluate facilities.

If your answer is "no," or you are undecided, turn to chapter 5, "Living in an Assisted Living Facility."

EVALUATING A RETIREMENT COMMUNITY WORK SHEET

By completing the following work sheet for each facility, your elder and family will be able to easily compare the cost of applying to each retirement community.

Name and address of retirement community

_____

_____

Contact person _____ **Telephone#** _____

The retirement community is a standard retirement community _____

continuing-care retirement community _____

It is: Accredited _____ Medicare-Certified in Health Center _____

Accepts Medicaid in Health Center _____

AVAILABLE FLOOR PLANS

studio apt. _____ one-bedroom apt. _____ two-bedroom apt. _____
three-bedroom apt. _____ townhouse condominium _____ cottage _____
single-family house _____ other _____

EVALUATING A RETIREMENT COMMUNITY continued

AVAILABLE LEVELS OF CARE

independent living _____

supportive services _____

assisted living _____

Alzheimer's/specialized units _____

nursing care in health center _____

FEES/AMOUNT OF FEES

Application fee $_____   Refundable _____ Nonrefundable _____

Entrance fee $_____   Refundable _____ Nonrefundable _____

First half due on _____

Endowment fee $_____   Refundable _____ Nonrefundable _____

Buy-in fee $_____   Refundable _____ Nonrefundable _____

Additional application fee $_____   Refundable _____

Nonrefundable _____

Total Entrance and Application Fees $_____

Monthly service fee $_____

Other _____   Fee $_____

Total Monthly and Other Fees $_____

QUESTIONS TO ASK ABOUT THE RETIREMENT COMMUNITY

Questions to Ask About Staff

1. How convenient is the facility to the nearest town or city?

2. Is bus/public transportation easily accessible?

3. What is the size/acreage of the retirement community?

4. Are the grounds well-maintained?

5. How many units are there?

6. Is there a waiting list for units in the retirement community?

7. How long is the waiting list?

8. Can you move into a temporary unit while waiting for your unit to become available?

9. What is the average length of stay among the residents?

10. What is the average age of residents?

11. Are most of the residents: female _____ male _____ married _____ single _____ divorced _____ widowed _____

12. Can you easily change from one floor plan to another?

13. Is there a fee for changing units?

14. Are there guest accommodations?

15. Can guests join the resident for a meal at mealtime?

16. Is there a charge for these accommodations or for meals provided during the guest's stay?

17. Are pets allowed in the residences or buildings?

18. Are children allowed to stay in the residences?

19. Is the facility staffed twenty-four hours a day?

20. What is the staff-to-resident ratio?

Questions to Ask About Services

21. Which services are included in the monthly fee? (See list of services on pages 90–92.)

22. Which services are subject to extra charges?

23. Who determines which supportive services are needed by a resident?

24. Which meals are included in the daily meal plan?

25. Are special diets provided?

26. If a resident has a temporary health problem, can her meals be delivered to her residence?

Questions to Ask About Health

27. Is nursing care available on the retirement community grounds?

28. Is a supplemental long-term health-care insurance policy required?

29. Does the retirement community have a contract or does it contract out to home health-care agencies?

30. Is there a policy on hiring temporary live-in help?

31. Can a resident receive skilled nursing care in the health-care center?

32. Can a resident receive intermediate care in the health-care center?

33. Is there a time limit for how long a resident can receive care in the health-care center?
    If yes, what is it? _____

34. Can a resident live on a permanent basis at the health-care center if she requires significant nursing care?

35. If a resident is hospitalized and requires moderate assistance or nursing care, can she return to her residence?

36. Is an evaluation by staff needed to determine the resident's ability to return to the residence after a hospitalization?

Retirement communities often require an evaluation of health-care needs at the hospital before allowing a resident to return to her residence. The evaluation may include talking with the nursing staff, a medical social worker, the primary-care physician, the family, and the patient.

The evaluation may focus on the mental and physical capabilities of the resident, including nursing-care needs, such as incontinence care, injections, and dressing changes and mobility, including the ability to get in and out of bed and walk safely to meals. For information on discharge planning from a hospital, turn to chapter 7, "Understanding Hospital Acute Care."

Questions to Ask About Cost

37. Is a financial report available for your review?

38. Can the monthly fee be increased?

39. What are the conditions for increasing the fee?

40. How often is the monthly fee increased?

41. Are residents responsible for paying property taxes?

42. Are there any hidden costs?

Additional expenses may include utilities, telephone service, medication, medical care outside the retirement community, garage or carport rental, additional meals or delivery of meals to your elder's apartment, excursions, and some transportation services.

Chapter 5

Living in an Assisted Living Facility

After living in a retirement community for a year, Marcy and her family decided it was not the best choice for her. Although she liked living in her own apartment, taking some of her meals in a communal dining area, and actively participating in social activities, she also found it increasingly difficult to get up in the morning without assistance. Although staff was supportive and other residents were helpful, her walk to the dining area became more difficult. The cost of hiring additional daily help placed a financial burden on Marcy's resources.

Marcy and her family looked at assisted living facilities designed to provide support and care to people no longer able to manage independently. These residences or apartments, typically for individuals aged sixty-five and older, provide twenty-four-hour supervision and assistance with personal care, bathing, dressing, grooming, toileting, medication management, and basic nursing care. Some facilities try to provide a higher level of care in supervised or specialized care units. These units are often an option for people with Alzheimer's-related illnesses.

Marcy and Her Family Decide to Learn About Assisted Living Facilities

As noted, after living for a year in a standard retirement community, Marcy and her family decided she was not able to live independently and safely without additional supervision and assistance. Several important factors helped them to make the decision to try a setting with greater supervision.

Although Marcy was able to walk, her problems with balance placed her at risk of falling during the long walk to the dining area. Because her retirement community provided only one meal a day under the monthly fee, extra meals meant extra fees on an already tight budget. As her forgetfulness increased, Marcy did not take her medication properly and missed several medical appointments despite reminders from her family and the doctor's office. Although the retirement community offered to provide a home health aide to help her, the additional cost made it difficult for her to afford to continue to live there.

Marcy and her family openly discussed moving from a retirement community to an assisted living facility, the next type of senior residence available on the continuum or chain of care provided by senior residences.

Is living in an assisted living facility the best choice for Marcy? This narrative raises several issues. Her loss of balance places her at risk of a fall on the way to the dining area, getting up at night to use the bathroom, or even tripping on the corner of a rug. Her memory loss places her at risk of becoming disoriented, being unable to recognize familiar people, wandering away from familiar surroundings, or forgetting to turn appliances off. Both of these make some homemaking activities, such as shopping for groceries and preparing meals. They also contribute to reduced health care, a result of missed medical appointments and taking incorrect medication. The extra fees place a greater financial burden on Marcy and her family.

When your elder's capacity to manage safely by herself places her at risk of harm, it may be time to consider an alternative setting that provides additional supervision and assistance. An assisted living facility can provide the needed supervision and assistance and, in addition, allow her to remain partially independent in her own apartment.

When your family and elder consider moving to an assisted living facility, you should know about licensing, levels of care, supervised or special-care units, admissions procedures, cost, insurance benefits, and available features and services. In addition, it is important to consider many of the factors you reviewed for retirement communities: location, environment, residents, and staffing. This information can help you make a realistic and informed decision, as well as determine if assisted living is the best choice for your elder.

Licenses and Regulation

In the continuum of care, assisted living facilities are one of several living options found between retirement communities and nursing-home care. This new alternative to nursing-home care is receiving praise from many but also raising concerns regarding the lack of standardized state or federal regulations governing these facilities.

Although more than one million elders now live in more than thirty thousand assisted living facilities nationwide, there is no uniform state or federal accreditation or licensing program. Some states may require specific training for staff, which includes certification to care for residents who need care and assistance. Others may have inadequately trained staff to provide this care. Some states may have regulations for building-code or fire-safety requirements. Others may not have any regulations regarding building or fire codes. Some facilities may comply with the Americans with Disabilities Act or be members of the American Health Care Association or a state health-care association. Others may not.

The Assisted Living Facilities Association of America (ALFAA) offers a free brochure and checklist you can use to help evaluate assisted living facilities. Ombudsmen, people who investigate complaints regarding facilities, may also offer additional insight.

Location

Many assisted living facilities situate themselves in areas close to hospitals and medical care, anticipating the need for medical services from a physician or hospital emergency room. Because many residents in these facilities are not fully independent and may rely on daily help and assistance, the proximity to a medical facility ensures prompt medical treatment when it is necessary.

Residents in these facilities may also need greater support from family, friends, and community agencies than those who live in a retirement community. Medical emergencies, visits to the doctor, and refilling prescription medications may necessitate regular trips by family. Family members may also find they are needed to assist their elder at mealtime or with the basic activities of daily living.

A location close to the family also ensures that your elder is checked on a regular basis. Too often, elders are left in their apartment units within the facility and not checked on by staff unless their absence during mealtime is noted. However, when family is nearby, members can regularly drop in to ensure their elder family member is well.

Environment

Assisted living facilities come in many shapes and sizes. Many resemble hotels, large private homes, high-rise apartment buildings, or one-level apartmentlike structures. In many facilities, the residents have a private apartment. These apartments should have safety features, including bathroom grab bars and an intercom system. A common area with books, television, games, and comfortable chairs and sofas may be shared with other residents. The dining area should be easily accessible to residents.

Some assisted living facilities are affiliated with retirement communities, which become available to residents when they are no longer capable of living independently but require significant assistance and/or supervision.

Small facilities may have five to eighteen residents; larger facilities may provide care for up to several hundred. When looking at these various settings, consider the types of residents, the staff members' professionalism, the resident-to-staff ratio, the physical environment (is climbing up and down stairs necessary?), and the level of care and assistance provided by each facility.

Residents

Many of the elders who choose to live in an assisted living facility may arrive directly from their homes or retirement communities. Physical-health problems, difficulties with basic-care needs, or deteriorating mental function may contribute to an elder's decision to change her living situation. As a result, many of the residents use walkers, canes, crutches, and occasionally a wheelchair. Yet, some facilities accept residents in wheelchairs only on a temporary basis.

Many residents may also require weekly visits from home health-care nurses to help them maintain their ability to live independently. The nurses may help them with medication management, check their blood pressures, pulse and respirations, and monitor their blood sugar or diabetes. Other home health personnel, such as a physical therapist, may make home visits to evaluate and treat them.

Residents who need durable medical equipment and supplies can obtain any necessary items while living in the facility. Sometimes a bedside commode or a raised toilet seat makes the difference between maintaining independence or being forced to move to a different level of care.

Other residents may be primarily independent; they may choose to live in an assisted living facility where they can receive meals and have easy access to social activities, care, and assistance, if needed.

Staff

A fair amount of interaction between the staff and the residents should exist. Expect the staff members to know the residents by their names. Expect them to become familiar with your family and to be aware of any medical problems your elder may have. Furthermore, the staff should be available to help your elder with her activities of daily living (bathing, grooming, dressing, toileting, eating), and if your elder has recently been in the hospital, they should be able to increase this assistance, at least for a short time.

Most families tend to visit at specific times and so may only know the staff on one or two shifts. But it is important to find out what the staffing is on each shift. Staff members usually work three different shifts. Administrators and other management may primarily work during the day shift (7 A.M. to 4 P.M.). Registered nurses, licensed practical nurses, social workers, and therapists tend to work the day shift and part of the afternoon shift (3 P.M. to 11 P.M.). During the night shift (11 P.M. to 7 A.M.), there may be only one registered or licensed practical nurse available, who receives additional support from a nurse's aide.

It is important to check the resident-to-staff ratio: How many staff members are available to help residents at mealtimes? How many staff members are available during the day or at night? Is there a high staff turnover? That may indicate poor or inconsistent care or inadequate management.

Cost

The cost of an assisted living facility is determined by several factors: the type of residential unit, the level of care, and the method of payment. For example, a person who receives level 1 care and resides in a studio apartment pays less than a level 1 person who resides in a one-bedroom apartment.

The level of care or the amount of supervision and assistance an individual needs to live independently and safely in her home is usually determined by an evaluation by the facility staff. The more help a person needs, the higher the monthly rate. For example, a person who receives level 2 care pays more than a person who receives level 1 care.

The method of payment refers to the way the monthly fee for assisted living is paid to the facility. Your elder may pay privately through her monthly Social Security or pension checks, or with funds from her investments. Or, if she has limited income, she may receive some financial support through Medicaid or through a long-term-care insurance policy. On average, assisted living facilities cost less than nursing homes, with their fees ranging from $850 to more than $2,000 a month. Some facilities also charge for supplies and other services.

Health Insurance

Most insurance policies do *not* pay for care in an assisted living facility, because the care provided in this setting is usually considered custodial or unskilled. Custodial care is general care and assistance with the activities of daily living, as well as supervision to prevent personal harm. This care can be provided by an unskilled person and is not considered medically necessary or essential to the treatment and diagnosis of an illness or injury.

Medicare does *not* pay for care in an assisted living facility.

Medicaid, in some states, provides coverage in an assisted living facility. To determine your elder's eligibility, contact the state area agency on aging or your local senior and disabled services office.

Private-insurance policies generally don't offer benefits for assisted living care. However, some long-term-care policies may provide limited benefits, which may cover part of the cost.

Veterans Affairs may have benefits that include care in an assisted living facility. Contact your nearest Veterans Affairs office to determine if it has these benefits in your area.

Levels of Care

If your elder chooses to move to an assisted living facility, she should be partially independent or able to care for herself without placing herself at risk of personal harm. The assisted living facility provides twenty-four-hour personal-care services, but your elder will also be alone in her apartment for significant portions of the day and night.

For example, although your elder can take a bath alone, a supervised bath by an assisted living staff member may be safer because your elder occasionally loses her balance. At the assisted living facility, an aide may be available to help her prepare for bed at night and help her bathe and dress in the morning. Staff may also provide medication.

The five levels of care available in an assisted living facility are:

1 basic care—independent, needs little or no care

2. level 1, or minimal care

3. level 2, or moderate care

4. level 3, or maximum care

5. supervised or special-care unit

Basic Care

To receive basic care, your elder should:

move independently, safely walk with a cane or walker, or self-propel a wheelchair

be able to easily and safely transfer from a wheelchair to a chair, bed, or toilet

not require assistance with her activities of daily living or the routine activities of everyday living, such as eating, dressing, bathing, and personal care

Base Monthly Rate for Basic Care	
semiprivate suite:	*$900–$1,400*
studio apartment:	*$1,360–$1,500*
one bedroom:	*$1,750–$1,900*
two bedroom:	*$2,200–$2,700*
additional person:	*$150–$450*

not require a special diet at mealtime (Some facilities prepare special meals, such as diabetic or low-cholesterol foods for residents at no charge or for a small extra fee.)

be able to take her medication properly

be alert and oriented to time of day, place (where she is), and person (who she is)

If your elder requires additional care, she may need a health evaluation by assisted living staff to determine the level or amount of care she needs. Because the levels of care vary in each facility, they should only be used as a guideline.

Level 1: Minimal Care Needs

To receive level 1 care, your elder should:

Level 1 Monthly Rate

semiprivate suite:	$1,130–$1,600
studio apartment:	$1,500–$1,785
one bedroom:	$1,750–$2,000
two bedroom:	$2,435–$2,500
additional person:	$200–$450

need occasional assistance with mobility or transfers (for example, your elder may need assistance walking to the dining area for her meals)

need minimal or occasional assistance with activities of daily living, such as bathing, dressing, or grooming

need an occasional reminder or assistance with personal hygiene

have occasional loss of control or incontinence of bladder or bowel

need a special diet

need occasional reminders or assistance to properly take medication

be alert and oriented, with minimal confusion or disorientation. Your elder should be aware of her surroundings and be able to understand information and make decisions on her own behalf.

Level 2: Moderate Care Needs

To receive level 2 care, your elder should:

Level 2 Monthly Rate

semiprivate suite:	$1,700–$2,100
studio apartment:	$1,750–$2,200
one bedroom:	$2,025–$2,400
two bedroom:	$2,700–$3,270
additional person:	$300–$685

need regular assistance with mobility or transfers

need moderate assistance with the activities of daily living

have frequent loss of control of bladder or bowel

need daily reminders and some assistance with personal hygiene

need daily assistance at mealtime

need daily medication management

need moderate medical and basic nursing care

be alert and oriented, with frequent episodes of confusion and disorientation

need daily supervision

Level 3: Maximum Care Needs

To receive level 3 care, your elder should:

need frequent intervention by staff

have an increased need for assistance with mobility

need continual assistance with bathing, dressing, grooming, and personal care

need constant supervision at mealtime

need constant supervision and monitoring of medication

need frequent medical intervention and basic nursing care

be moderately confused and disoriented

need constant supervision

Level 3 Monthly Rate

semiprivate suite:	*$1,700–$2,100*
studio apartment:	*$1,800–$2,300*
one bedroom:	*$2,100–$2,600*
two bedroom:	*$2,700–$3,200*
additional person:	*$415–$1,065*

Supervised or Special-Care Units

At some assisted living facilities, your elder can be placed in a twenty-four-hour supervised or special-care unit to prevent her from wandering from the facility and becoming lost. These special units may be ideal for people who suffer from the confusion, forgetfulness, and disorientation often associated with Alzheimer's. Many people with this disease do not have significant physical problems; however, mental confusion may contribute to problems with incontinence, poor hygiene, and inappropriate or unsafe behavior.

Three levels of care may be offered in a special-care unit at an assisted living facility. Each level provides twenty-four-hour supervision and personal assistance. The more time and care required by the resident, the higher the level of care and the cost of the service.

Level 1: Special Care Unit—Minimum Care

To receive level 1: special-care unit, minimum care, your elder should:

need minimal assistance with the activities of daily living

be capable of walking independently, or with a cane, walker, or wheelchair

experience occasional, short-term memory loss. For example, your elder may have difficulty remembering where she lives.

Average Monthly Rate

semiprivate: *$1,800–$2,500/month*
private room: *$2,000–$2,700/month*

experience some forgetfulness. Your elder may turn on the oven and forget to turn it off. Or she may not remember when or if she took her medication

have difficulty safely using standard household appliances. Your elder may have difficulty turning the knobs on the stove

have difficulty understanding information and making decisions on her own behalf

have difficulty remembering familiar people or places. Your elder may wander away from her room and not remember how to get back

experience occasional loss of control or incontinence with bladder and bowel

Level 2: Special-Care Unit—Moderate Care

To receive level 2: special-care unit, moderate care, your elder should:

Average Monthly Rate

semiprivate: *$2,200–$2,800/month*
private room: *$2,300–$2,900/month*

need moderate assistance with the activities of daily living on a daily basis

have a moderate amount of short-term memory problems

have difficulty following instructions, written or verbal

experience increased forgetfulness

not be safe with standard household appliances, such as the stove or microwave

have increased wandering and need for supervision

have increased difficulty recognizing familiar people and places

experience moderate loss of control or incontinence of bladder or bowel

Level 3: Special-Care Unit—Maximum Care

To receive level 3: special-care unit, maximum care, your elder should:

need maximum or total care for activities of daily living

have poor short-term memory and some long-term memory problems (for example, your elder may not remember what she ate for breakfast less than an hour before, or she may not remember the names of her family members)

Average Monthly Rate

semiprivate: *$2,500–$3,200/month*

private room: *$2,700–$3,500/month*

have difficulty with communication. Your elder may have difficulty organizing her thoughts in a coherent way.

be unsafe without constant twenty-four-hour supervision

be at risk of wandering greater distances

not understand information and be incapable of making a competent decision on her own behalf

not recognize familiar people or places

have total loss of control or incontinence of bladder and bowel

Please note: The monthly rates may vary from facility to facility. These figures are guidelines to help you estimate the cost of living in an assisted living facility with a specific level of care.

Basic Services in an Assisted Living Facility

Many of the services in an assisted living facility are similar to those offered in a retirement community. Basic services may include the following:

Three meals daily. In times of illness, many assisted living facilities agree to deliver meals to the room for a temporary period of time.

Transportation services. Many facilities have their own wheelchair van, which can be used for transportation to medical appointments and other excursions.

Apartment and ground maintenance.

Basic-care services as described in levels 1, 2, and 3.

Weekly housekeeping and linen service. This service may be provided once or twice a week, inclusive in the monthly fee.

Use of social and recreational areas. Many facilities have an activities director and monthly calendars of scheduled activities. Religious services may take place at the facility, or the facility may provide transportation to church or synagogue.

Features in a Typical Assisted Living Facility

A standard residence may be a studio or one-bedroom apartment, either semiprivate or private. All or most utilities are paid as part of the monthly fee. Discern which utilities are included in the monthly rental charge. Telephone services are usually not included.

Many of the residence have the following features:

use of convenient laundry rooms

individual heating and air-conditioning controls in each room

twenty-four-hour emergency call system

safety systems in each apartment unit

twenty-four hour a day staffing

can add own furniture to apartment

satellite television with local and cable stations

smoke detectors

soundproof construction

wall-to-wall carpeting

tiled bathroom with safety grab bars in the tub or shower

Social Activities

Depending on the level of care needed at the assisted living facility, a variety of activities may be available, including:

arts and crafts	bridge groups
bible studies	cards
bingo	ceramics

chapel	needlework
current events	pet therapy
discussion groups	photography
exercise room	recreational activities
game room	religious services
garden plots	shuffleboard
golf course	square dancing
health center	sports
indoor pool and spa	swimming
library	tennis courts
line dancing	theater
low-impact aerobics	water exercise classes
movies	woodworking shop
music	yoga classes

Admission Guidelines

Admission to an assisted living facility may depend on several factors:

the availability of a room

the level of required care

the source of payment

After your elder and family have visited a number of assisted living facilities and decided on the facility that will provide the best care, you must contact the facility's admissions office. A social worker or admissions coordinator will give you an application to complete, which includes information about your elder. Most of this information is on the Getting to Know Your Elder work sheet on page 18.

Because some facilities have a waiting list, it is important to ask about availability when you first visit the facility. Even if you have not decided on the best facility, it may be necessary to place your elder's name on the waiting list. This should not obligate your elder, but ensures that she will be notified when an opening becomes available. Some facilities will work with your family, placing your elder temporarily in a different room until her first choice becomes available. If the facility has a low turnover, this may give your elder priority; however, it may also cost more if the room is significantly larger.

The monthly fee is determined in part by room size and in part by the level of required care. The smaller the room, the lower the monthly fee. The lower the level of care, the lower the fee. As care needs increase, which is often the case in assisted living, the fee for living in the facility may also increase. Because of limited staffing, some facilities may not take residents with a high level of care needs. Or, they may feel that the resident should be placed in a higher level of care, such as a nursing facility.

When a resident has been in the hospital, many assisted living facilities will send a social worker, admission coordinator, or registered nurse to the hospital to review the resident's medical record and talk with hospital staff about her care needs. They may also determine from this information that the resident is no longer appropriate for their facility and refuse to take her back until she has reached a lower level of care.

Most people living in an assisted living facility are private-pay residents. As stated earlier, Medicare does not pay for this unskilled or custodial care. In some states, Medicaid will pay for assisted living costs for individuals who have very limited income and some care needs. In addition, some long-term-care policies may provide partial payment toward care in an assisted living facility. Veterans programs may also pay for honorable discharge and service-connected veterans to live in a facility when other options are limited.

EVALUATION

Do you feel living in an assisted living facility is the best choice for your elder family member?

If your answer is "yes," review chapter 3, "Getting Help in Your Home," chapter 10, "Using Home Health and Hospice Care," and chapter 11, "Your Guide to Resources."

If your answer is "no" or you are undecided, turn to chapter 6, "Living in an Adult-Care Home."

If you feel living in an assisted living facility is an option for your elder family member, use the evaluation form below when you visit facilities.

QUESTIONS TO ASK AT AN ASSISTED LIVING FACILITY

When you walk into an assisted living facility, look at the general appearance of the residence.

Outside Area

1. Are the grounds well maintained?
2. Is the residence taller than one story?
3. Are there ramps along the curb for easy wheelchair access?

Inside Area

4. Is a security guard stationed inside the door?
5. Is the lobby area empty, or are residents sitting around?
6. Is smoking allowed, or is there a designated smoking area?
7. Is the atmosphere formal or informal?
8. What are the visiting hours?
9. Are there standard visiting hours?
10. Are the hallways wide enough to accommodate a walker or a wheelchair?
11. Are handrails conveniently placed along the hallways?
12. Is there easy elevator access?
13. Do apartment units include a kitchen area?
14. Can residents provide their own furnishings?
15. Do apartment units contain handicap features such as emergency call buttons and grab bars in the bathroom?
16. Are pets allowed in the residence?

Staff

17. Are staff members professional and able to answer your questions?
18. How does staff determine the care needs of each resident?

19. Is your elder comfortable with staff members?

20. Does the facility have a care plan for each resident?

21. Is there a physician on the facility's staff?

22. How often does the physician visit the facility?

23. Can your elder's primary-care physician visit or continue to provide medical treatment for her?

24. Does the facility have an activities director?

Residents

25. Do residents remain in their rooms or do they visit in common areas?

26. Are residents active or inactive?

Care

27. Are residents allowed to self-administer their own medication?

28. Is medication management available to residents who have difficulty taking their correct medication at the proper time of day?

29. Do staff members keep health and medication records for each resident?

30. If a resident experiences a change in health, is staff available to provide additional assistance?

31. Is staff available to help with the activities of daily living such as:

bathing	transfers
grooming	shopping
personal hygiene	housekeeping
eating at mealtime	laundry
walking	

32. Can a resident hire a person to provide additional care in her apartment unit?

33. Do staff members encourage family involvement?

34. Are home health-care agencies available to provide basic nursing care?

35. Does staff help coordinate services with a home health-care agency?

Cost

36. What services are included in the monthly fee?

37. What services are *not* included in the monthly fee?

38. If a patient's care needs change, does this affect the monthly fee?

39. If a resident changes units or decides to leave the facility, what is the refund policy?

40. Does the facility accept Medicaid payments? (*This is an important question.* Some facilities do not accept Medicaid. Others may accept Medicaid's low reimbursement rate.)

41. What is the policy regarding residents if their funds run out? (*This is an important question.* Some facilities may discharge or evict a resident who is unable to pay for care. Others may try to work closely with your elder and family to prepare you for reduced funds. They may help your elder apply for Medicaid and financial assistance through the senior and disabled services office.)

42. If appropriate, will the facility help a resident apply for Medicaid?

43. Does the facility accept long-term health insurance? (Some long-term insurance policies will have limited coverage for assisted living.)

Transportation

44. Does the facility own a wheelchair van?

45. Does the facility provide transportation to medical appointments?

46. Is there a small fee for transportation services?

47. Are there excursions to other activities, such as plays, concerts, or movies?

48. Is the facility located close to shopping?

Visit several facilities *before* making a decision. Spend a day at the facility, dining and participating in activities. Take advantage of sleeping overnight in a guest unit. After talking with residents and staff members, sit down with other family members to discuss their impressions. Everyone may notice different details about the facility, but trust your instincts even if you are unable to pinpoint why you feel the way you do.

Chapter 6

Living in an Adult-Care Home

—————— ✖ ——————

Cast me not off in the time of old age;
forsake me not when my strength faileth

—Psalms 71:9

One of the most controversial types of care offered to semidependent adults is adult-care homes. These homes are also called *board-and-care homes, adult foster-care homes, domiciliary homes, personal-care homes, community residences,* or *rest homes.* These private homes fill a large gap in the types of care offered to seniors by providing assistance and support at a reasonable cost in a homelike setting. Each home may provide services to a specific population: older adults, people with physical or mental disabilities, people with mental retardation, or people with developmental disabilities. Other types of housing include *residential-care homes, congregate housing, shared housing, ECHO housing,* and *accessory apartments.*

This chapter's focus will be on older adults who have physical or mental disabilities. Your elder and family will learn how to locate and evaluate adult-care homes. You will also learn about the different levels of care, assistance, and services provided by these homes. General information regarding cost, insurance benefits, legal issues, and auxiliary community services, such as home health care and durable medical equipment and supplies, will also be discussed.

Because of the controversy surrounding adult-care homes, state licensing regulations, long-term care, ombudsmen programs, and the rights of residents, families, and care providers will be discussed. State and local resources to help you locate a desirable home are also addressed.

An adult-care home is a private home in which the owner of the residence, an employee, or a caregiver provides basic personal care and assistance with the activities of daily living (ADLs). The ADLs include grooming, bathing, dressing, personal hygiene, mobility, toileting, meal preparation and feeding, and supervision. Caregivers may also provide medication management and some basic nursing care.

It is important to note that adult-care homes often have an owner who does not live in the residence or provide direct care to the residents living in the home. These owners may still be responsible for supervising the hired caregivers and acting as a liaison between the resident, her family, the caregiver, and any community agencies, including home health-care agencies that provide services to the resident.

Marcy Considers Moving to an Adult-Care Home

After living in an assisted living facility for a year, Marcy's health began to decline. She lost weight due to her poor eating habits, wandered away from the facility and became lost, and was bruised after falling several times in her apartment. Although the assisted living facility provided twenty-four-hour supervision (meaning a staff person remained on duty for all residents), this was not exclusively for Marcy. If she decided to hire additional help in her apartment, she would be responsible for paying the additional charge.

The staff at the assisted living facility recommended she move to the supervised and locked Alzheimer's unit, which was designed for confused and wandering residents. With her increased need for care and supervision but her inability to pay additional charges for care, Marcy and her family decided to explore an alternative to living in an assisted living facility. Although they preferred to have her stay at the assisted living facility, they were concerned about the additional cost in the supervised Alzheimer's unit. The adult-care home was less expensive, maintained a smaller number of residents, and presented a more homelike setting. Marcy and her family decided to look at adult-care homes in their area.

Is an adult-care home the best living situation for Marcy?

When to Consider Living in an Adult-Care Home

When your elder and family begin to consider living in an adult-care home, it is important for you to review your elder's physical and mental condition, her current care needs, the location of the residence, its residents, the experience of the caregivers, the level of care offered, the available services, the physical and social atmosphere, and the cost of living in and receiving care in the adult-care home. It is also important to review the adult-care home's state license and the rights and responsibilities of residents, families, and care providers.

Warning Signs

Living in an adult-care home is usually not the first living situation a family would choose for another family member. When Marcy and her family decided to consider her living in an adult-care home, the assisted living facility had become increasingly difficult and unsafe for her. Her family recognized the warning signs before she had a serious accident. Those common warning signs included:

Poor eating habits, which caused a significant weight loss or gain due to an inadequate diet.

Frequent falls, which resulted in contusions, bruising, or abrasions and placed Marcy at high risk of a serious injury or accident.

Prolonged illness, injury, or a recent hospitalization, which resulted in the need for additional care and supervision that family, community agencies, and an assisted living facility are unable to provide.

Inability to manage medication, which resulted in an accidental overdose and caused confusion and disorientation.

Increased need for assistance with the activities of daily living and her inability to dress, groom, or feed herself, which resulted in daily assistance with mobility, toileting, and personal hygiene.

Increased social withdrawal or isolation from friends and family, whichresulted in low attendance at social activities and reduced visits from friends and family.

Significant depression, anxiety, or fears, which interfered with Marcy's ability to manage independently.

Increased mental confusion or disorientation, which resulted in her wandering from home and becoming lost. She was unable to recognize family and close friends and had impaired or faulty memory, which indicated a possible development of early dementia or Alzheimer's disease.

When Marcy's family noticed several of these warning signs, they decided to consider placing her in an adult-care home.

Licensing and Regulations

State licensing of an adult-care home is required in many states and is strongly recommended. However, it does not guarantee high-quality care or safety in the home. Inspections may be infrequent and enforcement of licensing requirements may be lax. A 1993 AARP study showed 32,000 U.S. licensed adult-care homes for older adults served more than 500,000 older residents. (Hawes et al., 1993). In addition, a U.S. House of Representatives Select Committee on Aging (1989) estimated 28,000 unlicensed homes, nationally.

Why is licensing so important? Those homes without a license have no regulated standards for providing physical care or a safe environment for their residents. They may not receive state funding from the Medicaid program to assist residents in paying the cost of care in the home. They may not have a state or watchdog agency checking on their facilities.

Those homes that are licensed demonstrated some responsibility in pursuing the state standards and upholding the state regulations and policies for providing care to older adults. They must meet structural and safety standards. In the event of fire, they must be able to evacuate residents in three minutes.

The caregiver or provider must complete a training program, pass a criminal-records check and be financially solvent and physically and mentally able to provide care to all residents. The home may have no more than five residents in the adult-care home at any one time.

The adult-care home should have a current state license and post it where it can be easily read by residents and families. The home should also provide a current summary of complaints, special conditions on the license, and a copy of the inspection report. If the adult-care home is reluctant or refuses to let your family view this information, you should consider a different facility. This information and a list of licensed facilities may be available at the local senior and disabled services office or state area agency on aging.

How to Choose an Adult-Care Home

When your elder and family begin to look for an adult-care home, you should consider many factors:

> the location of the residence
>
> the cost for room, board, and care
>
> the level of care provided at the home
>
> the accommodations
>
> the basic services
>
> the types of residents living in the home
>
> the home's physical and social atmosphere

Location

Adult-care homes may be located in many types of settings: an urban/city residential area, a suburban are, or a rural area. Many homes may be found in well-maintained neighborhoods; others may be found in run-down areas. In rural areas, the home may have some acreage and views.

When considering location, it is important to find a home that is convenient for your elder's family and friends to visit. It should also be close to a community with shopping, activities, and a church or synagogue for observing religious practices.

Factors in Determining Cost in an Adult-Care Home

The cost of living in an adult-care home is determined by several factors: the resident's required level of care and assistance, the type of accommodations, and the resident's financial situation.

Levels of Care

The level of care or the amount of physical care and supervision needed by each resident is determined by the owner and/or caregiver/provider of the adult-care home. By reviewing the activities of daily living with the resident and her family, the provider should be able to determine your elder's care needs. Or, if a state agency is involved and assisting with placement or payments to the adult-care home, a caseworker may review her care needs and determine the level of care she requires. The higher the level of care, the greater the cost for living in an adult-care home.

Each home is licensed to provide care at a specific level. The owner or caregiver and the state agency review the following care needs:

nutrition	bathroom activities and toileting
dressing and grooming	behavior management
personal hygiene/bathing	medication management
mobility and transferring	basic nursing care

A provider with a level I classification or license may accept residents who require assistance with up to four activities of daily living, routine oral medication management, and no skilled medical or nursing care. For example, your elder may require supervision due to confusion and wandering. If she is semi-independent with her activities of daily living and has no skilled medical needs, she may be considered level I.

A provider with a level II classification or license may accept residents who require assistance with all the activities of daily living. Routine nursing tasks may be assigned to the provider and qualified staff. If your elder requires significant assistance or is able to help the caregiver with her ADLs and has minimal medical needs, she may be considered a level II.

A provider with a level III classification or license may accept residents who are dependent on the caregiver with all the activities of daily living. However, the home may not accept more than one total-care or bedridden resident at a time. Skilled nursing tasks may be assigned to the provider and qualified staff only with approval from the resident's physician, a registered nurse, and the local state area agency on aging. If your elder is dependent or unable to help with her care and has some skilled medical needs or needs total or terminal care, she may be considered level III.

Because the guidelines for these levels of care vary from state to state, it is important to check with the nearest state area agency on aging or senior and disabled services office.

Accommodations

Accommodations may range from a private room with bath to a shared room. Private bedrooms may also be available to couples who choose to share a room. Most adult-care homes also have a common sitting area or living room. Your elder may be able to bring some of her personal belongings, such as a television, a radio, and sometimes furniture to the home to create a comfortable and familiar atmosphere. Some adult-care homes provide a telephone in each room, as well as cable service. Other facilities may include a patio, yard, gardens, and acreage.

The bathroom should be odor-free, clean, and close to the bedroom. There should be enough bathrooms to easily accommodate all the residents in the adult-care home. The bathrooms should be wide enough to easily accommodate a wheelchair or walker and should have high-riser toilet seats, safety grab bars, and shower stools in the bath or shower. If a resident is unable to easily use a bathroom, a portable commode chair should be available.

Hallways and rooms should also be clutter-free, making it easy for residents using walkers or wheelchairs to maneuver around the residence. This reduces the chance of an accidental fall and ensures easy access to exits in the event of an emergency. Grab bars and other assistive devices should be installed in the bathroom and hallways. Bars placed in the hallways also provide an additional safety feature for residents who need support for balance.

It is important to check the adult-care home's policy on smoking. Some homes allow smoking in designated areas only. Smoke detectors should be placed in each bedroom, in hallways, or in access areas. An emergency call system and periodic fire drills add to the necessary safety features in an adult-care home. A copy of the evacuation plan and a record of fire drills should be available for review.

Cost

The charge for living in an adult-care home varies depending upon location, level of required care, and the type of accommodation requested. Payment for an adult-care home may be made several ways: private pay, through the Medicaid program, or the Veterans Affairs office. Some financial support may also be offered through the Social Security Administration. Few long-term-care and private-insurance policies pay for care in an adult-care home.

Private Pay

The range of fees is $350 to $3,000 per month. Many of the homes are in the middle range of $850 to less than $2,000 per month. If your elder and family are considering an adult-care home in the high range, you may want to think of other alternatives, such as living in an intermediate-care facility or increasing services in an assisted living facility.

Medicare
Medicare does not pay for care in an adult-care home.

Medicaid
In some states, the Medicaid program helps supplement low-income seniors who need placement in an adult-care home. Caseworkers in the senior and disability services office will work with your elder and family to locate an adult-care home that would meet her needs. Although the state rates for care are lower than the homes' charges for private pay, many homes have a contract with the state stating they will accept the state rates. For heavy-care residents, the state may allow a higher allowance or rate to the adult-care home. To determine if your state provides this service, contact the nearest state area agency on aging.

Veterans Affairs
If your elder is a service-connected veteran, the Veterans Affairs (VA) office in his area may be able to help with care in an adult-care home or in a VA-sponsored domiciliary care program. Contact the nearest VA office and ask for the social work department to help determine the eligibility requirements. (This department should be able to answer any questions and/or direct your family to the appropriate department.)

Social Security Administration
In forty states and Washington, D.C., supplemental security income (SSI) may be used to make up the difference between the monthly room, board, and care fee and the resident's monthly income. This is called a state supplemental payment (SSP). This amount differs from state to state. Residents in an adult-care home may also keep a portion of SSI or SSP payments in the range of twenty to fifty dollars each month for personal needs.

Basic Services in an Adult-Care Home
The basic services offered in a typical adult-care home include room, meals, personal and medical care, supervision, and social activities. As noted, the rooms may be private or shared.

Meals may be served in a communal dining area. They should be tasty and nutritious and should meet the needs of special diets, such as low-salt and diabetic diets and cultural or religious regimens. Often, the owner or caregiver prepares the meals and eats with the residents. Snacks should be offered several times daily. If a resident has difficulty feeding himself, the caregiver should be available to assist him.

Personal care includes any assistance and supervision with the activities of daily living provided by the owner or caregiver.

Medical care is dependent upon the level of care offered by the adult-care home, the qualifications of the care provider to provide medical care, and the type of medical care needed. If temporary medical care is needed as a result of an accident, injury, or hospitalization, your elder's primary-care physician can request follow-up care at the adult-care home with a home health-care nurse or therapist to meet these temporary needs. They can also provide basic training to the caregiver at the adult-care home. The home's caregivers should work closely with the residents, family, and primary-care physician, arranging medical appointments and transportation as needed.

Social Activities and Atmosphere

Social activities vary in each adult-care home. Activities may depend upon the ability of the residents to actively participate in them. For example, your elder may not be able to play bridge due to her mental confusion. Adult-care homes with active social programs may offer outings to the theater and concerts, craft projects, pet therapy, supervised and planned projects at the home, exercise programs, and more. Many adult-care homes do not have an activities director.

The social atmosphere is important, because it can indicate the amount of stimulation and resident interaction offered by the home. If all the residents are in their rooms, your elder may have nothing to do and no one to talk with. It is important for her to continue to have contact with the other residents, your family, and the caregivers in order to remain as alert and active as possible.

Physical Atmosphere

The physical atmosphere of the adult-care home is important. If the home is not inviting to your elder and family, she will not be content to stay and live there. The adult-care home should be pleasing to the eye; the yard and physical structure should be well maintained. The home's carpet and furniture should be clean and in good condition. The home should be bright and cheerful. It should be easily accessible for wheelchairs and walkers. There should be a comfortable sitting area with a communal television or activities. Your elder and other residents should be able to choose where they sit from a variety of comfortable chairs.

It is important for residents to receive daily personal care and assistance with dressing. If residents are lounging about in their pajamas or bathrobes, the home may not be providing adequate staffing and care.

Types of Residents

The residents who live in the adult-care home are an important factor in choosing a home. If your elder is confused and requires supervision, she may do well in a home with other confused residents. For seniors who are alert and oriented but have physical disabilities and require care, a home with alert residents is more appropriate. This is especially important when your elder considers sharing a room. Your family should be sure her needs and personality are compatible with her roommate's.

Many adult-care homes provide care to difficult residents. A resident may be confused and may yell at all hours of the night. Or a resident may be incontinent and have no control over his bladder and bowel. Or she may have mental-health issues that make her unpredictable. Your elder and family should be sure to meet the home's residents before making a decision.

Disadvantages of Living in an Adult-Care Home

When your elder and family seriously begin looking into adult-care homes, you will hear about their negative aspects. It is important to remember that elders are vulnerable, and *many* abuses can occur in these facilities. The state licensing and regulations at this time are not fully adequate to guarantee quality care in all facilities. You should be alert for the following warning signs, which may indicate a substandard facility.

Overcrowded: There are too many residents in the home.

Limited caregivers: There are not enough caregivers to provide adequate care to all the residents.

Physical restraints or overmedication: The adult-care home uses these to keep residents calm and controlled.

Activities of daily living: Residents are not out of bed, dressed, or assisted with their personal hygiene on a daily basis.

Activity or social programs: No programs are planned during the day or evening. Residents watch television or remain in their rooms.

Safety: The adult-care home does not have a fire-emergency plan or drills. Hallways and rooms are cluttered, making emergency exit difficult. No grab bars are found in the bathrooms or hallways.

Cleanliness: The adult-care home does not follow basic sanitation policies. Commode chairs are not cleaned and emptied frequently, and incontinence diapers are not placed in a covered container. Precautions for infectious diseases, such as hand washing and needle disposal, are not taken. A pervasive odor may be present.

Licensing: There are special conditions stated on the license that directly relate to the risk of harm or potential harm to residents: for instance, that the provider is not in compliance with operation rules.

Abuse: This may include physical abuse or neglect, verbal abuse, and financial abuse. *Physical abuse* may involve bodily harm inflicted on a resident by a caregiver or other resident. In *verbal abuse*, words may be spoken to a resident for the purpose of causing emotional harm. Both may demonstrate a serious lack of control by the caregiver or an incompatibility with other residents at the home. *Financial abuse or mismanagement of funds* is a frequent occurrence. The owner of the adult-care home often assists the resident with her money management. Many residents endorse their monthly Supplemental Security Income or Social Security checks to pay for their care, and a portion of the check is then given to the residents to pay for personal needs. Unfortunately, in this situation, elders are vulnerable. Adult-care home owners may take advantage of residents by having them sign over property and other assets. It is important to ask other residents how they handle their financial affairs, and if the owner is responsible for their money management, how well they feel it is handled.

Other Types of Housing

In addition to adult-care homes, several other living options are available to seniors. These range from self-contained apartments to group-living situations. Some are designed for elders or disabled people; some provide services.

Accessory apartments are self-contained units located in a house in which other people live. It allows an elder to live independently without living alone. The advantages to living in this type of housing include income for the person renting the room in the home, as well as allowing your elder to live in a neighborhood close to friends and family. To live in an accessory apartment, your elder must be fairly independent and self-sufficient. If she is unable to care for herself, she may find several disadvantages to living independently. These may include having to shop for groceries, cook her own meals, clean her apartment, and care for herself without assistance.

Elder Cottage Housing Opportunity (ECHO) housing consist of small, self-contained units that can be placed in the back- or side yard of a single-family house. They are not the same as a mobile home. These are designed for elder and disabled people and are barrier-free and energy-efficient units. The cost for approximately five hundred square feet is less than twenty-five thousand dollars per unit.

Congregate housing has residents living in their own apartment independently. It is a group-living situation, with meals being shared in a central dining area, and includes services for heavy housekeeping, as well as social and recreational activities.

For information about these housing options, contact your local state area agency on aging or senior and disabled services office.

Where to Look for Information About Adult-Care Homes

There are many state and community agencies that can help your family find an adult-care home that is clean and safe and has a good reputation for care and management. Many agencies provide free lists of licensed homes, indicating the level of care they provide, whether they are owner-occupied, or if the owner hires a caregiver to provide services but lives in another residence. They may also indicate whether they are wheelchair accessible, prefer male or female residents, or accept fees from the state. These state fees may be less than what the adult-care homes normally charge.

When your elder and family decide to consider an adult-care home, you should obtain updated information about the homes in your area. There are several agencies to contact for assistance.

The State Area Agency on Aging (AAA)

This agency should have a list of adult-care homes. These homes should have operative licenses, which means occasional inspections by caseworkers from the AAA or senior and disabled services, a criminal-record check on the owner of an adult-care home, a level of care that the state feels is reasonable for the home, and a limit on the number of residents living in the residence at any one time. There may also be limitations on the number of difficult or heavy-care residents.

Be aware that although an adult-care home is on the state list, your family should still visit, meet the caregivers and owner, talk with residents, and have a meal at the home. You should also talk with a caseworker from the AAA who has been in the home. Ask about its reputation. Although the caseworker may not be able to directly state his opinion of the home, he should be able to support your decision as a good choice or suggest a different home. Additional services through the state area agency on aging include ombudsmen programs, caseworker support, and hands-on community services.

Senior and Disabled Services

This agency provides services to seniors and disabled persons. Each person served by the agency is assigned a caseworker who helps him obtain community services, such as homemakers; assistance with shopping and the activities of daily living, and applying for medical or financial assistance. The agency also investigates reports of abuse. It can guide your elder and family to the better homes and steer you away from the homes with marginal reputations or no licenses. Contact the state area agency on aging to find the office nearest you.

Adult-Care Home Associations

These associations can provide your family with information about choosing an adult-care home, the administrative rules of a home licensure, ombudsmen programs, and residents' rights and guide you through the difficult and time-consuming process of locating a good adult-care home.

Hospital Social Work or Case-Management Departments

The professionals in these departments usually work closely with the AAA and other community agencies, assisting with hospital discharge arrangements. Although they may not actually visit these homes, they are continually assessing residents who enter the hospital for medical reasons. They may contact the resident's family, the senior services caseworker, or other involved agency if there are questions regarding care at the adult-care home. If abuse is noted or suspected, these experts are instrumental in reporting it to the appropriate agency, and in addition, they can recommend additional support in the home by ordering necessary medical equipment and making referrals to community agencies, such as senior services or a home health-care agency, for follow-up care.

Home Health-Care Agencies

These agencies are an excellent resource, because the nurses, therapists, and social workers employed here actually visit residents in the homes on a regular basis. They are alert to care problems, poor hygiene, caregiver ability, medication management, and other health-care needs.

Private Agencies

Sometimes an individual helps families locate appropriate adult-care homes. Because these private caseworkers visit each home, they review the care provided to the residents and the type of residents in the home. They try to match the potential resident's needs and finances with the current residents, the caregiver, and the home. Sometimes a small fee is charged to the adult-care home or the family for this service.

Referral from Friends

Perhaps the best way to find an adult-care home with a good reputation is to ask a friend who has an elder parent or relative in such a setting if he is satisfied. Personal experience goes a long way when choosing a home for a loved one.

EVALUATION

Do you feel living in an adult-care home is the best choice for your elder family member?

If your answer is "yes," review chapter 3, "Getting Help in Your Home," chapter 10, "Using Home Health and Hospice Care," and chapter 11, "Your Guide to Resources."

If your answer is "no," or you are undecided, turn to chapter 8, "Understanding Nursing Facilities."

If you feel living in an adult-care home is an option for your elder family member, use the checklist on the following pages when you visit facilities.

Adult-Care Home Checklist

Visit several facilities before making a decision. Bring a friend with whom you can share your impressions. Spend a day at the home dining and participating in activities. After talking with residents and staff, sit down with other family members and discuss their impressions. Every person may notice different details about the home, but also trust your instincts even if you are unable to pinpoint "why you feel the way you do."

Your elder and family can visit an adult-care home anytime you wish to during regular working hours, usually 8 A.M. to 5 P.M. If you are interested in speaking with the owner, try calling in advance to set up an appointment. If you are interested in visiting the home, drop in and ask for a tour. Most homes should be able to accommodate you.

Use the questions on the following pages to keep track of your observations and responses to your questions.

QUESTIONS TO ASK AN ADULT-CARE HOME

When you walk into an adult-care home, look at the general appearance of the residence.

Date _____

Name and address of adult-care home _____

_____

Contact Person _____   **Telephone #** _____

Outside Area

1. Are the grounds well maintained?

2. Is the residence taller than one story?

3. Are there ramps along the curb for easy wheelchair access?

4. Does the neighborhood appear safe for walking?

Inside Area

5. Does the home have an odor?

6. Does the home appear clean?

7. Is the home air-conditioned?

8. Is the living room area empty, or are residents sitting around?

9. Are the hallways wide enough to accommodate a walker or a wheelchair?

10. Are handrails conveniently placed along the hallways?

11. If needed, is there easy elevator access?

12. Is smoking allowed in the home?

13. Is there a designated smoking area?

14. Is there easy access to a telephone?

15. Are exits clearly marked and easily accessible?

16. Does the home have regularly scheduled fire drills?

17. Is there easy access to a mailbox and postage stamps?

18. Is the atmosphere formal or informal?

19. Are there standard visiting hours?

Watch for:
bad odor
safety hazards
residents who are not dressed or are badly groomed
residents who remain in their rooms
residents restrained or tied in chairs. The law strictly limits the use of restraints, especially for convenience of caregivers.

Rooms

20. Are private rooms available?

21. How many residents can be in a room?

22. Must your elder family member share a room with another resident?

23. Will your elder family member have a compatible roommate? (*This is an important question.*)

24. Can residents provide their own furnishings?

25. Do rooms contain handicap features, such as emergency call buttons and grab bars in the bathroom?

26. Does each bed have a privacy curtain?

27. Does each room have a window or view?

28. Are pets allowed in the residence?

Nursing Care

29. What level of care is provided in the home?
    level I _____ level II _____ level III _____ terminal care _____

30. What therapies are available to residents? physical therapy _____
    occupational therapy _____ speech therapy _____
    respiratory therapy _____ other _____

31. Are residents allowed to self-administer their own medication?

32. Is medication management available to residents who have difficulty taking their correct medication at the proper time of day?

33. How are prescriptions filled? by a local pharmacy _____
    by a mail-order pharmacy _____ by family _____
      Some states require that all medications be prepared by a pharmacist in individual doses and placed in a bubble pack. Self-medication must be kept in a locked box or area.

34. Does the staff maintain health and medication records for each resident?

35. If a resident experiences a change in health, is staff available to provide additional assistance?

36. Is staff available to help with the activities of daily living (ADLs) such as:

bathing	transfers
grooming	shopping
personal hygiene	housekeeping
eating at mealtime	laundry
walking	

37. Can a resident hire a private-duty nurse to provide additional care?

38. Does staff encourage family involvement?

39. Can family bring medical supplies, such as incontinence diapers?

Caregivers

40. Is staff professional and able to answer your questions?

41. How does the staff determine each resident's care needs?

42. What is the resident-to-staff ratio?

43. How many caregivers are on duty during each shift?
    one _____ two _____ three _____ more than three _____

44. Does the home have a care plan for each resident?

45. Does staff cooperate with community agencies, such as home health-care agencies, medical-supply companies, and senior services?

46. Do your elder and family feel comfortable with staff?

47. Can your elder's primary-care physician visit or continue to provide medical treatment to your elder at the home?

48. Is there a private place for exams conducted by your elder's physician?

49. Staff should be:

warm	helpful
pleasant	affectionate
honest	courteous
cheerful	respectful
interested	encouraging

Watch for:

disgruntled staff	bad attitudes
yelling at patients	excessive complaining by staff
impatient staff	excessive time to respond to residents

Activities

50. Does the facility have an activities director?

51. Is there a posted schedule of activities?

52. Are activities:
    flexible _____ required _____ structured _____ optional _____

53. Are religious services observed:
    at the facility _____ at a local church or synagogue _____

54. Are community volunteers active at the home?

55. Is there a library at the home?

56. Is there a beautician or barber who visits regularly?

   Watch for:
   no scheduled activities
   a part-time activities program
   no stimulation
   excessive television watching
   residents not bathed or dressed

Transportation

57. Does the home own a wheelchair van?

58. Does the home provide transportation to medical appointments?

59. Is there a small fee for transportation services?

60. Is the home located close to shopping?

Cost

61. What services are included in the monthly fee?

62. What services are *not* included in the monthly fee?

63. Are there hidden fees?

64. If the care needs of a patient change, does this affect the monthly fee?

65. If a resident changes her level of care or decides to leave the home, what is the refund policy?

66. Does the home accept Medicaid payments? (*This is an important question.* Some homes do not accept Medicaid. Others accept the low Medicaid reimbursement rate.)

67. What is the policy regarding residents if their funds run out? (*This is an important question.* Some homes may discharge or evict a resident who is unable to pay for care. Others may try to work closely with your family to prepare them for reduced funds. They may help your family apply for Medicaid and financial assistance through your local state agency.)

68. Will the home help a resident apply for Medicaid?

Rights and Responsibilities of Residents in an Adult Foster-Care Home*

When individuals move into adult foster-care homes, they do not give up any of their civil rights or any rights granted to citizens of [their home state].

Rights of the Resident

to move

to feel safe and protected

to be involved in the care plan

to have a care plan

to decide which family member (or others) should be involved in care

to handle their own financial affairs

to decide who can visit them at the adult foster-care home

to negotiate to have arrangements made to meet special-care needs

to know what the provider expects

to know what to expect of the provider

to be needed, i.e., doing things around the home to feel useful

to make personal choices—clothing, hairstyle, etc.—to maintain their individuality

to understand the rules and have them explained

to self-determination

Responsibility of the Resident

not to make demands on others that are an infringement on the rights of others or that are harmful to self or others

---

Reprinted with permission, Oregon Department of Human Resources from the Senior and Disabled Services Division, Salem, Oregon.

Rights and Responsibilities of Providers

Rights of Providers

to expect timely payment for services

to receive the cooperation of family members to make the transition to adult foster care easier for the resident

same rights that any home owner has to privacy, i.e., knock before entering, call before you visit

to establish house rules that include topics such as

visiting hours

smoking

mealtimes

use of telephone for long-distance calls

pets

taking residents to and from functions outside the adult foster-care home

to deny access to visitor(s) if it would jeopardize the household's safe and secure environment

to set limits or charge for services that fall outside the normal scope of care or services, i.e., long-distance phone calls

Responsibilities of Providers

to explain the resident's bill of rights, house rules, and services contract to the resident and/or family member

to see that the care plan includes input from the resident and family, as well as specifying the role family members will play as part of the care team

to honor the resident's bill of rights and follow the principals of the social model of care

to keep family members informed of changes in the resident's condition

to maintain as much as possible an atmosphere of a family home

Rights and Responsibilities of Family Members

Rights of Family Members

> to be involved in the care plan unless otherwise specified by the resident

> to see facility records about their relative (with the resident's permission)

> to be informed of changes in care needs or the desires of family member receiving care

> to be given a thirty-day written notice prior to rate changes or requests to move the resident

> to have services provided as identified in the contract

> to have the peace of mind that their family member is well cared for

Responsibilities of Family Members

> to be involved in the selection of the care home, if it is desired by the relative seeking care

> to make the move to the care home as least traumatic as possible

> to visit the resident at reasonable times and to abide by the house rules

> to visit the resident on the promised day and time

> to help provider follow care plan, e.g., don't bring candy to a diabetic resident

> to inform provider of gifts and food being given to relative so provider can keep track of residents' personal belongings

> to give the provider reasonable notice of visitation plans

Chapter 7

Understanding Hospital Acute Care

————————— ❧ —————————

A hospitalization resulting from an accident, illness, or surgery can dramatically affect your elder's ability to care for himself. It may be necessary to consider a temporary higher level of care, provided either by family, community agencies, an assisted living facility, an adult-care home, or a nursing facility.

In this chapter, your elder and family will learn how to prepare for an admission to the hospital, approach hospital staff with questions, explore insurance coverage, and prepare an effective discharge plan.

❧ John Goes to the Hospital

While living with his family, John began to experience weakness on his left side and slurred speech. His son immediately called his father's primary-care physician. After hearing a description of John's symptoms, the physician recommended that he be brought promptly to the emergency room for an evaluation. His physician met them at the hospital.

In the emergency room, the ER physician examined John and ordered a CAT scan, which indicated that he had experienced a cerebrovascular accident, or stroke. In addition, the ER physician noted that John appeared to be confused and disoriented and was incontinent, or unable to control his bowels and bladder. He was also unable to verbally communicate with his family, the doctor, or the nursing staff secondary to his slurred speech and confusion.

After John was admitted to the medical floor of the hospital, his family discussed his medical-care needs with his physician, who felt it was too soon to know which services and placement options would be appropriate for John upon discharge. He encouraged the family to wait until all the tests and consultations were completed before making any plans or decisions.

During his hospital stay, John required assistance with feeding, using the toilet, transferring from his bed to a chair, and walking. As he stabilized, his physician ordered consultations from the physical therapist, occupational therapist, and speech therapist and assistance with discharge planning from the case manager or social worker.

The physician met with John and his family and recommended nursing-home placement for continued physical, occupational, and speech therapy. He also suggested that, following nursing-home placement, John be placed in a more supervised setting with twenty-four-hour nursing care.

How will John and his family prepare an effective discharge plan from the hospital? This brief narrative raises several issues:

How will John feel about his sudden change in health?

How will he feel about losing his independence and becoming dependent on nursing staff and family members for care?

How will he communicate his wishes to his family?

How does he feel about receiving care and therapy in a nursing home?

Are there other options to nursing-home care?

If it is needed, how will John's family find a good nursing home?

Will insurance pay for his care in the hospital, the nursing facility, or in his home?

Does he have adequate financial resources to pay for his care?

These are all important and reasonable questions and concerns.

Feelings About Hospitalization

Few people would choose to be admitted to a hospital for medical treatment. Rather, most use hospital services for emergency procedures, necessary or optional surgeries, or procedures and tests.

Outside the hospital, most people live independently, making their own decisions about what they eat, what to wear, and how to spend their day. In the hospital, this all changes. Instead of being independent, your elder may become dependent on nursing staff and other hospital personnel. He may have to share a room. He may need to eat a special diet of pureed food instead of hamburgers or he may need to call for help when he wants to go to the bathroom. Finally, he may have to wear skimpy hospital gowns with an open back, which provide little privacy. (Although he can ask for two gowns, one to cover the front and one to cover the back.)

Many seniors are private about their daily personal life and care. Simple but often necessary practices in the hospital, such as using a bedpan, may be difficult for them. Having a nurse who is a stranger bathe them may be a new and uncomfortable experience. It is important for your elder to share his feelings and concerns with the nurses who provide his care. This increases their awareness of his personal boundaries and needs, as well as enabling them to provide more compassionate care.

Encourage your elder to talk about his concerns regarding the future. The abrupt change in his ability to manage independently—to walk, eat, brush his hair, tie his shoes, button his shirt, use the bathroom, prepare meals, go shopping, or drive a car—presents a challenge. If he requires additional care and treatment after his hospitalization, he may feel he has even lost control over where he lives and who provides his personal care.

It is important for your elder to communicate his ideas and thoughts to your family and physician. If he is unable to communicate after the stroke or has undergone a change in his mental capacity, request a consultation with a speech therapist. A speech therapist is familiar with communication disorders and may have simple solutions or guidelines and information for his family.

Because supportive care in the home and in a care facility can be expensive, it is important for your elder and family to understand his insurance coverage and benefits for care in the hospital, in a care facility, or in his home. Insurance benefits may often determine the type of care available to your elder.

It may be necessary for your elder and family to discuss his monthly income and assets to determine which choices are financially realistic. Because discussing finances with a family member can be uncomfortable, consider which family member has the best relationship with your elder. Reassure him that the money will only be used to pay for his care. This confidential information may need to be shared with the hospital case manager or social worker.

Being Admitted to the Hospital

Your elder may be admitted to the hospital several different ways:

as a direct admission, with a physician's order for a planned surgery, procedure, or treatment

as a direct admission, with a physician's order secondary to sudden illness or an accident

through the emergency room

through outpatient services

Most hospitals have several admissions offices. For direct admissions during regular business hours (approximately 6 A.M. to 7 P.M.), your elder and family will be directed to the main admissions office.

If your elder is admitted through the emergency room, its admissions staff (usually located by the entrance to the ER and open twenty-four hours a day) takes the necessary information. Remember to contact your primary-care physician or specialist if you are going to the emergency room, because the ER doctor may need medical information or may need to consult with your doctor regarding your elder's medical history, condition, and treatment. If your elder has previously been a patient in the hospital, the ER admissions office will request his medical records from the hospital's medical records department.

If your elder is being admitted for an outpatient procedure, he will enter through the outpatient services admissions office or through the emergency room admissions desk. Some hospitals will use the ER admissions for both emergencies and outpatient procedures. Some patients are admitted to the hospital for observation following a procedure or surgery as an outpatient or twenty-three-hour stay.

The Admissions Interview

The admissions staff needs to verify information about your elder family member. Be patient, because they sometimes need to prioritize for emergency situations. In the emergency room, this information can be gathered after medical treatment is started. Normally, the admissions clerk asks for the following information:

elder's full name, address, and telephone number

elder's birth date

his place of employment, if applicable

his Social Security number

his spouse's name and place of employment

his spouse's Social Security number

next of kin

an emergency contact in the family or a close friend

known allergies and medications

his physician's name

presenting problem

insurance policies and numbers

It is important to bring the original or copies of the following:

medical and insurance cards

list of medications and dosages

copy of Social Security card

advanced directives*

Physician Orders for Life-Sustaining Treatment (POLST)

durable power of attorney for health care*

living will*

durable power of attorney

organ donor card

guardianship papers*

other pertinent legal documents

Each time your elder is admitted to the hospital, he is given a new account number, but the medical record number remains the same. It is necessary for him or someone in his family to sign the conditions of admission form and other documents.

---

*This is important: *Retain the original for your files, and give copies to the admissions office for the medical record, your elder's physician, his attorney, and any involved health-care facility or community agency.*

An advanced directive enables your elder to express his wishes for medical care during his illness. He has the right to change or cancel this document at any time. In this document he can:

appoint a health-care representative to direct his care if he is not able to.

complete health-care instructions regarding life support, tube feedings, and other limits of health care. (Life support means any medical procedures, devices such as ventilators, or medications that may be used to sustain life. *Tube feedings* include any food and water artificially supplied through medical means.)

choose to receive treatment, follow physician recommendations, or choose not to receive any treatments if close to death, permanently unconscious, suffering from an advanced progressive illness, or suffering extraordinary permanent and severe pain and using life support or tube feedings would only postpone death.

request a no code status be ordered by his physician. This is a Do Not Resuscitate (DNR) order. Or request a full code status, which means all medical means may be used to sustain life.

The Physician Orders for Life-Sustaining Treatment form, or POLST, is a newly developed voluntary physician order sheet for people who have serious health problems. It may be used to specify your elder's preferences and desires for life-sustaining treatment to his physician and other health-care providers. It is useful in various health-care settings, including long-term care, adult-care homes, home health care, hospitals, and emergency situations. Without the POLST form, emergency personnel are required to provide full treatment and resuscitation.

The bright pink POLST form must be signed by your elder's primary-care or attending physician but may be initiated by other health-care providers, your elder, or a family member. It may also be changed or canceled if your elder's treatment requires change. The original form should go with your elder whenever he is transferred or discharged from a health-care setting. Copies should be sent to the physician's office, appropriate health-care providers, and a member of your family.

The POLST is divided into five sections. Your elder may designate his treatment preferences in each:

Section A: Resuscitation means there is no pulse *and* no breathing.

Section B: Medical intervention, including emergency medical care, means there is a pulse *and/or* breathing. It describes the amount of medical treatment, intervention, and care requested by your elder.

Section C: Antibiotics. If no limitation is placed on the use of antibiotics, your elder will receive full treatment.

Section D: Artificially administered fluids and nutrition or the use of feeding tubes/IV fluids is designated if your elder is unable to take fluids by mouth.

Section E: Basis for physician orders states with whom the orders were discussed and summarizes the orders, signed by your elder's physician.

The POLST is a new and invaluable tool to ensure your elder's health-care decisions are followed during life-threatening situations. Although it summarizes the advanced directive, it is not a substitute for one. For information on acquiring a POLST form, see chapter II, "Your Guide to Resources," under Home Care and Hospice.

A *durable power of attorney for health care* enables your elder to appoint a health-care representative to make health-care decisions for him.

A *living will* is a document that expresses in writing your elder's wishes not to prolong life using extraordinary means or devices during terminal illness or a lasting comatose condition. It helps establish the no code status.

A *durable general power of attorney* allows your elder to appoint voluntarily someone to handle his real or personal property without advance notice or approval. These powers may continue to exist after he is declared incompetent, disabled or incapacitated. The power of attorney can also be limited (a limited power of attorney) to specific transactions and responsibilities, such as the payment of his bills. Your elder will not lose his right to manage his own affairs. This device simply allows him to choose another person to help him with these affairs.

An *organ donor card* can be completed at the time of admission. It expresses your elder's wishes to donate his organs at the time of death. There is no age requirement and no cost to his family.

If your elder and family have any questions or concerns regarding the documents listed above, consult an attorney. Free legal advice is available through some senior service agencies and state or county legal-service offices. A hospital social worker may be able to help you understand some of these documents.

Please note: Each state has different rules for advanced directives, a durable power of attorney for health care, and a living will. If your elder moves to another state, it is important to have him complete the above forms again while he can still make these decisions.

Financial Assistance

If your elder is unemployed, has limited or little income and limited or no insurance coverage, ask the admissions office for a confidential financial statement. It will request the following information:

responsible party

employment information

spouse information

dependents' names, relationship, and ages

sources of income

living expenses

payments due (credit cards)

list of medical and medication bills

comments to support your financial statement

The financial statement should be completed as soon as possible and mailed back to either the hospital's admissions or business office.

What to Bring to the Hospital Room

After the direct admissions interview, your elder is assigned a room. Hospitals usually require the patient to use a wheelchair when he is admitted. Once on the medical floor, nursing staff helps him to get settled in the hospital room.

If he is being admitted through the emergency room, the ER staff will bring him along with any pertinent medical records to his room. The ER registered nurse will also call or report necessary medical information to the nursing staff on the medical unit.

When your elder is admitted to the hospital, your family should bring:

bathrobe

nonskid slippers

pajamas

glasses

dentures

hearing aids

toiletries

important telephone numbers

reading material

Do *not* bring:

sentimental or personal items

jewelry

credit cards or cash

delicate clothing

dress shoes or clothing

medications from home

If your elder and family have specific questions regarding admission to the hospital, you should contact the admissions office.

Receiving Care in a Hospital

Most hospitals have many different departments, including administrative, human resources or personnel, admissions, medical records, business, nursing, rehabilitation services, outpatient services, case management or social work services, dietary, surgical, laboratory, X ray, pharmacy, engineering, and housekeeping.

The medical floors may be divided into units: medical, surgical, intensive care, emergency, short-stay, and skilled-plus or transitional-care units. Or, they may be divided by diagnosis: neurological, psychiatric, orthopedic, pediatric, maternity, cardiac, dialysis, cancer, rehabilitation, and general medical and surgical units. Other hospitals, for instance, teaching hospitals, may have additional specialty units.

When your elder and family complete the admission process, he is moved to a unit appropriate for his medical condition. If he is in critical condition, he may be transferred to the intensive- or critical-care unit (ICU or CCU). He will be assigned a registered nurse (RN), a licensed practical nurse (LPN), or a certified nurse's aide (CNA).

Hospital Staff

The *physician* is responsible for ordering the daily care, tests, treatments, medication, therapies, and consultations. These orders are written in the orders section of the medical record and then relayed, usually by the unit clerk or charge nurse, to the proper department. He may also write a general statement regarding the patient's treatment and progress in the "progress notes" section of the medical chart.

---

*If your elder requires physical therapy to increase his mobility,
his physician must write an order in "physician's orders,"
requesting physical therapy, evaluation, and treatment.
In the "progress" notes, he may write, "Patient still
experiencing moderate discomfort and pain when moved,
which is limiting transfers and ambulation."*

Many physicians make their rounds or visit patients early in the morning. If your family would like to speak with their elder's physician, ask the charge nurse to recommend a good time. A note may also be placed in the chart, informing the physician that your family would like to talk with him. It is important that you and your elder write down any questions, because physicians are often in a hurry, and it is easy to forget issues that seemed important previously.

Sometimes the registered nurse takes orders over the telephone from the physician, signs the doctor's name, registers the time of the order, and cosigns with her initials or signature.

If a registered nurse feels a pain medication is too strong for your elder, she can change the dosage only with a doctor's permission over the telephone or by written order.

Patients sometimes react strongly and unexpectedly to medications used in surgery or on the medical floor. They may experience visual or auditory hallucinations, intermittent confusion and disorientation, or changes in mental health, such as depression. If your family notices any unusual changes in your elder's mental condition, immediately notify the registered nurse who cares for your elder family member. She, in turn, will notify his physician.

It is important for your elder and family to communicate your wishes regarding extraordinary treatments, as stated in the advanced directives, and express your concerns to the physician. Likewise, your family should understand your elder's diagnosis, prognosis, treatment recommendations, and care needs. Physicians sometimes schedule an office visit to talk with family members about their elder's medical issues.

The *registered nurse* is responsible for medical care, monitoring IVs and dispensing medications, changing dressings, and more. The *licensed practical nurse* can assist the RN but cannot administer IVs or injections. The *certified nursing aide* can assist with personal hygiene, care, and mobility. Be aware that the nursing staff may change each day and each shift.

On admission to the medical floor, the RN talks with your elder and family to obtain pertinent social information and specific information about his medical condition and history and his ability to walk, transfer, feed, and care for himself. This nursing assessment is placed in the confidential medical record.

The charge nurse (the nurse in charge of the medical floor) receives information from many staff members, including physicians, nurses, medical social workers or case managers, therapists, and other hospital personnel. She is often responsible for tracking down doctors and obtaining orders for care. The charge nurse is usually aware of the ordered medical care, tests, and treatments for each patient on her floor.

Many nurses work twelve-hour shifts, three to four days a week. This means your elder may not have the same nurses during his hospitalization. This can disrupt the continuity of his care when his nursing care is given by a new nurse each day or shift. To remedy this disruption, the nurses give a verbal or taped report for the staff on the next shift.

An RN's professional expertise covers a wide range of services, including:

bladder and bowel training

blood and lab work

catheter care and family training

checking blood pressure and vital signs

chemotherapy

decubitus or bedsore care

diabetes management and education

dressing changes

electrolyte therapy

enteral nutrition and therapy

hydration therapy

intramuscular and subcutaneous injections

intravenous therapy (IVs)

medication management

pain control

patient education

total parenteral nutrition

wound, colostomy, and ileostomy care

Each hospital utilizes professional case managers, medical social workers, and discharge planners in different ways. All are patient advocates, but case managers are also hospital advocates; they review medical records to determine if patients meet acute-care hospital guidelines. All act as a liaison between the physician, nursing staff, therapists, dietitians, other hospital personnel, and your elder and family. All can help coordinate the medical care with the posthospital care to ensure a smooth transition from hospital to home or to a care facility.

Medical social workers in a social work services department have similar responsibilities to a medical case manager. The main difference is they are not utilization reviewers; they are primarily patient advocates who focus their expertise on counseling, evaluate family and home situations, address financial concerns, make referrals to community, state, and federal programs, and assist with placement in nursing-care facilities, adult-care homes, and assisted living facilities. In some hospitals, the medical social worker is primarily a counselor who talks to families about their personal concerns and feelings; these social workers may not be involved with discharge planning.

Case-management departments often combine social work service and utilization review departments. A *medical case manager* is usually a medical social worker or registered nurse with expertise in interpreting medical records and understanding insurance policies and benefits. They confer and share medical information with insurance companies to obtain necessary pre-authorizations for medical care in the hospital. In addition, they may provide counseling services, assist with referrals to community agencies, and help make arrangements for discharge from the hospital.

As utilization reviewers, case managers also review the elder's medical record to determine that the hospitalization is necessary and meets the insurance requirements for acute medical care. If they determine that your elder does not meet this requirement, they may notify his physician and request additional medical documentation in the medical chart. If your elder does not meet the guidelines for acute care, the utilization reviewer may send him and your family a letter advising that hospital benefits are being terminated. There is usually a grace period of one to two days. If your elder is not discharged during that time, his insurance may *not* pay for medical care in the hospital after the termination date.

Discharge planners primarily focus on helping the family to make discharge arrangements from the hospital. This may involve making referrals to nursing facilities, adult-care homes, and assisted living facilities, ordering durable medical equipment and supplies, obtaining home health orders, and arranging transportation.

Talking with a Case Manager, Social Worker, or Discharge Planner

When your elder and family decide it is necessary to speak with a case manager or social worker, you should have at least one extended family member or a friend present at the interview. In times of stress or anxiety, it may be difficult for your elder and family to remember all the important information being discussed. Having an additional person to talk with afterward may help you clarify the discussion and assimilate the information, which will result in a clearer and more thoughtful approach to your concerns. There are many ways to contact a case manager, social worker, or discharge planner.

your elder can ask his nurse to contact a case manager or social worker

a family member or close friend can ask to speak with a case manager or social worker

the physician can write an order for a case manager or social worker to see your elder and family

nursing staff can request a physician's referral

a community agency can request a referral

the case-management or social work department can screen the admission sheets and medical records to determine if your elder is a high-risk patient and see him without an order. High risk may be determined by:

no insurance information

age

an elder person in poor health who lives alone without family supports

specific medical diagnosis

cause of injury, such as an accident

drug or alcohol use

identified abuse issues

mental health issues, such as psychiatric history or depression

complaints by hospital staff regarding noncompliance or lack of cooperation during treatments

numerous emergency room visits

terminal illness and grief counseling

numerous repeat admissions over a short period of time

assistance with transportation for treatments, such as kidney dialysis, chemotherapy, radiation treatments, or outpatient physical or occupational therapy

possible financial concerns or low income

employment difficulties resulting from hospitalization

need for medical equipment or supplies

possible placement needs

Other Hospital Professionals and Nonprofessionals

Many essential hospital professionals and nonprofessionals work together to assure quality medical care. Although the nursing staff provides most of the physical care your elder receives, other hospital staff also play an integral role in providing comprehensive medical care.

The *pharmacist* is responsible for filling medication orders for patients. Some hospitals do not encourage families to fill prescriptions at the time of discharge at the hospital pharmacy. If your elder cannot afford the cost of the medication, talk with a case manager or social worker *before* his discharge. They sometimes can arrange financial assistance through the hospital pharmacy, one of the large pharmaceutical companies, or through a local social service agency.

The *dietitian* or nutritional therapist can assist with diet planning and educating and teaching patients about new diets, including a diabetic regimen. They consult with the physician about patients with poor nutrition or those who require feeding tubes. They can also help your elder to obtain dietary supplements, such as Ensure and Sustecal. The dietitian is usually available to meet with patients and their families in the hospital room. A dietitian can:

> enable families to have more control over their health by teaching them about the importance of diet
>
> make recommendations for dietary supplements and drinks, such as Ensure, Jevity, and Sustecal
>
> set up specific meal plans and diets
>
> make recommendations to your physician for medical problems, such as difficulty swallowing and poor food intake, and evaluate the need for nasogastric feedings

The *physical therapist* (PT) provides assessment, treatment, and rehabilitation of severe physical injuries or pain resulting from an injury or illness. A doctor's order is needed before a therapist can provide treatment. Your elder may benefit from physical therapy if he has:

> lost the use of his limbs or muscles in his arms or legs due to illness, accident, or injury
>
> a fractured hip

weakness due to a lengthy illness or injury

head or spinal cord injuries

stroke or cerebrovascular accident

neurological conditions such as multiple sclerosis and Parkinson's disease

The physical therapist can provide the following services:

assessment of rehabilitative and equipment needs and safety issues

assistance in obtaining durable medical equipment and supplies

therapeutic treatments, including hot packs, ultrasound and paraffin baths, or hydrotherapy

instruction for patient and family on safety, transfers, and bed mobility

balance and gait (walking) training

exercise programs

functional independence

endurance training

electrotherapy

transfer techniques

strengthening

physical restoration

prosthetic training

range of motion exercises

relaxation techniques

home safety evaluations

The *occupational therapist* (OT) may be needed following an illness or injury. By working closely with your elder, the OT can help him regain basic movements through strengthening and coordination exercises, increase his perception or ability to judge, and help him resume normal activities of daily living. The OT can assist with:

activities of daily living and self-care training. These activities include basic care and hygiene, including brushing hair and teeth, bathing or dressing, toileting, grooming, and meal preparation.

fine motor skills. These are precise movements, such as threading a needle or putting a key in a lock.

homemaking activities

orthotics and self-help device training. The OT can help by designing tools and gadgets to enable your elder to perform routine activities, such as tying a shoelace or buttoning a shirt, more easily.

transfer training or moving safely and independently from a bed to a chair

upper- and lower-limb exercises for strength, coordination, and range of motion

The *speech-language therapist* (ST) works with people who are recovering from an illness that has affected their ability to communicate. She can be beneficial to those who have had a stroke, head or mouth injury, neurological disorder, or surgery. The ST can help with:

assessment, diagnostic testing, evaluation, and treatment for speech and language disorders

relearning language skills

setting up easy-to-use communication systems

swallowing problems

The *respiratory therapist* provides direct services to those who have breathing problems. The respiratory therapist can assist by:

setting up respiratory equipment, monitoring oxygen levels, and giving breathing treatments

acting as liaison between the nursing staff, physician, home health-care agency, and medical-supply company

teaching proper use of equipment

ordering and supervising in-home set-up of equipment, such as oxygen and other breathing apparatus

providing follow-up services

The *X-ray technicians* are responsible for preparing patients for tests and X-ray treatments, transporting them to the proper department, and assisting the radiologist with the test. If your elder is unable to be moved, they can bring a portable X-ray machine to his room. For procedures involving large machines such as a CAT scan, your elder must be moved to the area where the test can be done.

The *lab technicians* are responsible for taking blood samples and running tests and screens in a timely manner. They can draw blood in your elder's room. These technicians are often called by nursing staff when they are having a difficult time drawing blood.

Paying for Your Hospitalization

Most people admitted to a hospital carry some type of insurance policy: Medicare, Medicaid, Medicare supplemental, Medigap, Medical HMOs, managed care, or veterans benefits. Occasionally, a person has no insurance but can qualify for Medicaid, or he "falls through the cracks" because he has no insurance, lacks income to pay for hospitalization, and has too much income to qualify for financial assistance.

As a Medicare beneficiary, your elder may receive medical services under the traditional Medicare fee-for-service program or through a managed-care or HMO plan that has a contract with Medicare.

Medicare

Medicare Part A hospital insurance pays for a semiprivate room and board, general nursing care, hospital services, and supplies for the first sixty days of hospitalization. Your elder's responsibility as of 2000 was a deductible of $776 per benefit period.

> The sixty-first through ninetieth day, Medicare pays all but $194 per day.
>
> The ninety-first through one hundred fiftieth day, Medicare pays all but $388 per day. These are considered lifetime reserve days and may be used only once.
>
> The one hundred fiftieth day and beyond, Medicare pays nothing. Your elder pays all costs.

(These deductibles may be paid by a managed-care, Medigap, or Medicare supplemental policy and will be discussed later.)

Medicare Part B medical insurance does not pay for hospitalization. It does pay for medical bills submitted by your elder's physician and for outpatient hospital care and medical services not covered under Medicare Part A. If your elder does not have Medicare Part A, he can buy the policy for a monthly premium of $301. For Medicare Part B, the monthly premium is $45.50. The deductible for Medicare Part B is still $100 annually.

Hospice care in the hospital is also covered under Medicare Part A as long as the doctor certifies the need for terminal care. It pays all expenses except a small fee for inpatient respite care and some outpatient medications. A patient can receive up to five days of care per admission, which gives family members respite care or a break in caregiving.

Unlimited blood is covered by Medicare Part A as long as it is medically necessary. Medicare will pay for the first 3 pints per calendar year. After 3 pints, your elder is responsible for either replacing or paying for the blood.

Blood is also covered under Medicare Part B medical insurance and again is unlimited if medically necessary. Your elder is responsible for the first 3 pints plus 20 percent of the approved amount and the $100 deductible. Medicare pays 80 percent of the approved amount after a $100 deductible and starting with the fourth pint of blood.

Outpatient hospital services treatment or therapy for an illness is covered under Medicare Part B. Your elder is responsible for 20 percent of hospital charges. This deductible may be paid under your managed-care, Medigap, or a Medicare supplemental policy.

It is important to remember that Medicare eligibility requirements, monthly premiums, and hospital deductibles change every year.

To apply for Medicare Part A or Part B, it is necessary to contact the nearest Social Security office, which can help your elder and family to determine if he meets the requirements for receiving or buying into a Medicare insurance policy. In addition, helpful brochures and information enable him to read carefully the eligibility requirements for Medicare benefits.

Medicare Supplemental and Medigap

These policies are designed to cover the "gaps" or "holes" in your elder's Medicare benefits. They may also pay for specific services not covered under Medicare. Some policies pay the Medicare deductibles and coinsurances. Medicare supplemental policies may have limits on benefits or exclusions for specific medical conditions.

Standard Medigap policies were developed by the National Association of Insurance Commissioners. The plans range from "basic" benefit packages to packages with additional options. The plans range from Plan A to Plan J; states are required to offer Plan A but are not required to offer additional Medigap policies. Medigap packages can help pay for:

- Medicare Part A coinsurance for the sixty-first through ninetieth day of hospitalization

- Medicare Part A coinsurance for sixty nonrenewable lifetime inpatient hospital reserve days

- Medicare Part A eligible hospital benefits at 100 percent after all Medicare hospital benefits are exhausted

- Medicare Part A and Part B coverage for the first 3 pints of blood

- Medicare Part B coinsurance for approved outpatient mental health services after the deductible is met

- Medicare Part A inpatient hospital deductible ($776 per benefit period in 2000)

- skilled nursing facility care daily coinsurance of $97 for the twenty-first through one hundredth day per benefit period in 2000

- Medicare Part B deductible of $100 per calendar year in 1998

- 80 percent of medically necessary emergency care in a foreign country, after a $250 deductible

- Coverage for home recovery, which includes up to $1,600 per year for home assistance with activities of daily living while recovering from hospitalization, surgery, illness, or accident. *Please note: This is a low allowance for home assistance when you consider the cost of hiring home help.*

- Coverage for preventative medical care. This benefit pays $120 per calendar year for physical examinations, serum-cholesterol screening, hearing test, diabetes screening, and thyroid-function tests. *Please note: This is a low allowance for these services. If your elder needs these tests, contact your local hospital or community health clinic. They often provide free or low-cost screening.*

- Basic prescription drug benefits, which cover 50 percent of cost for prescription drugs after an annual $250 deductible is met by the policyholder. *Please note: Some managed care, Medicare supplemental, and Medigap plans provide prescription drug coverage for a small deductible ($5*

to $20) or pay a percentage of each prescription. Because prescription med-
ications can be expensive, this is an important benefit.

Coverage for 100-percent Medicare Part B charges that exceed the
amount allowed by Medicare. *Please note:* The above benefits are available in the ten standard medicare-supplemental plans. For additional
information on purchasing Medicare supplemental and Medigap policies, contact your nearest state insurance department or state area
agency on aging.

Medicare HMOs = Managed-Care Programs

Medicare HMO programs were created to reduce the cost of health care and increase
the number of benefits to our nation's elderly. In reality, many of these programs have
significant limitations—some obvious, some "hidden" to the average person. They may
restrict which physicians a person can see or require pre-authorizations for services and
tests. An elder may need a referral from a primary-care physician to see specialists. If
the HMO determines the treatments, tests, or specialists are not medically necessary,
they may deny the referral or service. These decisions may actually be based on the service's cost rather than an individual's medical need. Some HMOs now exclude vital
services such as unlimited drug benefits (not covered under Medicare). In addition, an
HMO may use stricter guidelines for what constitutes emergency care or the need for
rehabilitation or skilled nursing care.

Managed care or HMO plans provide benefits within their own network of hospitals, physicians, and other health professionals. Your elder's primary-care physician

---

To qualify for a managed-care program a person must:

- *have Medicare Part B and continue paying Medicare Part B
  premiums, or live in the area serviced by the managed-care program*
- *not be receiving benefits under a Medicare-certified hospice*
- *not have permanent kidney failure at time of enrollment*

  Please note: Some managed-care programs have stricter guidelines than
  Medicare and may authorize shorter stays in hospital or nursing facilities or
  may not authorize treatment by a specialist outside the managed-care program.

---

selected through the managed-care program is responsible for hospital admissions, his medical care, and referrals to other health-care professionals and specialists.

Check with your elder's managed-care plan about its policy for receiving emergency care outside her local area, because some plans will try to have her transferred back to her area to receive necessary follow-up care, often at her own expense.

Your elder's managed-care or HMO plan must pay for her emergency care and the needed follow-up care, even if it is out of the service area. Pre-authorization for the emergency services should not be required. Doctors who are not affiliated with her insurance plan can provide the emergency care, and her HMO may not deny her claim for emergency services even if the medical emergency outcome is not a medical emergency.

Your elder and your family may also ask the hospital treating her medical emergency to negotiate a contract with the managed-care or HMO plan to keep her in the nonservice-area hospital until her condition is stable and she can be safely transferred to a participating HMO facility. If ambulance transportation is needed, negotiate with her HMO for assistance with the ambulance fee.

Do not transfer your elder until his attending physician indicates that his medical condition is stable, because a transfer before that time may place him at risk for harm or injury.

Some managed-care programs strongly prefer that your elder be treated in one of its facilities. Representatives may insist on transferring him before he is medically stable. Talk with his physician regarding his medical condition before agreeing to a transfer. Sometimes hospitals and your managed-care program can work out a onetime contract that allows your elder to continue to receive care in a nonaffiliated hospital. If the managed-care program insists on transferring your elder to its own hospital, be sure to discuss the safest way to transfer him and who will pay the transportation cost.

For example, Sam G. was hit by a car while on vacation three hundred miles from his home. He was admitted to the nearest hospital with a fractured pelvis, multiple contusions, and abrasions and placed in traction. He was unable to walk or move and considered medically unstable. Nonetheless, his HMO requested that Sam be transferred back to its hospital by commercial airline at the family's expense. When told he was not medically stable for transfer, his HMO's representatives asked for him to be transferred by medical air ambulance, again at the family's expense, at a cost of more than three thousand dollars. After many hours and days of negotiation, the HMO finally agreed to a contract with the treating hospital, which allowed Sam to stay and receive the necessary medical care.

For elders with veterans benefits, the hospital must contact the nearest Veterans Affairs office for authorization. Although the VA may choose to have the patient receive care in a non-VA facility, it may also request a transfer to a VA facility when he has been stabilized. The VA usually provides transportation for this transfer.

Other Programs

Medicaid is for those individuals who have limited income and limited assets. Medicaid pays for hospitalization if your elder does not have any other insurance that can pay for the benefits covered by the Medicaid program. It pays for deductible and coinsurance payments. Benefits vary from state to state, so it is important to contact the nearest state area agency on aging office or senior and disabled services office to obtain their guidelines and an application.

The Qualified Medicare Beneficiary program (QMB) can help low-income Medicare beneficiaries to pay their health-care costs by paying Medicare deductibles, monthly premiums, and coinsurance amounts for qualified people who have Medicare Part A. This program is regulated in each state, so the income limits may vary from these figures. If your elder's monthly income in 1999 was less than $691.01 for an individual, or less than $925 for a couple, and assets do not exceed $4,000 per individual or $6,000 per couple, he may qualify for this program.

The Specified Low-Income Medicare Beneficiary (SLMB) program is designed to help people who are entitled to Medicare Part A; these individuals have incomes slightly greater than (not more than 20 percent) the national poverty level. Under this program, qualified people have the state pay their Medicare Part B monthly premium. Your elder is responsible for the deductibles, coinsurance, and any other charges that are not covered by Medicare. To qualify, an individual's monthly income must be between $691.01 and $825; for a couple, their monthly income must be between $925 and $1,105.01.

(*Please note:* The eligibility rates for individuals and couples are approximate figures, because the monthly income limits for the QMB and SLMB programs change each year. Also, the monthly income limits in Hawaii and Alaska are approximately $200 higher than other states. For the specific monthly income eligibility requirements, call the Medicare hot line, at 1-800-638-6833.)

Hints About Hospital Insurance

It is important that your elder and family become familiar with hospital insurance coverage. By reviewing his policies, your family can identify areas that have gaps in coverage. Be sure that your elder has adequate coverage for the following benefits:

pays hospitalization deductible of $776 per benefit period in 2000

coverage for extended hospitalization coinsurance in case of lengthy hospitalization

skilled nursing facility coinsurance coverage for twenty-first through one hundredth day

prescription drug coverage

Watch out for policies that have:

exclusions for specific medical conditions. If your elder has a preexisting medical condition for which there is a strong probability that he will need medical treatment, do not sign any contract that states it will not pay for medical care related to that specific condition.

managed-care plans with strict guidelines that may override some of your Medicare benefits.

duplicate coverage of benefits.

inadequate policies. Do not cancel your elder's policy until it has been replaced with another policy. He does not want to find himself in an "insurance gap," without medical coverage.

limits on benefits. Some Medicare supplement policies (not Medigap policies) may have limits on what they pay for specific benefits. This allowable amount may be less than the Medicare-approved amount for hospital outpatient services or services provided by your physician.

Don't allow your elder to be pressured into buying a policy. Take the time to check with the Medicare hot line or the National Association of Insurance Commissioners. Use only a reputable company. Read the entire policy and write down any questions your elder does not understand.

Remember, these are only guidelines. To include all the information necessary to understand Medicare, Medigap, and Medicare supplemental policies more completely, you must read the available booklets and talk with knowledgeable professionals in the insurance and health-care field.

Planning Your Elder's Discharge from the Hospital

When your elder is ready for discharge from the hospital, your family may receive little or no warning. Each person in a hospital responds to medical procedures differently, so it is necessary to anticipate increased care needs and supervision following hospitalization.

Although some hospital discharges are straightforward, others can be more complex. When your elder and family consider all the changes he will experience in the hospital, it is easy to see why some elders do not quickly bounce back to their usual activities. Consider the number of tests, procedures, and surgeries, time in bed or in a chair, and changes in toileting and diet. All these variations from normal, everyday life can affect the amount of time it takes for an elder to recover from a hospitalization.

Although time in the hospital varies, each medical diagnosis has a standard predetermined length of stay. Assuming no complications arise, your family should be able to anticipate when your elder family member will be ready for discharge from the hospital.

Your elder may be able to return to his previous living situation or home, or he may need increased care in his place of residence or in an assisted living facility, adult-care home, or nursing facility. Or he may benefit from an inpatient or outpatient rehabilitation program.

How will your elder and family know what care or supervision is needed?

How will you know which community agencies or programs to contact?

How will you know the cost for services or care in a facility?

When your elder is soon to be discharged from the hospital, your family may want to speak with a social worker, case manager, or discharge planner about discharge plans. They will review his medical record and, with help from his family and information from hospital staff and his physician, discuss with his family all the reasonable care options. The social worker can provide your elder and family with helpful information and clearly lay out all the discharge options: returning home with community supports, home health-care services, and durable medical equipment and supplies; or living in a care facility. This means they may ask questions about your elder's current living situation, including:

the layout of his residence

the number of stairs inside and access to the bathroom

access to the bedroom area

his care needs and preferences

available financial resources

safety features in the home

medical equipment in the home or residence

availability of help from family, neighbors, and caregivers

names of community agencies or active caseworkers

If your elder was living alone prior to hospitalization, it may become necessary to contact community agencies for in-home support, services, and durable medical equipment and supplies. Or your family may decide to have someone stay with him or have him stay with family until he is able to resume independent living.

If your elder was living in a retirement or assisted living community, it may be necessary to increase help in his apartment or alert the retirement home or assisted living manager to his increased care needs.

If your elder is unable to safely return to any of these settings, your family may need to consider other options, such as adult-care homes and nursing facilities. If he is living in an adult-care home, your family should contact the home with an update of his medical condition. Some adult-care homes cannot care for a person who has extensive medical needs.

If nursing-home placement or an intensive rehabilitation program is a reasonable option, it is important to consult with your elder's physician, the medical social worker, or case manager regarding facilities in his area.

If your elder is transferred to a nursing facility, an adult-care home, or a rehabilitation center, the social worker may recommend that your family complete a Physician Orders for Life-Sustaining Treatment form; it should be signed by your elder's physician and remain with him whenever he is transferred or discharged from a health-care setting.

APPRAISING YOUR ELDER'S LIVING SITUATION AND CARE NEEDS

After leaving the hospital, your elder may need a different living situation or increased care and supervision for a short or longer period of time. To determine the appropriate living situation and care needs, please answer the following questions:

1. Where did your elder live prior to hospitalization?

2. Do you feel your elder can safely return to this living situation?

3. Do you feel some in-home supervision or assistance would be helpful?

4. Are you interested in exploring an alternative living situation while your elder recovers from his hospitalization?

5. Prior to hospitalization, how would you describe your elder's general physical health?

6. Prior to hospitalization, did your elder receive any assistance with personal or medical care?

7. Did your elder require care from a registered nurse, physical therapist, or home health-care agency?

8. Prior to hospitalization, how would you describe your elder's mental health?

alert	confused
oriented	disoriented
can make his own decisions	cannot make his own decisions
good memory	poor memory
easily follows directions	has difficulty following directions

9. Which alternative living situations would your family consider for your elder?
   retirement community _____ assisted living community _____
   adult-care home _____ nursing facility _____ other _____

10. Is your elder's monthly income adequate to private-pay for services in his home or placement in an alternative living situation?
high (exceeds $4,000/mo.) _____
moderate ($2,000–$4,000/mo.) _____
low moderate ($900–$2,000/mo.) _____
low (less than $900/mo.) _____

11. Does your elder have any assets? (stocks, bonds, CDs, bank accounts)
high (exceeds $35,000) _____
moderate ($15,000–$35,000) _____
low moderate ($5,000–$15,000) _____
low (less than $5,000) _____
If you marked low income and low assets, you may want to contact your local state area agency on aging or senior and disabled services office to help you determine eligibility for Medicaid benefits and programs.

12. Which insurance policies does your elder have?
Medicare Part A _____ Medicare Part B _____
Medicare supplemental _____ private insurance _____
Medigap _____ Medicaid _____ Managed Care/HMO _____
Veterans Affairs _____ no insurance _____
If your elder does not have health insurance, notify the hospital admissions or business office. If you need assistance completing an application or contacting an agency for a Medicaid application, talk with a hospital case manager or social worker.

13. Please check the services, activities, and medical care needed by your elder at discharge from the hospital.

Personal-Care Needs
___ bathing
___ brushing hair and teeth
___ dressing
___ bladder and bowel care
___ personal hygiene

Homemaking Activities
___ laundry
___ housecleaning

Nursing Care
___ blood-pressure check
___ dressing changes/wound care
___ injections
___ medication management
___ oxygen treatment
___ intravenous medication (IVs)
___ tube feedings
___ other _____

Mobility

___ walks without assistance

___ uses walker or cane

___ no problems with balance

___ problems with balance

___ uses furniture to maintain balance

___ uses wheelchair

___ bedridden

___ needs medical equipment and supplies

Meal Preparation

___ assistance with meal preparation

___ assistance with eating at mealtimes

___ meals-on-wheels needed

___ needs special diet

Supervision

___ daytime

___ nighttime

___ twenty-four hours per day

EVALUATION

You have looked at your elder's financial resources, insurance policies, physical and mental health, safety in the home and on the road, and activities of daily living to help you determine the type of care, assistance, and supervision she may need. Please answer the following questions:

Do you feel living at home is the best choice for your elder family member?

If your answer is "yes," or you are undecided, review chapter I, "There's No Place Like Home: Independent Living," chapter 2, "Living with Your Family," chapter 3, "Getting Help in Your Home," and chapter II, "Your Guide to Resources."

If your answer is "no," do you feel living with your family is the best choice for your elder family member?

If your answer is "yes," or you are undecided, review chapter 2, "Living with Your Family," chapter 3, "Getting Help in Your Home," and chapter II, "Your Guide to Resources."

If your answer is "no," complete Just the Facts, a comprehensive questionnaire found in chapter I, "There's No Place Like Home: Independent Living," or review chapter 4, "Living in a Retirement Community." Do you feel living in a retirement community is the best choice for your elder family member?

If your answer is "yes," or you are undecided, review chapter 4, "Living in a Retirement Community," chapter 3, "Getting Help in Your Home," chapter 10, "Using Home Health and Hospice Care," and chapter 11, "Your Guide to Resources." (This choice assumes your elder has moderate to high monthly income, moderate to high assets, and is in relatively good physical and mental health.)

If your answer is "no," do you feel living in an assisted living community is the best choice for your elder family member?

If your answer is "yes," or you are undecided, review chapter 5, "Living in an Assisted Living Community," chapter 3, "Getting Help in Your Home," chapter 10, "Using Home Health and Hospice Care," and chapter 11, "Your Guide to Resources." (This choice assumes that your elder has a moderate to high monthly income, low-moderate to high assets and good to fair physical and mental health. In some states, people with low monthly incomes and low assets may receive Medicaid benefits to pay for care in an assisted living community.)

If your answer is "no," review chapter 6, "Living in an Adult-Care Home," chapter 3, "Getting Help in Your Home," chapter 10, "Using Home Health and Hospice Care," and chapter 11, "Your Guide to Resources." Do you feel living in an adult-care home is the best choice for your elder family member?

If your answer is "yes," or you are undecided, review chapter 6, "Living in an Adult-Care Home," chapter 3, "Getting Help in Your Home," chapter 10, "Using Home Health and Hospice Care," and chapter 11, "Your Guide to Resources." (This choice assumes that your elder has a moderate to high income, low-moderate to high assets, and fair to poor physical or mental health. In some states people with low monthly incomes and low assets may receive Medicaid benefits to pay for care in an adult-care home.)

If your answer is "no," review the section on intermediate care in chapter 8, "Understanding Nursing Facilities." Do you feel living in an intermediate-care nursing facility is the best choice for your elder family member?

If your answer is "yes," or you are undecided, review the section on intermediate care in chapter 8, "Understanding Nursing Facilities." (This alternative will be influenced by the amount of care your elder requires, his financial resources, and, at times, insurance benefits. This choice assumes that he has a moderate to high income, low-moderate to high assets, and fair to poor physical or mental health. Care in an intermediate-care facility may be private pay or approximately twenty-five hundred to four thousand dollars per month. In some states, people with low monthly incomes and low assets may receive Medicaid benefits to pay for care in an intermediate-care facility.)

If your answer is "no," review the section on skilled nursing care in chapter 8, "Understanding Nursing Facilities." Do you feel temporary or long-term care in a skilled nursing facility is the best choice for your elder family member?

If your answer is "yes," or you are undecided, review the section on skilled nursing care in chapter 8, "Understanding Nursing Facilities," and chapter 7, "Understanding Hospital Acute Care." (This choice assumes that your elder has Medicare Part A or a moderate to high income, low-moderate to high assets and poor physical health. Care in a skilled nursing care facility may be private pay or approximately twenty-five hundred to four thousand dollars per month. In some states, people with low monthly incomes and low assets may receive Medicaid benefits to pay for care in a skilled nursing facility.)

If your answer is "no," review chapter 9, "Understanding Rehabilitation Centers." Do you feel temporary treatment in a rehabilitation center is the best choice for your elder family member?

If your answer is "yes," or you are undecided, review chapter 9, "Understanding Rehabilitation Centers." (This choice assumes that your elder has Medicare Part A and Medicare Part B or a moderate to high income, low-moderate to high assets, fair to poor physical health, and fair to good mental health. He must be able to participate in an intensive physical program and be able to follow directions. Private pay can be expensive. In some states, people with low monthly incomes and low assets may receive Medicaid benefits to pay for care in a rehabilitation center.)

If your answer is "no," review "Just the Facts," a comprehensive questionnaire found in chapter 1, "There's No Place Like Home: Independent Living," and talk with your physician and a medical case manager or social worker to help you assess your elder's medical-care needs.

Does your elder family member have a terminal condition or less than six months to live?

If your answer is "yes," or you are undecided, review chapter 7, "Understanding Hospital Acute Care," chapter 8, "Understanding Nursing Facilities," chapter 10, "Using Home Health and Hospice Care," chapter 3, "Getting Help in Your Home," and chapter 11, "Your Guide to Resources."

If your answer is "no," talk with your elder's physician and the case manager or social worker about hospice programs in his area.

Chapter 8

Understanding Nursing Facilities

———————— ❦ ————————

Did you know:

- 40 to 45 percent of everyone who turned age sixty-five in 1990 will stay in a nursing home at least once in his lifetime?
- of those admitted to the nursing home, half will stay less than six months?
- one-fifth will stay at least a year?
- only one-tenth will stay three years or longer?
- 5 percent of people older than sixty-five live in a nursing home?

When the health of an elder family member is affected by a long-term illness, injury, accident, surgery, or hospitalization, it may become necessary for your family to help make health-care decisions. These difficult and important decisions are often made under stressful conditions because they must be made quickly.

Many elders and their families view placement in a nursing facility in negative terms. It may be seen as the last resort for medical care and as a place to die. Although many elders do live and pass away in nursing facilities, it is important to remember that the majority do not. Most stay for a short period of time, receiving therapies and nursing care, and then return to their previous living situation or are placed in an alternative living situation.

Many elders move into a nursing home after an illness to regain strength, learn how to deal with their new medical condition, or receive intravenous antibiotics or close medical supervision. A short-term admission may last a few days or several weeks. For an elder who requires more extensive medical care, a long-term admission may mean several months.

It is also important to remember that your elder and family can always change their minds if they do decide nursing-home care is not the best choice. Other options, such as home health care, private-duty nursing, and in-home support from community agencies are also available to help provide care in the home. Alternatives to living in a nursing home can also include assisted living facilities and adult-care homes, depending upon your elder's medical needs.

However, if your elder has some rehabilitation potential, that is, potential to regain some or most of his physical abilities, it is strongly recommended that he pursue as intensive a program as the doctor recommends and that he is capable of handling.

John and His Family Consider Nursing-Home Care

For several years John lived with his family in their home. He was active, helping around the house with easy chores and caring for himself. At breakfast one morning, a family member noticed he was slurring his speech and having difficulty holding his fork. After consulting with his physician, he was taken to the hospital and admitted with a diagnosis of cerebrovascular accident, or stroke.

In the hospital, John and his family spoke with the doctor about his medical care. The stroke had affected his right side, weakening it and making it difficult for him to walk safely, maintain his balance, eat without assistance, and move independently from the bed to a chair. His speech was slurred and difficult to understand, frustrating him when he wanted to communicate with his doctor, nursing staff, or family.

The physician ordered evaluations by physical, occupational, and speech therapists. They all recommended follow-up therapy in a rehabilitation program, a skilled nursing facility, an outpatient therapy program at the hospital, or with therapists from a home health-care agency in his home. They suggested John begin a short stay in a skilled nursing facility, because they did not feel he could physically meet the requirements in a rehabilitation program. They also did not feel therapy as an outpatient or in-home with home health care was adequate.

To help John regain his ability to walk independently and to improve his speech, the doctor agreed with the therapists and recommended placement in a skilled nursing home. To help them with this process, he made a referral to the hospital case manager/social worker.

How will John and his family decide if placement in a nursing home is the best choice for him? What questions should his family ask about nursing homes? How will his family tackle the complicated process of admission to the nursing home? What observations should his family make when they visit nursing-home facilities? How will his family decide which facility will provide the best care for him? If John and his family are fortunate, a professional will guide them each step of the way, patiently reviewing relevant information, making recommendations when possible, and supplying them with handouts they can carefully read in a more relaxed setting. It is more common, however, to find that a family in this situation has limited guidance or information and an insufficient amount of time to make these difficult decisions.

What Your Elder and Family Need to Know

To gather the information necessary to make an informed decision about nursing-home facilities, it is important for your family to take some time to talk with health professionals. They will be able to guide you to appropriate nursing facilities and provide information about the different levels of care, the medical criteria for skilled nursing care, the types of insurance benefits through Medicare, Medicaid, and supplemental policies, private-pay rates, and admission procedures. They can also act as a liaison between your elder's family, the doctor, hospital staff, nursing-home staff, and community agencies.

Gathering the necessary information to make these decisions can be a lengthy and time-consuming process. Your family needs to know:

your elder's medical condition

doctor's treatment recommendations

how to get professional help

levels of care available in a nursing home

how to evaluate a nursing home

admission procedures

Medicare requirements for skilled nursing care

Medicaid requirements for skilled nursing care

insurance benefits and coverage

patient rights and responsibilities

Deciding If Nursing-Home Placement Is Needed

Medicare Requirements for Nursing-Home Care

To receive care in a nursing home with Medicare Part A coverage, your elder must meet several requirements. In addition, the nursing facility must participate in the federally managed Medicare program.

1. *Your elder must be admitted to a hospital as a full inpatient admission for at least three days,* not counting the day of discharge. *Please note:* If he is admitted as an outpatient and later changed to an inpatient, his outpatient days do not count as full/regular admission. Or, your elder must be admitted to the nursing facility within thirty days of discharge from the hospital. For example, if your elder family member was discharged more than thirty days before, he must be readmitted to the hospital for a three-day stay before his skilled nursing facility benefits can be used.

2. *Your elder's physician must certify that daily skilled nursing care is required* and can only be provided in a skilled nursing facility.

3. *Your elder must require skilled nursing care or rehabilitation services* that can only be provided in a skilled nursing facility.

4. *Your elder must require skilled nursing care on a daily basis* for a condition treated or occurring while he was in the hospital.

To help your family evaluate your elder's medical needs, please answer the following question: Does your elder family member have any of the following medical problems or physical-care needs? Please check any current physical problems.

_____ change in ability to walk

_____ paralysis

_____ amputation care

_____ daily dressing changes

_____ seizures requiring monitoring

_____ intravenous therapy(IV)

_____ severe or uncontrolled pain

_____ leg, arm, or body cast

_____ difficulty with speech or swallowing

_____ temporary or permanent tubes

_____ tube feedings

_____ total parenteral nutrition

_____ loss of consciousness

_____ loss of control with bladder or bowel

_____ oxygen therapy

_____ tracheotomy care/teaching

_____ new medications requiring injections or monitoring

_____ weakness from an extended illness

_____ severe weight loss

_____ other _____

Does your elder require assistance or instruction for any of these new physical changes? Do you feel that your elder will require care from a registered nurse or other health-care professional during his recovery period? Do you feel your elder would benefit from intensive physical, occupational, speech, or respiratory therapy? Do you feel your elder can participate in a daily therapy program? Do you feel your elder may need to spend some time in a nursing facility while he recuperates? Have you been informed by his physician that your elder has less than six months to live or has a terminal condition? Does his change in physical or mental health make it difficult or unsafe for your elder to return to his previous home situation?

If you answered "yes" to most of the above questions, your elder family member may need care in a nursing facility.

The Role of the Physician

The primary-care physician is the doctor chosen by your elder to coordinate medical care and services. He can be closely affiliated with a hospital, an insurance company, or an HMO or managed-care program, or he may maintain an independent practice. Referrals or requests to consult with specialists must be initiated by your elder's primary-care physician.

The attending physician is any other doctor who provides your elder with medical care. Either physician can make recommendations and referrals, request services, or write orders for medical care, prescriptions for medication, and orders for durable medical equipment for home use.

Your elder's physician can explain the kind of medical care needed, predict the length of time needed in the nursing home, and offer a prognosis. However, he may not know if your elder meets the Medicare requirements for skilled nursing care or the cost for private pay in a nursing facility. A medical social worker, case manager, or discharge planner is usually consulted for this information.

If your elder's doctor feels medical care or therapy in a nursing facility would be beneficial, his orders and instructions must specify skilled nursing care. He may also offer a referral to the social-work, case-management, or discharge planning department to help determine if nursing-home care is the best choice for your elder.

If your elder is transferred to a nursing home, his physician may or may not be able to continue to see him there. His physician must have privileges at the nursing facility to continue to see him as a patient while he receives care there. If his physician does not have privileges, the nursing home may have a house doctor who will agree to confer with your elder's physician and provide care as needed.

The house doctor becomes responsible for writing orders for medical care, or you may find a local physician with privileges at the nursing facility. His physician is required to see him in the facility only once a month. If additional medical care is needed, the nursing home can help make arrangements to transport your elder to the doctor's office for a medical appointment.

The Role of the Medical Social Worker, Case Manager, or Discharge Planner

The social worker/case manager is your elder's liaison between the physician, the hospital, the nursing homes, the insurance companies, and community agencies. The social worker can explain the admission procedure in the nursing home and insurance benefits, arrange transportation for transfers to the nursing home, and provide emotional support and counseling. They review the medical record to determine Medicare eligibility for skilled nursing care, contact the admissions coordinator at the nursing home to determine bed availability, and discuss the skilled nursing care needs. If necessary, the case manager can also contact his insurance company to obtain preauthorization for skilled nursing care. If Medicaid coverage is needed, they can help your elder start an application or refer your family to the appropriate community or state agency.

Social workers may not be able to recommend a nursing facility to your elder and family, but they may make strong suggestions to lead you to better facilities. It is important for your family to visit the nursing facility before you make a decision. For example, three different families may visit the same three nursing home facilities on the same day and each may have a different preference.

Licensing

The Health Care Financing Administration certifies approximately sixteen thousand nursing homes that receive Medicare and Medicaid funds. The state survey or inspection report, published every twelve to fifteen months, tells you what is going on inside the nursing home. These reports are based on unannounced visits to the nursing facility and describe patient care, safety, health, quality of life, incident reports, and the list of deficiencies in the last state survey. It should be displayed or available upon request for your family to read. If the nursing home is reluctant to show this report, contact the local state ombudsmen program.

Long-Term-Care Ombudsman

An ombudsman is a person hired by the state to advocate and investigate complaints filed by a nursing-home resident or by a concerned family member, friend, or visitor on behalf of a nursing-home resident. *An ombudsman is not a legal representative.*

Established by the Older Americans Act in 1975, the state requires that ombudsmen regularly visit nursing facilities, talk with residents, investigate complaints, and gather information. They keep records of the initial complaints and results of the investigation. Although ombudsmen are not allowed to recommend a nursing facility to you, they can provide your family with helpful information. Information about the ombudsmen program should be posted, sometimes near an exit or elevator, for families to easily see.

Nursing Facilities and Their Levels of Care

There are three basic types of nursing facilities available to provide medical care, personal care and assistance, and supervision for your elder family member: hospital-based skilled-plus nursing units; community-based skilled nursing facilities; and intermediate-care nursing facilities. Each type of facility has specific eligibility requirements, insurance benefits, and admission procedures.

This section will outline the basic information your elder and family should know when considering placement in a nursing facility. It will explain the different levels of medical care and whether insurance will cover therapies and nursing care. The five levels of care are:

1. skilled-plus care in a hospital-based nursing facility
2. skilled nursing care in a community-based nursing facility
3. intermediate care
4. terminal care/comfort measures
5. custodial care

Hospital-Based Skilled-Plus Nursing Units/Transitional Care Units

A hospital-based skilled nursing unit provides skilled-plus nursing care within the hospital complex. It is used for patients who no longer meet the acute or critical level of care in a hospital but still require a high level of medical care. The patient's medical-care needs may also exceed the amount of skilled care available at a non-hospital-based facility. A patient receiving care in a skilled-plus facility must receive at least two types of treatments at least three times daily.

The primary-care physician is instrumental in determining if your elder is a candidate for skilled-plus care. The physician may feel your elder requires skilled medical care and services and supplies that are medically necessary or essential to the diagnosis and treatment of his illness or injury. If the treatment or diagnosis is complicated, he may feel it requires a high degree of monitoring and skilled care available in a hospital.

Insurance companies often review the prescribed treatment, services, and recommendations of a physician and can determine that the medical treatment could have been provided in a different way and/or at lower cost. It may be necessary to receive permission and guarantee of payment before specific medical treatment can be started. With the assistance of a medical case manager, pre-authorization or -approval is obtained from the insurance company before a transfer is made to a skilled-plus or transitional-care unit. Skilled-plus care costs less than acute care and inpatient rehabilitation but more than care received in a community-based skilled nursing facility.

To find out more about the cost of skilled-plus care, contact the medical case manager or the business office in your local hospital.

Appropriate Diagnosis for Treatment in a Skilled-Plus or Transitional-Care Unit

If your elder has been hospitalized with a serious or complicated illness, skilled-plus care, if available in your local hospital, may be appropriate for him. Listed below are a few skilled-plus care diagnoses:

infectious diseases such as AIDS, hepatitis B, staph infection, active tuberculosis, and other contagious conditions

multiple skilled needs such as a comatose condition, severe decubitus, contractures, tracheotomy care, tube feedings, intravenous feedings, oxygen and respiratory treatments, and complex sterile dressing changes

conditions requiring highly technical equipment, such as ventilators

other diagnoses, such as stroke, congenital deformity, amputation, major multiple trauma, fractures, brain injury, polyarthritis and rheumatoid arthritis, and neurological disorders, such as multiple sclerosis, Parkinson's disease, and polyneuropathy

Advantages and Disadvantages of Skilled-Plus Care

The advantages of placing a patient in a hospital-based skilled nursing unit or TCU include:

a higher level of skilled care

an extension of the continuum of medical care begun in the hospital

an alternative to comprehensive inpatient rehabilitation units

lower cost than a rehabilitation unit

easier access to doctors and emergency care

easier access to X rays, scans, test procedures, and lab work

easier transfer to skilled-plus unit, eliminating need for ambulance transportation

a smoother and easier transition for the patient

The disadvantages of placing a patient in a TCU include:

higher cost than a skilled nursing facility

shorter stay in unit if condition improves

Nursing Care at a Community-Based Skilled Nursing Facility

This type of nursing facility may offer several levels of care: skilled nursing care, intermediate care, terminal care/comfort measures, and custodial care. *Skilled nursing care* is medical care that requires the services of skilled health professionals, such as a registered nurse or physical therapist, to provide necessary medical services and therapies.

Covered and Noncovered Care

The medical services covered or noncovered may vary in each type of nursing facility. Covered care means Medicare, a federal health insurance program for people sixty-five and older and disabled people, pays for the specific medical care ordered by the doctor and provided by the nursing home. Noncovered care means Medicare does not pay for the specific medical procedure.

Please note: Some managed-care programs may override your elder's Medicare benefits and not pay for care usually covered under Medicare. Also, Medicaid, a joint federal- and state-regulated program for people with low incomes and limited assets, sometimes pays for medical care considered noncovered by Medicare.

Skilled services provided at this level of care may include:

Skilled observation. Professional medical staff appraise a person's medical condition to determine his skilled care needs. Short-term Medicare and Medicaid benefits may cover this service.

Foley catheter care. If catheter care is the primary reason for nursing-home care, it may be considered a noncovered service. However, if catheter care is needed due to a diagnosis such as bladder cancer, which requires irrigation and considerable medical care, it may be covered.

Wound care/dressing care. Extensive dressing changes and care at least three times daily that require the services of a professional registered nurse may be considered covered care.

Decubitus/bedsore care. Large, deep, and draining bedsores that require the services of a professional registered nurse may be considered covered care. They must be: multiple stage II on the trunk of the body, similar to a shallow crater, blister, or abrasion; stage III, which presents as a deep crater; or stage IV, which shows extensive damage to tissue, muscle, bone, tendons, or joints. Treatment for these three stages may be covered for up to one hundred days.

Diabetic observation. For people who have unstable diabetic conditions and are insulin-dependent on an injection, this may be a short-term covered service that requires medical supervision.

Teaching and administering intramuscular and subcutaneous injections. Conditions that require a skilled professional to administer or teach the individual or family how to administer medication may be a covered or noncovered service. It is necessary to talk with the admissions staff at the nursing home to determine the condition's status.

Teaching and administering insulin/diabetic care. For new diabetics or insulin users who require medical supervision and teaching, this may be considered a covered service until the family or person is able to competently perform the necessary care. This is covered by Medicare only once.

Administering intravenous feeding. This service requires the skills of a professional registered nurse and is considered a covered service.

Teaching ostomy/ileostomy/conduit care. For people who have new or complex ostomies, teaching and care may be considered a covered service.

Teaching/administering tube feedings. For a person who requires medical supervision and teaching, this may be considered a covered service until the family or person is able to competently perform the necessary care. Nasogastric tube feedings may receive one hundred days of coverage. New gastro tubes may only receive fourteen days of coverage.

Teaching/administering tracheotomy care. For people requiring medical supervision and teaching, this may be considered a covered service until the family or person is able to competently perform the necessary care. Daily suctioning must also be required.

Teaching/administering respiratory/inhalation treatment. For people who have an unstable respiratory condition that requires medical supervision and teaching or high oxygen needs, this may be considered a covered service until the family or person is able to competently perform the necessary care. Medical nebulizer treatments needed four times daily may also be covered. Noncovered care may include patients with chronic respiratory problems, such as emphysema. They can receive treatment at home with the assistance of a home health-care agency.

Teaching and care of terminally ill. Terminal illness may be a covered service for people with a limited prognosis. Be aware, however, that some managed-care plans override the Medicare coverage and may deny payment if they determine there is no skilled care needed. Care of the dying is often referred to as *comfort measures*, where the emphasis is placed on comfort and pain control and not on providing skilled services.

Insert/maintain feeding tube/gastrostomy tube. For people who require medical supervision and teaching, this may be considered a covered service until the family or person is able to competently perform the necessary care.

Suctioning care/teaching. For people who require medical supervision and teaching, this may be considered a covered service until the family or person is able to competently perform the necessary care.

Ventilator support. Although this may be considered a covered service, it may be difficult to find a facility that can provide adequate medical care and support.

Physical therapy (PT). This therapy is considered a covered service for people who are recovering from long-term illnesses that require some physical restoration, which includes strokes, fractured hips, femurs, and other specific fractures, amputation, some neurological disorders, and multiple traumas. You must receive it on a daily basis five times per week.

Deferred therapy. To receive coverage for deferred therapy, a person should be unable to bear weight on his legs or torso for six weeks. After receiving three to five days of covered Medicare benefits for physical therapy, the nursing facility may move a person to an intermediate-care unit with room and board as private pay. Therapy would continue to be covered at 80 percent under Medicare Part B. After six weeks, the person may be moved back to the skilled-care unit with Medicare benefits for physical therapy. The thirty-day rule for Medicare benefits for skilled nursing care after hospitalization is exempted as long as your elder's physician writes orders for "deferred therapy related to weight-bearing status."

Routine physical therapy may continue for a small fee, covered by Medicare, after a person has reached a plateau or is no longer improving if they have another skilled need.

Restorative therapy that is less than twenty days and utilizes a skilled therapist is covered by Medicare. The restorative aide program is not chargeable to Medicare; it is considered private pay. When restorative therapy is provided by a rehabilitation aide, HMOs and managed care may not cover this therapy.

Occupational therapy. This treatment is considered a noncovered service unless specific therapy is ordered by the physician. When used in collaboration with physical therapy—a skilled service—it is usually covered.

Speech and language therapy. This therapy is considered a covered service when skilled medical care and supervision are required.

Social-work and case-management services. The social workers in nursing homes provide an invaluable service by helping families understand insurance requirements, providing counseling, and arranging transportation, assistance from community and home health-care agencies, and in-home services at time of discharge. This noncovered service is usually provided free of charge.

Intermediate-Care Facilities

Intermediate-care facilities provide routine nursing care to elders who need some medical supervision and assistance with the daily activities of living, such as bathing, dressing, grooming, and personal care. Residents may have difficulty with transfers, getting in and out of bed or a chair. Or they may be confused and disoriented, unable to remember who they are, where they are, or the time of day. They may not recognize close family members and friends. As a result of this confusion, they may require twenty-four-hour supervision for safety.

On the continuum of care, intermediate care falls between care provided by an adult-care home and skilled nursing care. It is an excellent alternative for people with senile dementia, Alzheimer's disease, mental deficiency or retardation, or psychological conditions. Some facilities, however, may hesitate to accept a patient who places other patients at risk or who presents a severe behavior problem.

Intermediate care may be provided in a licensed nursing facility staffed twenty-four hours a day by nurses and certified nurse's aides. Programs in physical and occupational therapy and an activity program may also be offered, usually for an additional fee.

Intermediate care may be available in a skilled nursing facility as one of its lower levels of care or in a facility designated exclusively for intermediate or custodial care. The nursing staff can provide the following nursing care:

    routine Foley catheter care and incontinence issues

    medication management excluding IVs and insulin injections

    physical therapy three times weekly

    occupational therapy three times weekly

    general skin care, simple dressing changes

    assistance with feeding

    basic oxygen/respiratory care

    difficult behavioral issues

    assistance with the activities of daily living, including personal hygiene,
        bathing, grooming, and dressing

Terminal Care/Comfort Measures

Terminal care refers to the medical care and support needed by a person with a life expectancy of six months or less. *Comfort measures* refer to care designed to make the person as comfortable and pain-free as possible in their final days. In a skilled facility, it may be covered by Medicare or Medicaid. In an intermediate-care facility, it may be covered by Medicaid or private pay.

Medicare Part A may pay for palliative terminal care in a skilled nursing facility designed to provide temporary pain relief or alleviate symptoms but not necessarily effect a cure. Medicare coverage may include care for pain management using injections or intravenous medication, nutrition, and skin care. If aggressive or extraordinary measures are used to prolong life, the person may not qualify for Medicare benefits under terminal care.

Managed-care programs may have stricter interpretations and may consider terminal care a nonskilled service and therefore noncovered under its plan. This means the family or elder family member is responsible for payment of services received in the nursing facility. Check your policy for speciic information.

Some long-term-care policies may have limited coverage for terminal care.

Other Options for Terminal Care

There are other options to receiving terminal care in a nursing facility.

A hospice program with an interdisciplinary team of health-care professionals and supportive personnel can provide emotional support and medical care to your elder and family when it has been determined that your elder has a limited life expectancy. If your elder is in the hospital but no longer requires acute hospital care, it may be possible to move him to a hospice bed within the hospital for pain control, symptom management, and supportive services, instead of to a nursing facility. Your family may want to discuss this option with his physician or a hospital social worker. An inpatient hospice facility can also provide supportive care, focusing on pain relief and comfort.

Some hospitals work closely with a home health-care agency to provide hospice care. They can designate a bed for hospice care under Medicare Part A for a limited period of time. Home health-care agencies can also provide hospice care in your home. That can mean extensive services, such as respite care, in-home supports, and even twenty-four-hour availability to your elder and family.

Custodial Care

Custodial care is general care and assistance for the activities of daily living, such as eating, dressing, bathing, grooming, and personal hygiene, as well as supervision that prevents personal harm. This care may be provided by an unskilled person and is not considered medically necessary. It is not covered by Medicare or private insurance companies.

When custodial care is provided in a nursing facility, it is considered private pay. People with Alzheimer's disease who display mental confusion and disorientation, wander, and require twenty-four-hour supervision are considered candidates for custodial care. Some nursing facilities have a special locked Alzheimer's unit designed to ensure a person's safety by preventing them from wandering or inadvertently injuring themselves. Medicaid and some long-term-care insurance policies may provide limited coverage for this care.

Insurance Benefits in a Nursing Facility

Medicare Benefits for Skilled Nursing Care

If your elder meets the Medicare requirements for nursing-home care, he will receive the following coverage:

> The first 20 days in the skilled nursing facility will be covered 100 percent.

> The next 80 days in the skilled nursing facility will be covered except for a daily coinsurance of $97 per day in 2000. (*Please note:* This coinsurance changes every year.)

> Your elder is responsible for all costs after 100 days. Some long-term-care insurance policies may provide additional skilled nursing facility benefits, extending the coverage beyond 100 days.

If there is a change in your elder's medical condition during his stay in the skilled nursing facility and he no longer meets the requirements for skilled nursing care, Medicare benefits may no longer cover the nursing-home stay.

If your elder is admitted to the hospital from a skilled nursing facility, it must keep his bed as long as the bed is paid for. Your family must let the nursing facility know you would like him to return to the nursing home after his hospitalization. Often, a hospital social worker or case manager will contact the nursing facility and provide it with medical updates, enabling it to anticipate a readmission date.

Managed-Care Policies

A managed-care policy may override your elder's Medicare benefits if it is a primary insurance or the first insurance billed by the nursing facility. A managed-care case manager may evaluate your elder's medical needs to determine if he requires skilled nursing care. This determination may be based on stricter guidelines than those used by Medicare.

For example, terminal care in a skilled nursing facility is often covered by Medicare. Under managed care, terminal care may be considered a nonskilled service, and therefore not covered under Medicaid's plan. Or under Medicare guidelines, twenty days of physical therapy following a stroke may seem reasonable and medically necessary. Under a managed-care plan, using stricter guidelines, they may determine that only ten days are reasonable and medically necessary.

Medicare Supplemental Insurance/Medigap Policy

A private-insurance or Medigap policy complements Medicare benefits by paying for deductibles and coinsurances not covered by Medicare. A deductible is the amount your elder must pay before Medicare begins to pay for covered services. Coinsurance is the Medicare-approved amount your elder is responsible for.

These policies work with Medicare, covering some costs not covered by the program. Each policy has different benefits, so it is important to look at your elder's insurance policy or to call the insurance carrier to determine his supplemental benefits.

In a skilled nursing facility, these policies may pay the daily coinsurance if your elder meets the Medicare eligibility requirements for benefits. Or some policies may pay a specific amount on admission to the nursing facility and/or a percentage of the charges not covered by Medicare.

For example, in 2000, the daily coinsurance after twenty days in a skilled nursing facility was $97 per day. Your elder would be responsible for paying this amount, or a Medicare supplemental policy could pay the daily coinsurance as long as he continues to meet Medicare requirements for skilled nursing care.

Long-Term-Care Insurance

This insurance is usually purchased before people become ill or later in life, when they realize they have large gaps in their medical benefits. These policies sometimes provide additional skilled nursing home benefits. In addition, there may be benefits for lower levels of nursing-home care, such as intermediate care or care in an assisted living facility or an adult day-care center.

Purchasing long-term-care insurance as an elder with medical problems can be expensive. There are many policies offered, so it is best to research them carefully before making a decision. The National Association of Insurance Commissioners and the Health Care Financing Administration of the U.S. Department of Health and Human Services issue excellent free publications, including "The Guide to Health Insurance for People with Medicare."

Medicaid

The Medicaid program is designed for people who have low-income and limited assets. Medicaid eligibility varies from state to state, with different requirements for financial eligibility and medical care. To determine if your elder qualifies for Medicaid benefits in a skilled nursing facility, it is necessary to contact the local state area agency on aging for the state eligibility guidelines. They can direct your elder and family to the nearest office, which can assist you with your elder's application. Or if your elder is in a hospital or skilled nursing facility, the social workers or case managers can help you contact the appropriate agency to complete an application.

For your elder to receive Medicaid benefits, the nursing facility must participate in the Medicaid plan. A good nursing facility will talk with your family about Medicaid before it is needed and will accept the Medicaid payments when it becomes necessary. It is important to note that since Medicaid pays a much lower reimbursement rate to the nursing facility, some nursing homes may be reluctant to accept Medicaid patients. They may only accept Medicaid payments if your elder first pays for care for a specific period of time.

For example, the nursing facility may ask for private-pay rates for six months before it will change your elder's coverage to Medicaid.

In many states, a Medicaid-approved nursing facility must accept a Medicaid patient if it has an available bed. It may, however, state that it is unable to accept a Medicaid patient if it determines that his care needs are too great for the staff.

Ask the nursing facility about its policy for patients whose Medicare benefits expire. Will it help the family apply for Medicaid? Will it transfer the patient to another facility or discharge them home? Does it require private-pay payments for additional care?

In some states, preadmission screening, or PASSAR, is required for Medicaid patients before they can be admitted to a nursing facility. This is a federally regulated guideline that ensures people receive the correct level of care in a nursing home. Many nursing facilities require a completed PASSAR from a hospital social worker at the time of admission.

If your elder is admitted to the hospital from a skilled nursing facility, the nursing facility must keep his bed available as long as the bed is paid for. If he is a Medicaid resident, the program usually pays for the bed to be held for a few days.

Private Pay

When a family decides to private-pay for skilled nursing care in a nursing home, it may be because they have used up their Medicare and supplemental insurance benefits and do not financially qualify for Medicaid benefits. Or they may feel that nursing-home care is needed, because they cannot comfortably provide the necessary medical care at home or in another facility. This medical care may not meet the Medicare requirements to receive benefits for skilled nursing care.

When applying for Medicaid, bring:

- *birth certificate or marriage license*
- *proof of citizenship*
- *three months of bank statements and other financial assets*
- *copies of bonds, stocks, other assets*
- *copies of Medicare, Social Security, and other insurance cards*

Private pay is expensive. Rates range from approximately twenty-five hundred dollars per month to over four thousand dollars per month. In addition to the daily rate charge, there are additional charges for supplies, medication, phone services, special diets, and therapies.

Many patients enter a nursing home as private pay and then, when their financial resources are depleted, become eligible for Medicaid. Again, be sure the nursing home accepts Medicaid and will accept your elder under the Medicaid terms.

Veterans Affairs

For skilled nursing-care services, the VA may use a fee-basis or contract out to skilled nursing facilities or private home health-care agencies for skilled nursing care. These contracts are often negotiated on a time-limited basis, which is determined by the VA physician.

To be eligible for care-in-a-skilled-nursing-facility benefits from Veterans Affairs (VA):

Your elder must have a service-connected disability. This means he is receiving money for an injury sustained while in the military service. He should have been receiving compensation for this injury since discharge from the service. Occasionally, a veteran with a nonservice-connected disability can receive services.

Your elder requires pre-authorization from Veterans Affairs.

For information about VA services and benefits, please contact your nearest Veterans Affairs Social Work Services department.

Worker's Compensation Programs

Each state runs its own program and may have different allowable amounts of compensation and services. If your elder has recently applied for Worker's Compensation because of a work-related injury, it is necessary to contact his local claim office regarding skilled nursing-care benefits.

Look under State Office in the telephone directory for the nearest Worker's Compensation program or contact the personnel office at his place of employment.

Insurance Benefits for Intermediate Care

Neither Medicare nor Medicare Supplemental Insurance pays for intermediate care in a nursing facility. Some long-term-care policies may provide limited coverage for intermediate care. Check the long-term-care policy to determine what benefits, if any, are designated for intermediate care.

Medicaid may pay for intermediate care in a nursing facility. Medicaid requirements vary from state to state. Contact your local state area agency on aging for information regarding eligibility requirements.

Veterans Affairs may pay all costs if care is approved by the VA.

Private pay for intermediate care can be expensive, from twenty-five hundred to four thousand dollars per month.

On page 201 is a summary of insurance coverage and benefits in a nursing facility.

Nursing Home Staff

Nursing homes are staffed by professionals and nonprofessionals. Their responsibilities vary with their area of expertise. All, however, play an important role in providing patient care in a nursing facility. You may note that many of these job descriptions are similar to those held by hospital staff members.

The *registered nurse* (RN) provides skilled nursing care to the patient, following orders prescribed by the physician. She may act as a liaison between the physician and patient, discussing changes in the patient's condition, requesting additional therapies, and remaining alert to reactions to medication and reporting these to the physician. A

SUMMARY OF INSURANCE COVERAGE AND BENEFITS IN A NURSING FACILITY

	Skilled-Plus Care	Skilled-Nursing Care	Intermediate Care	Custodial Care	Terminal Care
Hospital-Based	X				X
Community-Based		X	X	X	X
Medicare You must meet Medicare requirements for care	Medicare Part A pays 100 percent for 20 days. Pays 80 percent for 80 days. Your pay $97 coinsurance per day.	Medicare Part A pays 100 percent for 20 days. Pays 80 percent for 80 days. Your pay $97 coinsurance per day.	Does not pay for intermediate care.	Does not pay for custodial care.	May pay for terminal care depending on care needs.
Medicaid Federal and state program for persons with low income and assets.	Must be Medicaid recipient to receive benefits. Payment varies state to state.	Must be Medicaid recipient to receive benefits. Payment varies state to state.	Must be Medicaid recipient to receive benefits. Payment varies state to state.	Does not pay for custodial care, but area agency on aging may be able to provide free or low-cost services.	Must be Medicaid recipient to receive benefits. Payment varies state to state.
Medicare Supplemental	May provide additional coverage.	May provide additional coverage.	Does not pay for intermediate care.	Does not pay for intermediate care.	May pay for terminal care.
Managed Care/HMOs	Eligibility and benefits determined by medical case manager.	Covers skilled care based on its guidelines; may override Medicare benefits if it is your primary insurance.	Does not pay for intermediate care.	Does not pay for custodial care.	May have stricter guidelines than Medicare for eligibility. May not pay for terminal care.
Long-Term-Care Insurance	May pay for care after Medicare benefits have expired.	May pay for care after Medicare benefits have expired.	May pay for some limited intermediate-care services.	May pay for limited custodial care in home, adult day care or assisted living.	May pay for limited terminal care.
Veterans Affairs	Federally regulated. May pay all costs if approved by the VA. Must meet eligibility guidelines for VA.	Federally regulated. May pay all costs if approved by the VA. Must meet eligibility guidelines for VA.	Federally regulated. May pay all costs if approved by the VA. Must meet eligibility guidelines for VA.	Does not pay for custodial care but may help with supportive services.	May pay for limited terminal care.
Private Pay	If you have no insurance or do not meet the requirements for skilled-plus care, you may private-pay.	If you have no insurance or do not meet the requirements for skilled nursing care, you may private-pay.	You may private-pay for this care.	You may private-pay for this care.	You may private-pay for this care.

registered nurse must be on the premises of the nursing facility at all times. The charge nurse, however, can be a registered nurse or a licensed practical nurse. As in a hospital, the nurse provides care according to the physician's orders. Review chapter 7, "Understanding Hospital Acute Care," for more information regarding the role of the registered nurse.

The *licensed practical nurse* (LPN) can provide some of the nursing care under the supervision of a registered nurse. They can hang IVs but may not administer medication or antibiotics.

The *certified nurse's aide* (CNA) can assist with bathing and personal care under the supervision of an RN. She may also assist with:

exercises

light housekeeping

assistance at mealtime

self-administered medications

The *physical therapist* (PT) in a nursing facility continues the assessment, treatment, and rehabilitation begun in the hospital. The PT receives treatment orders from the physician as he works to increase your elder's mobility and strength. Review chapter 7, "Understanding Hospital Acute Care," for more information regarding the role of the PT.

The *occupational therapist* (OT) may be needed following a hospitalization. In the nursing facility, the OT may receive orders from his physician to continue working with your elder on the basic activities of daily living, enabling him to increase his independence when he returns to his home or other living situation. Review chapter 7, "Understanding Hospital Acute Care," for more information regarding the role of the occupational therapist.

The *speech-language therapist* (ST) often continues to follow your elder when he is receiving care and rehabilitation in a nursing facility if he is still experiencing speech or swallowing problems. Many STs have a contract with the nursing facility. Review chapter 7, "Understanding Hospital Acute Care," for more information regarding the role of the ST.

The *social worker/case manager* is your elder's liaison between the physician, hospital, nursing homes, insurance companies, and community agencies. She can explain the admission procedure in the nursing home and insurance benefits, arrange transportation for transfers to the nursing home, and provide emotional support and counseling. In addition, she reviews the medical record to determine Medicare eligibility for skilled nursing care, contacts the admissions coordinator at the nursing home to determine bed availability, and discusses skilled nursing-care needs. If needed, she can also contact your elder's insurance company to obtain pre-authorization for skilled nursing care. If Medicaid coverage is required, she can help your elder start an application or refer your family to the appropriate community or state agency.

> *For example, three different families may visit the same three nursing-home facilities on the same day, and each may have a different preference.*

Social workers may not be able to recommend a nursing facility to your elder and family, but they may make strong suggestions to lead you to better facilities. Again, it is important for your family to visit the nursing facility before you make a decision.

Once in the nursing home, a social worker or admissions coordinator works with your family to ensure that your elder receives the proper care and, later, a well-thought-out discharge from the nursing facility to home or an alternative setting. The coordinator can also help make any arrangements for equipment or referrals to other community agencies. Review chapter 7, "Understanding Hospital Acute Care," for more information regarding the role of the social worker and case manager.

The *respiratory therapist* provides direct services to those who have breathing problems. He can assist by ensuring that the proper equipment is ordered for follow-up care at the nursing facility. Any necessary equipment or treatments must be ordered by the primary-care or attending physician. Review chapter 7, "Understanding Hospital Acute Care," for more information regarding the role of the respiratory therapist.

A *nutritional therapist* or *dietitian* can help your family with information about special diets and nutritional supplements. She can make recommendations to the physician and nursing-home staff regarding your elder's nutrition and diet. Review chapter 7, "Understanding Hospital Acute Care," for more information regarding the role of the dietitian.

The *activities director* arranges and directs state-required activities and programs for patients in the nursing facility. These may include arts and crafts, pet therapy, music therapy and entertainment, dance and movement programs, and social activities and excursions.

Admissions Procedures

When your elder's family decides to transfer him to a nursing home, you must deal with the admissions process, which usually involves meeting with an admissions coordinator or social worker and completing an admissions contract and personal-information sheet.

The social worker may act as a liaison between your elder and family, the hospital, and the nursing admissions office. She will coordinate the time of transfer, arrange transportation, and prepare your family for transfer to the nursing home.

When your family meets with the nursing-home admissions coordinator, you should bring insurance and financial information. If you are also applying for Medicaid, additional information may be requested. This information may include:

Medicare card

Medicaid card

other insurance cards

living will*

advanced directives*

POLST form (Physician Orders for Life-Sustaining Treatment)*

power of attorney for health care*

power of attorney or guardianship paper

the name, address, and phone number for the primary-care physician*

list of medications/allergies*

The nursing facility also needs to know the name of the physician who will be responsible for following your elder's care and writing orders and prescriptions. This physician needs privileges at the nursing home to provide his care. If your elder's physician is not affiliated with the nursing home, he may need to find a physician who has privileges at the facility, or he can accept the care of the designated medical doctor for the nursing home. It is important to remember that cardiologists, pulmonologists, and surgeons, for instance, usually won't visit and provide medical care to a patient transferred from a hospital to a nursing facility. They may continue to see your elder only in their office or when he needs their specialty care in the hospital.

If your elder is being admitted to the nursing facility directly from a hospital, the above information may be supplied by the hospital and sent with him when he is transferred to the nursing facility.

WHAT TO BRING TO A NURSING FACILITY

Each nursing facility has a list of things to bring with you at the time of admission. Use this checklist to help you pack.

___ four changes of clothing for day and night

___ nonskid washable slippers or slip-on shoes

___ one-week supply of socks and underwear

___ bathrobe

___ one to two sweaters/light jacket/sweatshirt

___ personal toiletries

___ a touch of home

Hints:

Sweatshirts and sweatpants with an elastic band are easy to pull on and off. They do not have zippers or buttons and are very comfortable.

Bring permanent-press clothing, because nursing facilities usually do not iron clothing.

Do not bring delicate fabrics.

Family can choose to do personal laundry instead of using the laundry service available at the nursing home.

Mark clothing and personal items with a permanent marker or label.

Check with the nursing facility to see if you can bring incontinence diapers or other medical supplies. It is often less expensive to have family provide these items.

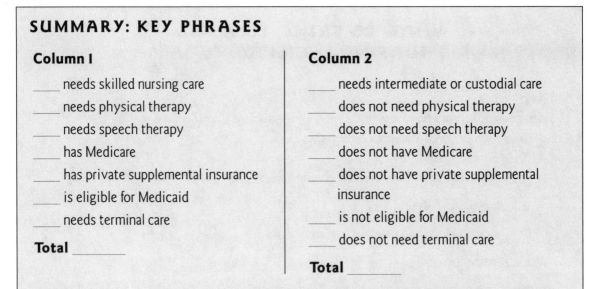

SUMMARY: KEY PHRASES

Column I

_____ needs skilled nursing care

_____ needs physical therapy

_____ needs speech therapy

_____ has Medicare

_____ has private supplemental insurance

_____ is eligible for Medicaid

_____ needs terminal care

Total _____

Column 2

_____ needs intermediate or custodial care

_____ does not need physical therapy

_____ does not need speech therapy

_____ does not have Medicare

_____ does not have private supplemental insurance

_____ is not eligible for Medicaid

_____ does not need terminal care

Total _____

If most of your responses checked are in column I, your elder should be able to go to a nursing facility for skilled nursing care with insurance benefits. If he qualifies for Medicaid, it may also pay for care.

If most of your responses checked are in column 2, your elder may _not_ be able to go to a nursing facility for skilled nursing care with insurance benefits. If he qualifies for Medicaid benefits, intermediate care may be covered.

EVALUATION

Do you feel a nursing facility is the best choice for your elder family member?

If your answer is "yes," review chapter 7, "Understanding Hospital Acute Care."

If your answer is "no," or you are undecided, review chapter 9, "Understanding Rehabilitation Centers," and chapter 10, "Using Home Health and Hospice Care," or talk with a medical social worker or your elder's physician.

Nursing-Home Checklist

Visit several facilities before making a decision. Bring a friend with whom to share your impressions. Spend a day dining and participating in activities at the facility. Take advantage of sleeping overnight in a guest unit. After talking with residents and staff members, sit down with other family members to discuss their impressions. Every person may notice different details about the facility. Trust your instincts even if you are unable to pinpoint why you feel the way you do.

You can visit a nursing facility anytime you wish to during regular working hours, usually 8 A.M. to 5 P.M. If you are interested in speaking with the admissions coordinator or a social worker, call in advance to set up an appointment. If you are interested only in visiting the facility, drop in and ask for a tour. Most facilities should be able to accommodate you. Use this questionnaire to keep track of your observations and responses to your questions.

The following nursing-home checklist will help you evaluate the nursing facilities you visit.

QUESTIONS TO ASK WHEN YOU VISIT A NURSING HOME

When you walk into a nursing facility, look at the general appearance of the residence.

Date _____

Name and address of nursing home:

_____

_____

Contact person _____   **Telephone #** _____

Outside Area

1. Are the grounds well maintained?
2. Is the residence taller than one story?
3. Are there ramps along the curb for easy wheelchair access?

Inside Area

4. Does the nursing facility have an odor?
5. Is the nursing facility clean?
6. Is the nursing facility air-conditioned?
7. Is there a security guard stationed inside the door?
8. Is the lobby area empty, or are residents sitting around?
9. Are the hallways wide enough to accommodate a walker or a wheelchair?
10. Are handrails conveniently placed along the hallways?
11. Is there easy elevator access?
12. Is smoking allowed in the facility?
13. Is there a designated smoking area?
14. Is there easy access to a public telephone?
15. Are fire exits clearly marked and easily accessible?
16. Is there easy access to a mailbox and postage stamps?
17. Is the atmosphere formal or informal? formal _____ informal _____
18. Are there standard visiting hours? The visiting hours are:
    Monday–Friday: _____ Saturday–Sunday:_____

Watch for:

bad odor

safety hazards

residents who are not dressed or groomed

residents who remain in their rooms

residents who are restrained or tied in chairs (The law strictly limits the use of restraints, especially for convenience of nursing staff.)

Rooms

19. Are private rooms available?
20. How many residents can be in a room?
    one _____ two _____ three _____ more than three _____
21. Will your elder need to share a room?
22. Will your elder have a compatible roommate? (*This is an important question.*)

23. Can residents provide their own furnishings?

24. Do rooms have handicap features such as emergency call buttons and grab bars in the bathroom?

25. Does each bed have a privacy curtain?

26. Does each room have a window or view?

27. Are pets allowed in the residence?

Nursing Care

28. What levels of care are available in the nursing facility?
    skilled nursing care _____ intermediate care _____
    terminal care _____ custodial care _____

29. What therapies are available to residents?
    physical therapy _____ occupational therapy _____
    speech therapy _____ respiratory therapy _____ other _____

30. Are residents allowed to self-administer their own medication?

31. Is medication management available to resident who have difficulty taking their correct medication at the proper time of day?

32. How are prescriptions filled? (The state requires that all medications be prepared by a pharmacist in individual doses and placed in a bubble pack. Self-medication must be kept in a locked box or area.)
    on the premises _____ by a local pharmacy _____
    by a mail order pharmacy _____ by family _____

33. Do staff members maintain health and medication records for each resident?

34. If a resident experiences a change in health, is staff available to provide additional assistance?

35. Is informed consent signed for medical tests?

36. Is staff available to help with the activities of daily living, such as:

bathing	transfers
grooming	shopping
personal hygiene	housekeeping
eating at mealtime	laundry
walking	

37. Can a resident hire a private-duty nurse to provide additional care?

38. Does staff encourage family involvement?

39. Can family bring medical supplies, such as incontinence diapers?

Nursing-Home Staff

40. Is staff professional and able to answer your questions?

41. How does the staff determine each resident's care needs?

42. What is the resident-to-staff ratio?

43. How many registered nurses are on duty during each shift?
    one _____ two _____ three _____ more than three _____

44. Does the facility have a care plan for each resident?

45. Does staff help coordinate services with community agencies, such as home health care and medical-equipment companies, at time of discharge?

46. Do you feel comfortable with the staff?

47. Is there a physician on the facility's staff?

48. How often does the physician visit the facility?

49. Can the primary-care physician continue to provide medical treatment to your elder?

50. Is there a private place for exams by your elder's physician?

51. Staff should be:

affectionate	interested
cheerful	pleasant
courteous	respectful
encouraging	responsive to calls for assistance
helpful	warm
honest	

Watch for:

disgruntled staff	excessive complaining by staff
yelling at patients	excessive time to respond to call
impatient staff	light by staff
bad attitudes	

Activities

52. Does the facility have an activities director?

53. Is there a posted schedule of activities?

54. Are activities: flexible _____ required _____
structured _____ optional _____

55. Are religious services observed:
at the facility _____ at a local church or synagogue _____

56. Are community volunteers active at the facility?

57. Is there a library at the nursing facility?

58. Is there a beautician or barber who visits regularly?

Watch for:

no scheduled activities
a very part-time activities director

Transportation

59. Does the facility own a wheelchair van?

60. Does the facility provide transportation to medical appointments?

61. Is there a small fee for transportation services?

62. Is the facility located close to shopping?

Cost

63. What services are included in the monthly fee?

64. What services are not included in the monthly fee?

65. Are there any hidden fees?

66. If the care needs of a patient change, does this affect the monthly fee?

67. If a resident changes his level of care or decides to leave the facility, what is the refund policy?

68. Does the facility accept Medicaid payments? (*This is an important question*. Some facilities do not accept Medicaid. Others accept Medicaid payments but may be reluctant to accept their low reimbursement rate.)

69. What is the policy regarding residents if their funds run out? (*This is an important question.* Some facilities may discharge or evict a resident unable to pay for care. Others may try to work closely with the elder's family to prepare them for reduced funds. The facility may help your family apply for Medicaid and financial assistance through a state agency.)
70. Will the facility help a resident apply for Medicaid?
71. Does the facility accept long-term-care health insurance?

Please rate the nursing facility.

OVERALL RATING WORK SHEET

How would you rate this nursing home?

Date _____

Name and address of nursing home

_____

_____

	Excellent	Very Good	Good	Fair	Poor	Comments
General environment						
Room set-up						
Care						
Staff						
Activities						
Transportation services						

Patient's Rights and Responsibilities in a Nursing Facility

You have the right to respect and dignity.

You have the right to manage your own money.

You have the right to make your own decisions regarding care and treatments.

You have the right to assist in preparing your care plan.

You have the right to participate in and be informed of medical care.

You have the right to refuse medication and treatments.

You have the right to see your physician.

You have the right to privacy.

You have the right to keep private property and belongings.

You have the right to receive and send mail.

You have the right to make and receive phone calls.

You have the right to social services, counseling services, and assistance with discharge planning.

You have the right to not be restrained against your will.

You have the right to be free of verbal, mental, or physical abuse.

You have the right to complete an advanced directive.

You have the right to complete a power of attorney for health care.

You have the right to be informed of your rights and rules and regulations in the nursing facility.

You have the right to receive visitors during reasonable hours.

You have the right to review your medical records.

You have the right to refuse transfer to another room in the facility.

You have the right to contact a long-term-care ombudsman with concerns or complaints.

You have the right to share a room with your spouse.

You have the right to refuse discharge from the nursing facility unless:

you are a safety hazard to others or yourself

the nursing home cannot provide adequate care

nursing-home care is not needed

no payment has been made for services

the nursing home is closed

Chapter 9

Understanding Rehabilitation Centers

———————— ❦ ————————

Most people take for granted that they will be able to get up in the morning, brush their teeth, brush and comb their hair, shave, button their shirt, tie their shoes, and put on a skirt or a pair of pants. They assume they will be able to prepare breakfast, set the kitchen table, and eat their meal with a fork and knife. After breakfast, they may expect to drive a car to work, run errands, exercise, or clean their house.

When an unexpected medical event or crisis occurs—an accident, injury, or a severe illness—a person's life can be turned upside down. It can affect their ability to perform these normal, everyday activities and may dramatically change their life and the lives of their family and friends. They can go from being independent to being partially or completely dependent on others. The future, once clear, may now be confusing and frightening.

What Your Family Should Know

Before your family decides if treatment in a rehabilitation center would benefit your elder family member, it is important to know the following:

Does the current medical condition or event justify care or treatment in a rehabilitation program?

What are the doctor's treatment recommendations?

To what extent can your family participate in your elder's rehabilitation treatment program?

What types of rehabilitation centers are located near you?

What are the requirements for admission to the rehabilitation program?

What are the specific insurance benefits for treatment in a rehabilitation program?

How do you choose an appropriate rehabilitation program?

How will your elder and family decide which rehabilitation program can provide the best treatment?

What are the options for care after completing a rehabilitation program?

What questions should your elder and family ask about rehabilitation programs?

John Considers Treatment in a Rehabilitation Program

Following his hospitalization for a stroke, John spent two weeks in a subacute community skilled nursing facility, where he received nursing care and physical, occupational, and speech therapies. Although he made progress, his therapists and physician recommended a short stay in an inpatient rehabilitation program to further assess his strengths, weaknesses, physical limitations, and range of motion. In addition, they recommended a swallowing evaluation to help determine why he was continuing to have difficulty with eating.

When his physician felt that John had made significant progress and increased his endurance, he referred him for an evaluation by staff from a hospital-based rehabilitation program. The program required at least three hours of active participation in daily therapy. In addition, the rehabilitation staff requested family participation in education, training, and discharge planning.

John and his family were told that the rehabilitation staff would meet to discuss John's progress and medical-care needs in the subacute setting in order to set realistic goals, as well as to determine a tentative length of stay in the rehabilitation program. They would also meet with interested family members to discuss the program objectives, treatment plan, and any family concerns. The rehabilitation staff felt that John was a good candidate for their program.

John continued to improve his mobility, balance, range of motion, and speech in the subacute setting, but he still was not considered to be safe for independent living. The case manager met with John and his family to discuss all the options: receiving treatment in the intensive rehabilitation program and returning home with supervision and the help of community services, including home health care, or moving John to a supervised setting, such as an assisted living facility or an adult-care home.

How will John and his family decide if treatment in a rehabilitation center is his best choice? This narrative makes several important points:

John continued to make progress in the subacute setting.

John continued to need skilled medical care in the subacute facility.

Even with his progress, John was still considered unsafe for independent living.

John needed a referral from his physician before he could be considered for the rehabilitation program.

He also needed an evaluation by the rehabilitation team before he could be admitted to the rehabilitation program.

Other discharge options were also available to John and his family.

Because most people who need rehabilitation are already in a hospital or subacute (or skilled nursing) setting or have lived with a chronic illness for years, the transition to a rehabilitation center should be fairly smooth.

If your elder is living at home but experiencing increasing difficulty managing everyday activities, your family may want to make an appointment with his physician to discuss the feasibility of admitting him to an inpatient or outpatient rehabilitation program to improve his life skills and functioning.

To gather the information necessary to make an informed decision about rehabilitation centers, it is important for your family to talk with your elder's physician, therapists, and a medical social worker or case manager. They will be able to begin the process needed to determine if a rehabilitation program is appropriate. They can also verify insurance information and review the benefits for inpatient or outpatient rehabilitation, home health nursing care, durable medical equipment, and more. The more information your family has about available rehabilitation programs, the clearer the guidelines for admission will be.

When a Rehabilitation Program Is Needed

Treatment in a rehabilitation program may be needed for a variety of reasons. Your elder may have been living with a chronic illness or recently had an accident, is in a hospital, or had surgery. Listed below are some of the frequent diagnoses treated in a rehabilitation program:

cerebrovascular accident, or stroke

major multiple traumas

debilitating arthritis

spinal cord injury

amputation or loss of a limb

neurological conditions

congenital or hereditary deformities

severe orthopedic conditions, such as fractures or replacements

brain injury, trauma, or dysfunction

cognitive or mental changes

chronic illnesses, such as multiple sclerosis, Parkinson's disease, amyotrophic lateral sclerosis (ALS or Lou Gehrig's disease), and Huntington's chorea.

Most people enter a rehabilitation program during or after a hospitalization. However, rehabilitation can begin at any point on the continuum of care. This means it may start during the acute-hospital stay, during subacute or skilled care at home, with follow-up by therapists and nurses from a home health-care agency, or during a subacute rehabilitation program at a skilled nursing facility.

For many of these conditions, especially head, brain, and spinal cord injuries, it is important to begin treatment during the acute phase of the injury, even in the intensive- or critical-care unit. Other times, it won't begin until the acute medical problem has been resolved or stabilized.

People living at home with multiple sclerosis or Parkinson's disease, for instance, who experience a decreased level of functioning may also benefit from a rehabilitation program if they require comprehensive services, such as self-care training, mobility assessment and training, and some rehabilitation nursing, for example, monitoring heart rate, respiration, blood pressure, and bowel and bladder training.

Your elder family member may need rehabilitation if:

He is having difficulty with mobility and balance or experiencing a deterioration in his physical abilities.

He is having increased difficulty thinking rationally and making decisions, or is experiencing significant memory impairment. However, he must be able to follow some directions and commands.

He has impaired learning but retains the ability and potential to relearn.

He has neurological complications or cognitive deficiencies that could benefit from constant and consistent intervention.

He is recovering from a recent illness, accident, injury, or debilitating chronic illness.

He has difficulty maintaining adequate nutrition secondary to difficulty swallowing.

He has difficulty functioning due to a significant nerve or sensory loss.

He is at risk in his home and may need home-safety modifications that require an evaluation and the expertise of skilled rehabilitation staff.

He is at risk of being placed in an institution or other setting.

He has complicated lower- or upper-extremity orthotics needs.

He has nursing-care needs at a higher level of care than can be provided in a subacute setting.

He has daily physiatry (nonsurgical treatment of pain or disability) needs.

He has low endurance for physical activity or is severely deconditioned.

Types of Rehabilitation Programs

When your elder family member needs rehabilitation, it is important to work closely with the physician and other health professionals involved in his care. They will help your family determine the appropriate rehabilitation setting for your elder.

There two basic types of rehabilitation facilities: hospital affiliated and free-standing. In a hospital-based program, the facility is within the hospital complex or works closely with the hospital. Most of these facilities can provide inpatient acute, postacute, or subacute rehabilitation. Hospitals may also offer outpatient therapies and follow-up when the inpatient rehabilitation program is completed. Often, the same therapists and physician are able to continue the treatment, thus providing continuity of care.

A freestanding facility may not be directly affiliated with a hospital and may not be able to provide acute rehabilitation. However, it may be more cost-effective, because it may maintain access to medical services without the expensive cost of hospital care. These facilities may also refer more difficult and complex cases to a hospital-based program.

Acute rehabilitation may begin as soon as your elder is medically stable, sometimes as early as the intensive-care unit. The treatment emphasis is directed at assessing the physical level of functioning by looking at strengths, weaknesses, limitations, and the level of cognitive or mental functioning. After being evaluated by the rehabilitation team, a patient may remain in acute care during the hospitalization while receiving treatment from the rehabilitation team. If additional long- or short-term treatment is deemed necessary, the patient may be transferred—when ready—to an inpatient unit for a more intensive program. The acute-rehabilitation programs tend to admit patients with more complex cognitive, neurological, and disabling conditions.

Subacute rehabilitation usually begins after your elder has been discharged from the hospital and is commonly called the postacute phase of rehabilitation. Subacute rehabilitation is usually provided in a skilled nursing facility or hospital-based transitional-care unit. Freestanding subacute rehabilitation programs may work closely with a hospital but may not be hospital-based. The length of stay is determined by the amount of progress made by the patient during physical, occupational, and speech therapies. In a subacute unit, nursing needs are less complex, neurological problems are minimal or less complex, and physician visits are less frequent.

Transitional rehabilitation may be found in both acute and subacute programs. A community group home may also be used. The emphasis of this rehabilitation program is on preparing the patient for reentry into the community. These programs emphasize the basic living skills necessary to become independent in the community. They also emphasize compensation or increasing the functioning of an unimpaired but similar body part versus restoring use of the body part that no longer adequately functions.

Long-term rehabilitation or extended rehabilitation may be needed after the first year of rehabilitation to fine-tune newly learned skills and to continue to maintain some level of progress. By this time, although improvement is continuing, it may have considerably slowed. This treatment may be found in hospital- or community-affiliated rehabilitation programs.

Coma treatment rehabilitation programs are specialized rehabilitation programs for patients registering at the lower end of the *Ranchos Los Amigos Guide to Cognitive Levels* (see guide on page 236), which determines cognitive functioning for patients with traumatic brain injury. The testing is usually performed by a neuropsychologist or neurologist. A low score indicates no response or a limited response to stimulation. Patients who require this care should receive extensive physical, occupational, and stimulation therapies in addition to skilled nursing care. Many rehabilitation programs do not include this type of care. If your elder family member needs it, talk to your physician, a rehabilitation social worker, or case manager for additional information.

Outpatient rehabilitation programs may be affiliated with either hospital-based, freestanding, or community-based facilities. The treatment is usually a continuation of therapies begun in an inpatient program. Outpatient care may be needed as follow-up therapy after an inpatient rehabilitation program or as an alternative to therapy in a skilled nursing facility or from a home health-care agency.

Choosing a Rehabilitation Program

Because family involvement and participation are important for helping your elder gain optimum benefits from his program, it is necessary to consider where his program is located. If you are in a major metropolitan area, you likely have a choice of facilities and programs. If you live in a smaller city or town, your options may be more limited. For elders who have specialized needs, it may be necessary to travel to another state. For example, a coma treatment patient in Oregon may need to go to Washington or California for a comprehensive rehabilitation program.

It may be difficult to choose a rehabilitation program without the expertise of involved physicians, therapists, and case managers who work with people with disabilities on a regular basis. Therefore, it is *strongly* recommended that if your elder meets many of the criteria for admission to a rehabilitation center, your family should work closely with the these health-care professionals to ensure an appropriate program geared to his disability and medical-care needs. When it is necessary to choose a rehabilitation program, look for the following:

accreditation of the rehabilitation program

a physician familiar with rehabilitation programs who is also easy to talk with

a comprehensive program that meets the recovery needs of your elder

a rehabilitation facility approved by your elder's insurance company

rehabilitation staff members who are compassionate, flexible, and well trained

Accreditation

Rehabilitation programs affiliated with hospitals often have accreditation with the Joint Commission of Accredited Hospital Organizations (JCAHO). In addition, many seek accreditation with the Commission on Accreditation of Rehabilitation Facilities. (CARF). CARF is a private, nonprofit organization that establishes standards of quality care in rehabilitation facilities. Rehabilitation facilities that seek CARF accreditation must meet these strict standards and guidelines when they are examined on-site by rehabilitation professionals. Programs that receive accreditation earn a certificate of accreditation and are included in the *Directory of Accredited Organizations*.

Approaching Admission to a Rehabilitation Program

Before your elder family member can be admitted to a rehabilitation program, he must:

obtain a referral from his primary-care physician and/or a neurologist or physiatrist (a physician who specializes in physical medicine and rehabilitation)

meet the criteria for admission

have his insurance benefits reviewed and, if needed, obtain pre-authorization for treatment

have a definitive or potential discharge plan in mind

Usually, a rehabilitation case manager or other member of the rehabilitation team obtains medical information and a copy of the medical transcript *before* accepting a person for admission. They also look at the discharge plan, the patient's current functional status, and his ability to learn and participate in the program. Admission is not black and white; it allows for extenuating circumstances and is flexible.

However, because insurance guidelines are growing more stringent, it is becoming harder for rehabilitation programs to justify admissions. At one time, uncomplicated strokes could be readily admitted to an acute-rehabilitation program. Now they are referred to subacute programs. Patients who have suffered strokes must be able to demonstrate multiple medical issues and medical necessity.

Getting a Referral

To enter a rehabilitation program, it is necessary to get a referral from a primary-care physician. Or a referral may be made by a neurologist or physiatrist actively involved in treatment, who then recommends admission to a rehabilitation program. When the rehabilitation staff members receive the referral, they may send members of the team to meet your elder and evaluate his physical and cognitive capabilities. If it is decided—usually by a physician—that your elder could actively participate in the program and would benefit from it, he may be considered for admission to it.

Once admitted into the rehabilitation program, the physiatrist or neurologist may become the primary physician. Upon discharge from the program, the regular primary-care physician may resume responsibility for your elder's basic care.

Referrals can also come from other acute-care hospitals, rehabilitation facilities, nursing facilities, physicians, nursing staff, therapists, home health-care agencies, community agencies, or family members.

Meeting the Criteria for Admission

To enter a rehabilitation program, there must be *a defined rehabilitation need,* that is, not only one medical need but a comprehensive group of needs that require the skills of the rehabilitation team and skilled nursing care.

The person entering the program must have the *endurance and tolerance* to actively participate daily in the program, sometimes for as long as three hours or more. If they do not have the endurance to participate, subacute or skilled care is often recommended prior to admission. Following subacute care, a person may then be transferred to a more intensive rehabilitation program.

When your elder is admitted to a rehabilitation program, he will be evaluated by a physiatrist, registered nurse, neuropsychologist (or neurologist), physical therapist, occupational therapist, and a speech-language or communication-disorder therapist. These evaluations and assessments are shared at weekly, biweekly, or bimonthly case conferences, after which realistic individual goals are set. A tentative discharge date may also be recommended at that time. The typical length of stay in any of the above programs varies from region to region and program to program. They may range from three days to several months; the average length of stay is three to six weeks. These goals and lengths of stay are usually flexible and may change depending on the progress or lack of progress made by your elder.

Checking Insurance Benefits

Entering a rehabilitation program without insurance benefits can be expensive, which is why it is important to have your elder's insurance benefits checked *before* he is admitted into a program. Usually, a rehabilitation case manager, an admissions official, or a business office representative contacts the insurance company.

Rehabilitation benefits may be limited by the number of days (standard is thirty to sixty) or a monetary amount or may have unlimited benefits determined by medical necessity. Medical necessity includes the medical care, services, and supplies essential to the treatment and diagnosis of an illness or injury. Insurance companies may require pre-authorization and review the physician's prescribed treatment, services, and recommendations. They can determine that the medical treatment could have been provided in a different way and/or at lower cost. The physician may recommend a preferred provider program (a program which he may have a contract or agreement with) or a different option, such as subacute, outpatient, or home health-care therapies, before agreeing to admission to an intensive and more expensive rehabilitation program.

Private-Pay Rates

Many programs charge more than one thousand dollars per day, which may include all therapies. Your elder must still meet all the criteria for admission.

Medicare Rates

Inpatient rehabilitation benefits are covered under the hospital benefits for physical, occupational, and speech therapies. Medicare determines the rate of reimbursement based on a complicated formula called TEFRA rates. Some programs indicate that if an individual's length of stay exceeds nine to ten days, the rehabilitation program begins to take a financial loss. However, if he continues to meet the admission criteria, rehabilitation programs will keep a Medicare patient as long as needed.

Outpatient rehabilitation therapies in a hospital are covered under Medicare Part B. Medicare pays 80 percent of the approved amount after a onetime annual one-hundred-dollar deductible has been paid.

If your elder has Medicare through a managed-care or HMO program, the program may override Medicare benefits if, after reviewing the medical records, it determines rehabilitation care in a hospital-based program is not medically necessary. The HMO may prefer care in a less expensive subacute or skilled facility, an outpatient program, or a home setting with home health-care therapies.

Medicaid Rates

Medicaid pays a much lower reimbursement rate than Medicare or commercial/private insurance. Pre-authorization or approval from the Medicaid program is usually required before a patient can be admitted to a rehabilitation program.

Medicaid pays for most physician fees, therapies, nursing care, orthotics, and medical equipment in the rehabilitation program. It may also provide out-patient services, good supportive care at discharge, assisting with transportation, home health care, durable medical equipment for home use, and homemaker support, which includes housecleaning, shopping, and meal preparation.

Commercial/Private Insurance

Because each individual commercial policy may provide different benefits, it is important to carefully review your elder's policy for inpatient rehabilitation services, outpatient rehabilitation services, and subacute or skilled nursing-care services. Most commercial plans limit the amount of money paid out or the number of allowed treatments. In addition, check the coverage for home health-care services and durable medical equipment, because these may be needed for follow-up care after the rehabilitation program. Pre-authorization is usually required.

Managed Care/HMOs

Many HMOs and managed-care programs contract with the rehabilitation facility to determine the daily cost of admission. Or, they may be willing to negotiate a rate with a facility. However, many HMOs may prefer to use subacute rehabilitation, because it is more cost-effective.

In some policies, rehabilitation must start within a period of two consecutive calendar months per episode of care. Different illnesses or medical conditions may justify an additional two-month benefit period. This benefit may be renewed each calendar year.

Pre-authorization is needed, and often the HMO only authorizes treatment for one week at a time. In these cases, the rehabilitation case manager or responsible person acts as a liaison, providing the insurance company, the patient, the family, and the rehabilitation team with medical updates.

Check with your HMO regarding benefits for inpatient rehabilitation, subacute or skilled nursing care, outpatient therapy, durable medical equipment and orthotics, and home health-care services. Ask your HMO if it has contracts with any rehabilitation facilities in your area. Ask if it prefers to admit patients who have rehabilitation needs to subacute facilities or hospital-based rehabilitation programs.

Long-Term-Care Insurance Polices

Some people purchase long-term-care policies for extra coverage. Be aware that skilled nursing care (subacute care) is already covered under Medicare or Medicaid. This policy should primarily provide benefits for care *not* covered under other policies, including custodial care, intermediate care, and nonskilled care. Look carefully at the premium to determine if it is worth purchasing. Check your elder's insurance policy for:

inpatient rehabilitation coverage

limitations on rehabilitation treatments

the number of days of rehabilitation benefits for inpatient treatment

the out-of-pocket or co-pay cost to you, especially for outpatient therapies

Please note: Co-pays may often be per treatment. For example, especially in outpatient programs, each treatment with a therapist may cost a co-pay of $10. Many programs recommend follow-up care three times a week with each therapist, sometimes for four to six weeks. This means that if your elder receives treatments from a physical therapist, an occupational therapist, and a speech therapist, the cost is:

at $10 per visit with a physical therapist X 3 visits per week
= $30 per week

at $10 per visit with a occupational therapist X 3 visits per week
= $30 per week

at $10 per visit with a speech therapist X 3 visits per week
= $30 per week

Total: $90 per week
$90 per week X 4 weeks = $360
$90 per week X 6 weeks = $540

The total co-pay cost for home visits from physical, occupational, and speech therapists three times weekly for four weeks is $360. Or for six weeks of therapies, the cost is $540.

What to Bring to the Rehabilitation Program

Upon admission, your elder and family will provide personal, medical, and insurance information. A copy of his most recent medical transcript with a history and physical, consultations, medications, X-ray and lab reports, therapy notes, and other significant information will be requested by the rehabilitation admissions coordinator or case manager. If your elder is already in the hospital receiving acute care, his medical records may be transferred directly to the rehabilitation unit. You may need to sign a release of information, which gives them permission to obtain these data. It is important to bring the original or copies of the following:

medical and insurance cards

copy of Social Security card

organ donor card

living will*

advanced directives*

Physician Orders for Life-Sustaining Treatment (POLST)

durable power of attorney for health care*

a durable power of attorney

guardianship papers*

other pertinent legal documents*

list of medications and dosages

If your elder has just been in the hospital, this information may be provided in the transfer summary prepared by the nursing staff.

To participate in the rehabilitation program and therapy sessions your elder needs at least three sets of clothing including:

loose-fitting clothes; those that are easy to get on and take off, including
sweatpants, leggings, sweatshirts, and, for women, front-fastening bras

---

*This is important: *Retain the original for your files, and give copies to the admissions office for your elder's medical record, her primary-care physician, her attorney, and any involved health-care facility or community agency. Your family may want to review chapter 7, "Understanding Hospital Acute Care," for more information about advanced directives, living wills, durable power of attorneys, and organ donor cards. If you elder has just been in the hospital, this information may be provided in the transfer summary prepared by the nursing staff.*

(Avoid zipper tops, because they may scratch or be difficult to manage with an upper-body disability.)

jacket for outside therapy

tennis shoes or comfortable flat nonskid shoes

sleep attire, such as bathrobe, pajamas, and nonskid slippers

toiletries, including hairbrush, comb, and makeup

personal items, including glasses, dentures, hearing aides, personal bed pillows, important telephone numbers, or a picture of your family

leisure activities, including books, games, and knitting your elder may have potential to perform

Do *not* bring:

sentimental or personal items

jewelry

credit cards or cash

delicate clothing

dress shoes or clothing

After your elder has been admitted to the rehabilitation program, he is entering a new environment. Although similar to a hospital in many ways, the treatment program is different from an acute-care hospital setting. In a hospital, the emphasis is on treating an acute medical problem. The nurses do everything for the patient. In a rehabilitation program, your elder is expected to do as much as he can. Here, the emphasis is on restoration or giving the patient an improved or compensatory level of functioning. The goal is to make your elder as independent as possible within realistic expectations.

On Admission to the Rehabilitation Program

On admission, your family and elder meet with a social worker. She will interview both of you extensively, asking about medical history and problems; current abilities; family history and support system; family dynamics; the living situation, including steps within the home and bathroom accessibility; transportation assistance; the splitting of household chores; vocation and education; interests and activities; finances and insurance; family and patient goals and expectations; and other practical considerations. In addition, she will ask about the discharge plan and any anticipated problems.

Your elder family member is expected to participate in a fairly strenuous therapy program three to six hours daily. Basic activities taken for granted for many years will present new challenges. Walking, standing, sitting, buttoning shirts, tying shoelaces, dressing, grooming, holding utensils, speaking, thinking, reasoning, remembering, visualizing, and comprehending may be difficult for your elder when he begins the program.

A schedule of activities, therapies, and appointments may be posted in a general living area or by the door to your elder's room. This enables staff, visitors, and family to plan their day so they can attend important therapy sessions and meetings. Although schedules change, usually a brief phone call can confirm any modifications.

Each member of the rehabilitation team—except for nutrition and social work—assesses your elder's abilities by using the *Functional Independence Measure*, or *FIM*. In addition, the neuropsychologist or neurologist may use the Rancho Los Amigos Guide to Cognitive Levels to determine cognitive functioning after a traumatic brain injury.

Family Involvement

Family involvement, support, and encouragement are instrumental for a successful rehabilitation program. The extent of family involvement may differ with each individual patient. Most families are unfamiliar with the specific objectives and goals of rehabilitation programs. They may not understand that quality of life at the completion of the program may be improved but not necessarily to its previous state before the medical event. They may not understand how the medical event or condition affects the physical body, and they may not be aware of the cognitive or mental changes that may occur.

While some elders may initially be distracted and unable to focus on their therapies when family is present, others may find that family makes them feel more secure and motivated. Many rehabilitation programs encourage family participation if they feel it will be beneficial to the patient.

The more positive your family approach and interaction are with your elder, the more likely he will feel encouraged and develop a more positive attitude. A favorable attitude may enable him to cope more easily with his disability and work harder in the rehabilitation program. The more hopeful and realistic your family is about recovery, the more empowered your elder will feel. The more your family compliments your elder's progress—even if it is in small steps—the more confident your elder will feel about his progress.

It is common for patients with new and severe limitations to feel frustrated, discouraged, depressed, helpless, angry, confused, disorganized, or agitated. If these feelings remain during participation in the rehabilitation program, they can directly affect your elder's ability to relearn coping skills and adapt and adjust to his new limitations.

It is important to maintain realistic expectations: Your elder may not completely recover all his lost abilities. He may recover only some, or only in some areas. However, any progress he makes moves him from dependence on family, caregiver, or community to increased independence.

Your family may become an advocate and intermediary for your elder. You may be asked to participate in caregiver training and rehabilitation education. The sooner the training begins, the greater the comfort level your family will have providing the necessary help or care.

Beginning the Program

Many different types of programs are offered by a rehabilitation center. The one your elder chooses depends on several factors: the nature of his disability, including the ability to actively participate in the program, the location of the rehabilitation facility, and the physician's recommendations. Each member of the rehabilitation team independently works with your elder and works collaboratively with the rest of the rehabilitation team.

The Goal of a Rehabilitation Program

The goal of a rehabilitation program, according to the Western Unabridged Dictionary, is "to restore the rights, authority, dignity and former capacity" to an individual by using the skills of an interdisciplinary team of physicians, health-care professionals, therapists, family, friends, and community.

Each individual who enters a rehabilitation program is there for similar reasons: their ability to function, that is, think, perceive, feel, cope, move, behave, or manage in their daily life, has changed. They may experience new emotional changes that affect their ability to reason and to make rational decisions. New physical limitations may also occur. They may lose control of movement in their arms, legs, and upper body and bodily functions, including bowel and bladder control. Activities once taken for granted may become difficult or impossible to perform. However, with comprehensive rehabilitation, training, and education, a person can relearn her living skills and develop new skills to help her adapt to her new life.

Each person who is admitted to a rehabilitation program may meet with staff to determine her specific goals and most effective course of treatment. The goals may be dependent on her physical or cognitive limitations, home environment, or dependence on others.

Measuring Your Elder's Capabilities

A patient can enter a rehabilitation program at various levels of functioning or capabilities. In many facilities, each member of the rehabilitation team—the registered nurse, neuropsychologist, physical therapist, occupational therapist, and speech-language therapist—uses the FIM to assess each patient. These scores are updated weekly, at discharge, and during follow-up visits. Total scores can range from 18 to 126. The higher the score, the greater the patient's level of independence. Patients are scored in the following areas:

self-care, including eating, grooming, bathing, dressing upper and lower body, and toileting

sphincter control, including bladder and bowel management

mobility, including safely performing transfers from bed, chair and wheelchair, toilet, and tub or shower

locomotion, including safely walking, using a wheelchair, and going up and down stairs

communication, including auditory and visual comprehension, vocal and nonvocal expression

comprehension, including the patient's ability to ask for any needed help with the daily activities of life

social cognition, including social interaction, problem solving, and memory.

Social interaction includes getting along with others in various situations. Problem solving includes the ability to make good decisions regarding finances and social and personal interactions, as well as solving problems in a timely and correct manner. Memory includes verbal and visual recognition of people, using learned information, and remembering daily routines.

The FIM scoring looks at the following in each discipline:

7. complete independence, timely and safely without aid

6. modified independence with a device but without aid

5. supervised, with helper

4. minimum assistance, or patient can help more than 51 percent of the time

3. moderate assistance, or patient can help 50 percent or more

2. maximum assistance, or patient can help 25 percent or more

1. total assistance, or complete care needed

No helper means the patient is capable of safely performing the specific task without assistance or set-up. *Helper* means the patient needs some supervision, assistive or adaptive device, or set-up help.

Programs and Classes

Each rehabilitation program has different names for specific treatment programs. Although these programs and life skills may seem trivial to a healthy person with two functioning arms, two functioning legs, and no cognitive problems, imagine the difficulty a person in a wheelchair may have reaching a countertop, preparing a meal, or using a wall telephone. Imagine shopping for goods that are several feet higher than your reach. When cognitive, reasoning, and organizational skills are not adequate, how do you make appointments, write a shopping list, manage your finances, or communicate?

Many health-care professionals with a multitude of skills work together on a treatment plan, so the program should provide some consistency, continuity, and momentum geared toward discharge from the program at a higher level of functioning.

The rehabilitation staff will work with your elder on basic life skills, including meal preparation, adaptation skills, community socialization, and activities of daily living.

Meal Preparation

This can include planning and preparing a simple or complex nutritious meal; preparing a shopping list; budgeting the meal; and using appropriate assistive or adaptive devices. Meal preparation may involve social interaction skills, organizational and coordination skills, the ability to focus and remain focused on a task, the ability to solve problems, and awareness of safety issues and increasing stamina. Practice sessions may be held with a occupational therapist in a kitchenlike setting in the rehabilitation facility.

Adaptation Skills

Your elder will relearn and adapt to performing common, everyday tasks. Emphasis may be placed on improving range of motion, strength, coordination, balance, and endurance. Learning how to adjust with cognitive, perceptual, or sensory losses, including hearing, seeing, and touching, may also be addressed.

Community Socialization

Your elder will learn how to appropriately interact with staff, family, and other patients. He will learn how to behave appropriately in public, recognize inappropriate behavior, accept redirection, and acknowledge activities that are difficult for him to do. He will also rebuild relationships, maintain social boundaries, recognize emotions, and accept and acknowledge physical, emotional, and personal losses.

Activities of Daily Living

Your elder will focus on relearning basic living skills: doing household chores, preparing meals, dressing, selecting clothes, grooming, toileting, managing simple finances, following a budget, writing a check, and balancing a checkbook.

Exercise Class

Your elder will work on strengthening muscles and improving his joint flexibility, endurance, range of motion, and mobility.

Pool or Aquatic Class

Water exercises may be used for patients who are unable to stand on their own in order to increase muscular strength and joint flexibility. They may also be used to help decrease anxious, defensive, edgy, and excitable behavioral tendencies.

Pet Therapy

Dogs, cats, and birds may be brought to the facility. As patients interact with the animals, they strengthen their social skills, increase their endurance and whole-body movement, decrease depression and feelings of isolation, develop responsibility as they care for the animal, and increase their own senses and orientation to the real world.

Peer Counseling Program

Some rehabilitation programs arrange for former patients to talk with current patients experiencing similar problems. Sometimes talking with someone who has already been through the program helps allay fears and concerns regarding the ability to participate in the program or about their future. For example, a patient who has had a traumatic amputation of his leg may feel hopeless and depressed following surgery. Seeing a former amputee patient walk into his room on two legs, using a prosthesis, may give the rehabilitation patient hope and motivation. Peer counselors should participate in a training program before speaking with patients and should also respect confidentiality.

Sexuality Program

Following a major accident, injury, or disability, many patients have questions and concerns about their sexuality. What can they do? What has changed? In many rehabilitation programs, a staff member is assigned to a patient to discuss these important issues. In others, group sessions may be held with other patients and interested family members.

Day or Weekend Passes

Some facilities have in-house programs that provide real-life challenges within the rehabilitation complex, including a realistic post office or grocery store where your elder can practice his newly acquired skills. However, as your elder nears discharge, he may be encouraged to use a weekend pass to go home or to take a short car ride. A home visit with a therapist may also be recommended, because it may increase your elder's confidence and self-esteem as he moves toward increased independence. Or, it may highlight specific problem areas and allow therapists and staff to focus on them prior to discharge.

Each rehabilitation facility and program has different requirements for obtaining a pass. They may offer one pass at different times during the program, with specific individuals, or during specific hours only. Most require a release form signed by the patient and the responsible person during the visit.

If, after a home visit, your family does not feel able to care for your elder, that's not unusual. The case manager may recommend hiring a caregiver or placing your elder in a supervised setting, such as an adult-care home. If a caregiver is hired to help provide in-home care following the rehabilitation program, they will be encouraged to actively participate with the therapies and attend caregiver training. Often, adult-care home providers will attend these training sessions.

Rehabilitation Staff

The Role of the Physiatrist

The physiatrist, a physician who specializes in physical medicine and rehabilitation, is trained to work with injuries related to the spine, muscles, nerves, and joints. In addition, he may work with people who have disabilities arising from neurological disorders and traumatic injuries to the brain and spinal cord.

In some rehabilitation programs, the physiatrist may not be the primary physician to monitor the patient's care or lead the interdisciplinary team. Instead, a physician acting as medical or clinical director, a licensed psychologist, a social worker, or a psychiatrist may be primarily responsible for managing and coordinating patient care. The advantage in using a facility with a physiatrist is the extensive training and education these professionals bring to the program.

For example, if your elder had a severe heart problem, would you want him to be treated by a family practice doctor or by an experienced cardiologist?

The Role of Nursing

The nursing staff is responsible for providing all the necessary care required by your elder. Upon admission to the rehabilitation program, they sit down with your elder (and family, if needed) and complete a thorough nursing assessment that looks at your elder's abilities and medical-care needs. They may provide assistance with self-care, bowel and bladder management, medication management, and skilled nursing care, including administering injections and intravenous solutions, changing dressings, and maintaining skin tone. Unlike the registered nurse in the hospital, the rehabilitation nurse encourages your elder to perform as much of his own care as possible. The registered nurse is often assisted by a certified nurse's aide who is trained in rehabilitation care. The nursing staff should be available in the rehabilitation program twenty-four hours a day.

The Role of the Neuropsychologist

The neuropsychologist is trained to study the behavior of the brain. He looks at how it functions, as well as how thinking, personality, mood, memory, and perception are affected—especially after a stroke or brain injury.

Many rehabilitation programs maintain a contract with a local neuropsychologist instead of having him on staff. When he is iassessing a patient, his views, opinions, and recommendations become an integral part of the interdisciplinary treatment plan.

The neuropsychologist or neurologist may also assess cognitive functioning after a traumatic brain injury by using the Rancho Los Amigos Cognitive Guide. His assessment is scored by using the following scale:

Rancho Los Amigos Cognitive Guide

I	no response
II	generalized response
III	localized response
IV	confused and agitated
V	confused, inappropriate, and nonagitated
VI	confused and appropriate
VII	automatic and appropriate
VIII	purposeful and appropriate

Because this testing is extensive and complex, it is best to speak directly with the neuropsychologist about your questions or concerns.

The Role of the Physical Therapist

The physical therapist works with your elder on exercises and activities to improve his strength, conditioning, mobility, and endurance, as well as to increase range of motion and reduce pain. The physical therapist may also provide caregiver training to ensure proper techniques are used in lifting, transferring, mobility, and exercises. He works primarily with patients who:

are recovering from a stroke

have had knee- or hip-replacement surgery

have orthopedic disabilities, such as fractures, muscle sprains, or strains

have chronic and potentially debilitating illnesses, such as multiple sclerosis, Parkinson's disease, Huntington's chorea, and amyotrophic lateral sclerosis (known as ALS or Lou Gehrig's disease)

have had a leg or arm amputation

experience disabling pain from arthritis

experience problems with balance

are weak and incapacitated as a result of a medical illness

are recovering from a trauma

need training and education in body mechanics and ergonomics

The physical therapist may use massage, soft-tissue mobilization, biofeedback, personalized exercise programs, ultrasound, electric stimulation, transcutaneous electrical nerve stimulation (TENS) units for pain relief, hot and cold compresses, gait retraining, and more. He may also order prosthetics and specialized adaptive devices. Certified and trained physical therapy aides may assist the physical therapist.

The Role of Orthotics

With an order and prescription from the physician, the orthotics staff member designs and constructs adaptive equipment, such as braces and wheelchair seats, for patients who have lost the ability to function due to illness, injury, or chronic disease. Not all rehabilitation programs have an on-site orthotics person. The facility may need to request a consultation or contract out to one working locally.

The Role of the Occupational Therapist

The occupational therapist focuses on your elder's ability to perform everyday activities. He may also review the home environment and develop adaptive equipment for individuals. He works with patients who:

are recovering from a stroke

have limited cognitive skills as a result of a head injury or trauma

are recovering from a spinal cord injury

have orthopedic injuries, including fractures and surgical replacements

have a chronic illness or condition such as multiple sclerosis (MS), Parkinson's disease, arthritis, and amyotrophic lateral sclerosis (ALS)

are at risk for contractures or stiff joints, which severely limit range of motion

The occupational therapist helps patients to develop a sense of how their body parts relate to one another and organizational, problem-solving, discriminating, and perceptual skills. Using Peg-Board, toys, balls, marbles, puzzles, blocks, arts and crafts, games, and other interactive activities, the occupational therapist helps your elder develop skills through simple playlike activities.

The Role of the Speech-Language Therapist

The speech-language therapist focuses on improving communication, speech, and comprehension. She also evaluates swallowing disorders and may recommend communication aids and devices. She works with patients who:

have had a laryngectomy

have a chronic illness or condition, such as ALS, MS, Parkinson's disease, or Huntington's chorea

have head or neck cancer

are recovering from a stroke and have lost all or part of their ability to communicate

have swallowing difficulties

have difficulty with auditory comprehension, speech production, or articulation due to muscle paralysis or lack of coordination around the mouth area, including the jaw, tongue, and lips

The Role of the Nutritionist or Dietitian

In many rehabilitation programs each patient is seen for consultation by a nutritional expert. This health-care professional reviews the patient's dietary habits and restrictions and makes recommendations for a well-balanced meal. For patients who have swallowing difficulties, she may recommend specific foods and diets. For patients who have weight problems, she may recommend ways to increase or decrease weight. In addition, she may have handouts that feature recipes and other dietary hints.

The Role of the Social Worker or Case Manager

The social worker often acts as your family's liaison between the rest of the interdisciplinary rehabilitation team. They are usually available during regular working hours (7 A.M. to 6 P.M.) to talk with your elder and your family about concerns, expectations, hopes, finances, family relationships, employment concerns, and discharge planning.

He may also help with arranging family conferences, follow-up appointments, and community referrals; he may provide information regarding appropriate support groups, assist or arrange ordering of durable medical equipment, and act as a liaison between your elder and the insurance company. In addition, he can help your family with emotional issues and guide you to a reasonable and safe discharge plan for your elder family member.

The social worker can empower your family by giving you the necessary tools you need to explore other options. He can help your family recognize your roles as an advocate and intermediary. The social worker can:

arrange in-home services and care

provide lists of agencies and individuals who offer caregiver assistance

order medical equipment and supplies

make referrals to supportive community agencies and home health care

suggest sources for financial assistance

provide transportation assistance

assist with Social Security Disability (SSDI) or Supplemental Security Income (SSI) applications

provide emotional support and individual and family counseling services
for issues such as:
grief and loss
alcohol and drug abuse
family relationships
fear of death

depression and self-esteem

domestic violence

make referrals to individuals or clinics for counseling services

The social worker may recommend referrals to support groups focusing in areas such as:

caregiver support

depression

stroke

specific illnesses (MS, ALS, Parkinson's)

brain injury

spinal cord injury

widow/widower support

grief and loss support

Information and Referral

The social worker may contact or encourage your family to contact community agencies on your elder's behalf to arrange in-home support services. She may also provide information about appropriate, available resources. The most common referrals are made to agencies that provide:

home-delivered meals

durable medical equipment and supplies

transportation

financial assistance

alternatives to living at home

drug and alcohol treatment

free services such as transportation and loaner equipment

In chapter 3, "Getting Help in Your Home," you will find helpful work sheets: Keeping Track of Services, Sample Schedule Guide, and Hiring Help in Your Home.

Discharge Planning

When your elder family member enters a rehabilitation program, his ability to deal with basic life activities may be greatly impaired. His mobility, reasoning, coordination, and bodily functions may not work as they once did. He may not be able to live safely and independently in his home or another homelike setting without assistance and supervision.

Community Support

Community support is any assistance given to your elder by a community-based agency. Many of these agencies are nonprofit or have specific eligibility guidelines. A social worker or case manager can guide you to the appropriate agencies.

Some of these programs provide: financial assistance, home health aides, home-making support for shopping and meal preparation, transportation, prescription and medical-equipment assistance, and assistance applying for Medicaid, Social Security Disability (SSDI), or Supplemental Security Income (SSI).

Review chapter 3, "Getting Help in Your Home," for more information.

Home Health Care

Many patients who return home or to other homelike settings, such as assisted living facilities or adult-care homes, are referred by their physician to a home health-care agency for follow-up care. The home health-care agency can provide physical, occupational, and speech therapies in addition to skilled nursing care if your elder is considered homebound, that is, unable to easily leave his home.

Because physical and speech therapies and skilled nursing care are considered skilled services, Medicare and most commercial insurance carriers provide benefits for these services. Once a skilled service is in place, insurance benefits pay for secondary services, such as occupational therapy, social workers, and home health aides who can visit the home.

If your elder is referred for home health care, have the case manager check the agency's scheduling to determine if it is overbooked or maintaining a waiting list due to a heavy volume of patients or staff shortage.

More information regarding home health-care agencies is provided in chapter 10, "Using Home Health and Hospice Care."

Durable Medical Equipment and Supplies

During your elder's admission interview, the social worker and therapists may ask about the layout of your elder's home where she will be discharged at the end of her program. They may ask about stairs, railings, ramps, tubs and showers, safety grab bars, current medical equipment and supplies, access to kitchen counters and appliances, and the width of doors and hallways for wheelchair or walker access.

As the rehabilitation team evaluates and assesses your elder's needs and limitations, mentors may recommend specific medical equipment to support the treatment program. With a prescription from the physician, the therapist will contact the appropriate vendor regarding the equipment's design, special features, and specific information, such as your elder's body measurements, weight, and height. Sometimes rehabilitation facilities are equipped to make prosthetics, orthotics, adaptive aids, and other devices; other times, they need to make a referral to a medical-supply company or an orthotics specialist.

Insurance information is also reviewed to ascertain how the equipment or device will be paid for. If insurance does not cover the equipment, the case manager or social worker may be able to investigate community resources or obtain financial assistance. If your family is responsible for payment, the caseworker or therapist will review the costs with you. Pre-authorization may also be needed, since approval of durable medical equipment is directed by medical necessity.

For example, an amputee may need a prosthesis or artificial leg. Or a stroke patient may need an assistive device to help him button his shirt or hold a fork. More frequently, medical equipment needs include:

bedside commode

high-rise toilet seat

shower or tub bench

safety grab bars

flexible shower hose

walker or cane

Please review the chart in chapter 2, "Living with Your Family," regarding insurance coverage and cost of frequently used medical equipment. With special rehabilitation needs, equipment that may not usually be covered may be covered secondary to diagnosis and special need.

Services in a Rehabilitation Program

Depending on the specific program, your family may find a wide range of services in a rehabilitation program. Many of these services may be geared to specific disabilities or age groups.

For example, it is unlikely that an eighty-year-old who has recently suffered a stroke would be asked to participate in vocational counseling or job placement. These services may include:

activities of daily living (ADL) skill training	neuropsychological testing
	nursing/medical management
aquatic therapy (in facilities with easy access to a pool)	occupational therapy
	physical therapy
arts and crafts	psychiatric treatment
behavioral management	recreation and leisure therapy
caregiver training	safety training
case management	sexuality classes
cognitive therapy	speech-language therapy
medical services	vocational counseling/ job placement and counseling
music therapy	

Less common services in a rehabilitation program include:

ceramics	equestrian instruction
computer instruction	group psychotherapy

Discharge from a Rehabilitation Program

When your elder family member nears completion in her rehabilitation program, she will be prepared for life outside the facility. To make the transition from program to home or another homelike setting as smooth as possible, the rehabilitation staff will work closely with her and with your family.

Before your elder is discharged from the rehabilitation program, your family will have a definite discharge plan that encompasses:

where your elder will live

who will provide any necessary care and thus receive the necessary
caregiver training

ordering and delivery of any durable medical equipment or supplies

where outpatient therapies will occur (either at home with home health
care, in an outpatient clinic, or in a subacute facility)

referrals for transportation assistance and other helpful community
agencies

There are many choices and care options for elders completing a rehabilitation
program. The most common discharge plans include:

from inpatient acute rehabilitation to home with family support and referrals to
home health care or outpatient therapies, durable medical equipment companies,
and community agencies.

from inpatient acute rehabilitation to home with hired caregiver support with
referrals to home health care or outpatient therapies, durable medical equipment
companies, and community agencies.

from inpatient acute rehabilitation to home with home health care, followed by
outpatient therapies.

from inpatient acute rehabilitation to an assisted living or an adult-care home
with referrals to home health care for outpatient therapies, durable medical
equipment companies, and community agencies.

from inpatient acute rehabilitation to a subacute or skilled nursing facility,
with referral for durable medical equipment

from inpatient acute rehabilitation to a different acute-rehabilitation facility,
which can provide specific rehabilitation needs not available at the initial rehabilitation facility

So much information will be given to your family and elder in a short period of
time that many families have a difficult time remembering it. After talking with you,
many social workers will give handouts and brochures that spell out resources, support
groups, team recommendations, the treatment plan, the discharge summary, follow-up

care and appointments, important telephone numbers, and addresses of medical-equipment suppliers.

Home Visit

A home visit is a way for the rehabilitation team to evaluate your elder in her home environment. Many people, especially elders, are drawn to the familiar surroundings and feel safer in their own homes. This "feeling of safety," however, can cause unexpected accidents. Items around the house that were safe before the change in physical or cognitive health may no longer be secure.

By visiting the home with your elder prior to discharge, an occupational or physical therapist can evaluate the home, such as accessibility to bathrooms, hallways, bedrooms, and stairs, and make recommendations that improve the home's efficiency and safety.

Recommendations may be made about specific equipment needs and other ways to make the home safe, including removing throw rugs, extra furniture, or clutter and changing the locations of telephones, appliances, or storage units to facilitate access to essential items. A ramp or handrail may also be recommended.

Caregiver Training

Prior to discharge, your family, a hired caregiver, or an adult-care home provider may be asked to attend a series of caregiver training sessions. In these sessions, therapists will review the safest and best ways to assist with transfers, walking, using the bathroom, performing dressing and grooming activities, responding to cognitive deficits, and more. They will review how to put on braces and other adaptive devices. They will try to prepare the caregiver for the essential-care needs of your elder.

Nursing staff may review medication management and bowel and bladder care, as well as other nursing-care needs.

Family Conferences

A family conference with the rehabilitation team may be recommended prior to discharge to address additional questions and concerns. Your elder and any interested family members may attend these meetings to ask questions and express concerns.

In some cases, the physiatrist, neuropsychologist, social worker, or therapist may request a session with the family or caregiver; in others, the family may request a meeting. In these meetings, each member of the rehabilitation team may review the progress your elder has made, noting areas where he has achieved his goals and those in which he needs additional support and encouragement.

A family conference may be instrumental in helping your family to understand the goals and process of the treatment program. It would also enable your family to introduce themselves to the staff. It is much easier to talk with someone you are acquainted with about a problem or concern.

Discharge Summary

At discharge, a discharge summary may be given to your elder and family. It reviews the goals and progress made in each discipline. It also contains treatment recommendations, follow-up appointments with the doctor, and outpatient therapies.

The social worker also lists any referrals made, pending applications, appropriate support groups, and the names of medical-supply companies if equipment was ordered. A copy of the discharge summary remains in the chart as part of the original medical record.

EVALUATION

Do you feel a rehabilitation facility is the best choice for your elder?

If your answer is "yes," review chapter 7, "Understanding Hospital Acute Care," and chapter 8, "Understanding Nursing Facilities."

If your answer is "no" or you are undecided, review chapter 8, "Understanding Nursing Facilities," and chapter 10, "Using Home Health and Hospice Care," or talk with a medical social worker or your elder's physician.

REHABILITATION FACILITY CHECKLIST

If you have the opportunity, visit the facility before your elder is transferred to the rehabilitation unit. Bring a friend with whom you can share your impressions. Talk with residents, other families, and staff.

Many rehabilitation programs have specific hours for visitors and tours. If you are interested in speaking with the admissions coordinator or a social worker, call in advance and set up an appointment. Most facilities should be able to accommodate you. Use this questionnaire to keep track of your observations and responses to your questions.

Date _____

Name and address of rehabilitation facility

_____

_____

Contact person _____ **Telephone #** _____

Admission

1. How are patients screened for admission to the rehabilitation program?

2. Are there special admissions requirements to enter a rehabilitation program?

3. Is a physician referral needed?

4. Can a patient be admitted directly from home?

5. Can a patient be admitted from the hospital, a nursing facility, or other alternative home setting?

Rehabilitation Program

6. Is the rehabilitation program for inpatients, outpatients, or both?

7. Are there specialty programs, such as brain-injury rehab, spinal cord rehab, or stroke rehab?

8. Does each resident have an individualized rehabilitation program?

9. How many hours a day is the patient expected to participate in the rehab program?

10. Are individual daily schedules posted in an easily accessible area?

11. What is considered a normal length of stay?

12. What are the rehab facility's goals?

13. Who decides on appropriate goals for each patient?

14. How are the goals for each patient determined?

15. If a resident has a difficult time meeting the program goals, are the goals revised?

Patients

16. What are the types of limitations most common to patients in the rehabilitation program? mobility _____ self-care _____ communication _____ cognitive disability _____ physical disability _____ bowel/bladder care _____ skin care _____ other _____

17. What is the average number of patients in the rehabilitation program?
1–5 _____ 5–10 _____ 10–15 _____ more than 15 _____

18. Do the patients all have similar disabilities?

19. If no, what are the most common disabilities?

20. What is the staff-to-patient ratio?

Staff

21. How does the staff determine the care needs of each resident?

22. Does the rehab facility have a care plan for each resident?

23. How many registered nurses are on duty during each shift?

24. Is staff professional and able to answer your questions?

25. Does staff help coordinate services with community agencies, such as home health care and medical-equipment companies, at time of discharge?

26. Are you comfortable with the staff?

Therapies and Services

27. What therapies and services are available in the rehab program?
nursing _____ nutrition _____ social services _____
psychological services _____ orthotics _____
occupational therapy _____ physical therapy _____
speech and communication disorders _____
other _____

28. Do therapists work on the weekends?

29. How many patients does a therapist see daily?
fewer than 5 _____ more than 5 _____ more than 10 _____

30. How long are the daily therapy sessions?
less than a half hour _____ less than 1 hour _____
less than 2 hours _____ more than 2 hours _____
flexible, dependent on the level of ability _____

31. What happens if a patient cannot actively participate in therapy?
nothing _____
therapy is geared toward the patient's endurance _____
patient is asked to leave the program _____ other _____

32. Are nursing responsibilities on a rehabilitation unit different from those in an acute-care hospital setting?

Family

33. What is the family's role in a rehabilitation program?

34. How much family, parent, or partner participation is needed?

35. Do caregivers/family receive training prior to the patient's discharge?

36. If you have questions, is it possible to meet with all or most of the staff to hear their evaluations and to obtain answers?

37. Are there resources available for family to read?

Facilities

38. As an inpatient, what facilities does the rehab unit include?
dining area _____ kitchen area _____
exercise and therapy room _____ cognitive therapy room _____
independent living and training area _____ other _____

39. Is smoking allowed?

40. What are the visiting hours?

41. Do patients share a room or have a private room?

42. Can small appliances, such as a radio or tape player, be brought to the rehab unit?

43. Is laundry done by the rehabilitation unit, or can family launder the patient's clothing at home?

Cost

44. Does Medicare pay for participation in a rehabilitation program?

45. Does Medicaid pay for participation in a rehabilitation program?

46. Does private insurance pay for participation in a rehabilitation program?

47. Is pre-authorization needed from the insurance company?

48. If yes, who obtains the authorization?

Home Visits and Passes

49. Are home visits or weekend or day passes encouraged?

50. What are the rules for passes and home visits?

51. Is special family or caregiver training, such as care transfer training, needed prior to a pass?

Discharge from the Rehabilitation Unit

52. Will the home be evaluated for modifications prior to discharge from the rehabilitation program?

53. Who will perform the evaluation?

54. How will necessary medical equipment and supplies be ordered?

55. If my elder cannot return to his home, who will help him find a place to live?

56. How is the date of discharge determined?

57. Will there be follow-up care in the home or as an outpatient?

58. Are support groups or programs available for patients or families after discharge from the rehabilitation program?

Please rate the rehabilitation facility.

OVERALL RATING WORK SHEET

How would you rate this rehabilitation facility for meeting the needs of your elder family member?

Date _____

Name and address of rehabilitation facility

_____

_____

	Excellent	Very Good	Good	Fair	Poor	Comments
General environment						
Room set-up						
Nursing care						
Therapies						
Programs						
Supportive services						
Activities						
Staff						
Transportation services						
Cost						

Chapter 10

Using Home Health and Hospice Care

————————— ❧ —————————

When Marcy moved into an adult-care home, her physician felt that she needed continued medical supervision. When John completed his rehabilitation program, his physician felt that he would benefit from continued therapies in his home. Both physicians made referrals or requests for services to a home health-care agency.

In this chapter your family will learn how to effectively use a home health-care agency. In many ways, involvement with home health may be a determining factor when your family must make decisions regarding medical care, supervision, assistance, and alternatives to living at home.

Home health care is skilled or professional nursing care and therapies your elder receives in his home. When health-care professionals from a licensed public or private home health-care agency visit your elder's home and provide specific skilled nursing care and therapeutic services, including physical therapy, these services are considered home health-care services.

Home health care can also be viewed as an alternative to extended hospitalization, nursing homestays, and frequent visits to the doctor's office by providing continuity of care and treatment in your elder's home or place of residence.

When to Use a Home Health-Care Agency

A home health-care agency can provide essential medical services in your elder's home. A referral may be made:

- for follow-up skilled medical care after hospitalizations, accidents, and illness

- when your elder is homebound and unable to easily get to a doctor for medical care

- following new diagnosis or treatments that may require monitoring, teaching and skilled nursing care. For example, a new diabetic may need to learn more about his illness, including how to give a self-injection and monitor his blood sugars.

- for assessment following a general change in health or a lengthy illness. For example, your elder may be weak after an illness such as the flu. If he is bedridden or unable to leave his home without great difficulty, he may benefit from a physician's referral to a home health-care agency for a nursing assessment and physical therapy in his home.

Patient and/or Physician Benefits

There are many benefits to your elder when he receives services from a home health-care agency. Because the home health staff may also act as a liaison between your elder, your family, and the physician, a smoother progression of medical treatment may occur. Some of the benefits include:

Availability. Most home health-care agencies are open seven days a week, with emergency service available twenty-four hours a day

Skilled patient monitoring and prompt feedback from health-care professionals

Strong medical liaison between the physician, patient, and home health-care agency

Fewer necessary office visits to the physician

Improved continuity of medical care—a smooth transition of medical care and information from a physician, hospital, or medical facility to another medical organization

Direct billing to Medicare, Medicaid, and other insurance carriers

Cost savings: Medicare Parts A or B pays 100 percent of charges. (Please note: This could change to 80 percent of charges under new Medicare reform.)

Improved quality of life

Licensing and Accreditation

A home health-care agency must obtain a license, as required by each state, to become Medicare-certified or an approved provider of skilled nursing care and therapeutic services to homebound elders. The home health-care agencies that provide these services are governed by state and federal laws and should be accredited by the Joint Commission on Accreditation of Healthcare Organizations (JCAHO).

Locating a Home Health-Care Agency

There are many ways to locate information about a home health-care agency. The easiest and most efficient ways are:

Using the index in your local yellow pages. Under the letter "H" you can locate Home Care Equipment and Supplies and Home Health Services. Under the letter "S" locate State Offices, Social Service Agencies, and Senior Citizen's Services. Listings under State Agencies may include Senior and Disabled Services Division and the Veterans Affairs Department.

Speaking with your elder's physician

Contacting an area hospital, medical clinic, or VA facility

Calling the nearest state area agency on aging (AAA) or senior and disabled services office

Contacting adult day-care centers and seniors centers

Calling the Eldercare Locator, a national information center of aging services. Call 1-800-677-1116. Have your elder's zipcode when you call.

Getting a Home Health-Care Referral

A referral or request for home health-care services can be made by your elder, family, friends, health professionals, or primary-care physician. The primary-care physician is the medical doctor responsible for coordinating the medical care with other physicians, hospitals, and health-care agencies. For insurance to pay for these services, the primary-care physician must write an order for home-care services, stating his treatment plan and the type and duration of the services needed.

Choosing a Home Health-Care Agency

Begin by checking for JCAHO accreditation and Medicare certification. If a home health-care agency is *not* accredited and Medicare-certified, you may want to contact another agency. Each can be contacted by an individual. However, because of the need for a physician referral and orders, as well as extensive medical information, it is recommended that your family work directly with a health professional and the doctor's office. There are three types of home health-care agencies: hospital-based, private home, and county pubic health agencies.

Hospital-Based Home Health-Care Agency

This home health-care agency is affiliated with one or more hospitals. It may use hospital discharge planners, case managers, or social work departments to coordinate services and arrangements for home health care. Doctors and hospital staff work closely with the home health-care agency, ensuring continuity of care and providing a smooth transition from hospital to home. They can assist with ordering medical equipment and supplies, such as hospital beds and wheelchairs. In addition, the home health-care agency can serve as an outpatient extension of services.

For example, a stroke patient who receives physical therapy in the hospital can continue to receive physical therapy in his home with a physical therapist from a home health-care agency. Once the patient has made significant improvement, if needed, he can move from his home program to a more intensive outpatient physical therapy program or, sometimes, into a rehabilitation program.

Private Home Health-Care Agency

A private home health-care agency works closely with physicians and hospital staff. It can coordinate physicians' orders and home health-care services and receive medical information and records by telephone and fax. Some agencies visit a patient in the hospital to determine his medical needs prior to making a home visit. They provide similar services to hospital-based agencies and sometimes have additional, although nonreimbursable, services available.

County Public Health Agency

County public health agencies usually focus on general health in the community, with an emphasis on well-baby clinics, infection control, and other public health issues.

For a person who doesn't have insurance or who has limited finances, a telephone call to your county health department to check out local services is recommended.

Home Health-Care Visits

For insurance purposes, a home-care visit is defined as *each service* a home health-care agency delivers to a person in her home. For example: If a registered nurse visits twice a day to give an injection, this equals two home-care visits. If a physical therapist visits once a week, a home health aide visits twice a week, and a medical social worker visits once, this constitutes four home-care visits.

Reaching the Physician

Many people become frustrated trying to reach their primary-care physician when they have a medical question. Calling the physician's office often results in being placed on hold for many minutes, and then being informed that the doctor or his nurse will call you back as soon as they are available.

Try to understand the physician's work schedule and his staff's increasing responsibilities. With the constant changes due to health-care reform, the physician and his staff are spending more time on insurance calls, billing, and obtaining pre-authorization for treatments. Their medical responsibilities to their patients are changing, because managed-care plans require them to submit requests for specialists instead of simply sending their patients to see another physician. Some ways to be helpful to the physician and simultaneously expedite a quick response are:

> *Give your elder's name and the name of his physician.* For example: "Hello, this is John Hilt. My father is a patient of Dr. _____."

> *Describe your elder's current problem to the person who answers the phone.* This may be a receptionist who may not have the authority or the medical knowledge to help you. If your elder's physician is unavailable, ask to speak with the nurse. For example: "My father has an appointment tomorrow at 9 A.M. with Dr. Jones to have his blood sugar and blood pressure checked. However, he is feeling nauseous and weak and unable to come to the doctor's office. Can I get a home health nurse to come to his home to check on him instead?"

> *Try to provide helpful medical information,* including a description of your elder's symptoms. If you feel you have an emergency, inform the doctor's office.

For example: "This is an emergency. My father woke up this morning because of a sharp pressure in his chest. He also noticed a slight numbness in his fingertips." Offer to be placed on hold to wait for the doctor or his nurse. If you have an emergency, stay on the line.

If you are told, "The doctor is with a patient. He will call you as soon as he is available," try to set a short time limit. For example, say, "Please have the doctor call me in ten minutes," or ask, "Should I call an ambulance or go to the hospital right now?"

If you do not hear from your physician within a reasonable time, call back.

If you do not have an emergency, try to be patient with your doctor's office. Your physician or his nurse will call you as soon as possible. If you do have an emergency, call 911 or get to the nearest hospital emergency room.

Insurance and Home Health Care

Medicare

Because many private agencies are not Medicare-certified, they may not bill Medicare for their services. One reason they may not accept Medicare is that Medicare reimbursement rates are only 76 percent of the agencies' normal charges.

A Medicare-certified home health-care agency can bill Medicare Parts A or B for an unlimited number of home-care visits provided that your elder meets the following eligibility requirements:

1. She must require at least one of the following skilled home-care services:

   skilled nursing care

   physical therapy

   speech therapy

   If she meets the eligibility requirements listed below, Medicare Parts A or B pays 100 percent of the cost for her home health-care services. This reimbursement rate may change in response to Medicare reform.

2. She must be homebound, which means that she is unable to leave her home without considerable difficulty but is not necessarily bedridden. If

she does leave her home, it must be for a brief period of time, infrequently, and primarily for medical treatment. If she is able to shop, drive a car, or take short walks or wheelchair strolls, she is not homebound.

3. She must be under the care of a physician who determines that she needs home health care and sets up a home care treatment plan for her. Your elder's physician will provide the following information to the home health-care agency:

> medical information including your elder's diagnosis, medical history, and medications

> orders for specific home-care services

> the length of time these home-care services may be needed. Your elder's physician can extend the time allowed for home-care services if he feels continued medical care is needed.

4. The home health-care agency that provides services should be a participant in the Medicare program.

Medicaid

Eligibility for Medicaid is based on monthly-income limits and poverty-level guidelines. If eligible, Medicaid pays 100 percent of the cost for home health care. Some private home health-care agencies do *not* accept Medicaid reimbursement rates, because they tend to be less than half the agency's standard rate for services. Medicaid regulations vary from state to state, so check with your local senior services office for benefit information. Pre-authorization for home health services from your elder's case-worker may be required. (Please note: Medicaid reimbursement and benefits can change in response to pending Medicaid reform.)

Managed Care and HMOs

Most of these insurance programs provide benefits for home health care. They may require pre-authorization before your elder can receive services in his home.

Private-Insurance Coverage

Each individual private-insurance policy must be checked. Information about benefits may be found in your elder's policy under the section *Home Health Care*. There is a wide range of benefit plans. Most will need pre-authorization or pre-certification. The primary-care physician and his staff or the home health-care agency may have to contact the insurance company's pre-certification unit before your elder can receive services. If the insurance company feels that the visits are medically reasonable and necessary, it can authorize a specific number of visits and services for a limited period of time. Benefits may range from 100 percent coverage to no home health-care benefits.

(*Please note:* The home health-care benefits provided by your elder's private insurance company may differ from his Medicare benefits. These benefits may be secondary to his Medicare benefits. The home health-care agency can contact his insurance company and provide him with specific information about his home health-care benefits.)

Veterans Affairs Coverage

To be eligible for Veterans Affairs (VA) coverage:

> *Your elder must have a service-connected disability.* This means he is receiving money for an injury received while in the military service. He should have been receiving compensation for this injury since being discharged from the service. Occasionally, a veteran with a nonservice-connected disability can receive services.

> *Your elder will require pre-authorization* from the Department of Veterans Affairs.

For information about VA services and benefits, please contact the nearest Veterans Social Work Services department. (*Please note:* In regard to services supplied directly from the VA, not all VA hospitals and facilities have home health-care services. Services may be limited to homemakers, home health aides, and certified nurse's aides. For skilled services, the VA may use a fee-basis or contract out to private home health-care agencies for skilled nursing care. These contracts are often negotiated on a time-limited basis determined by the VA physician.)

Worker's Compensation (WC) Programs

Each state runs its own program and may have different allowable amounts of compensation and services. If your elder has recently applied for Worker's Compensation due to a work-related injury, it is necessary to contact his local claim office regarding home health-care benefits.

Look under State Offices in your telephone directory for your nearest worker's compensation program, or contact the personnel office at your elder's place of employment.

Hospice Care

Many home health-care agencies provide hospice services for elders who are terminally ill and their families. An interdisciplinary hospice team of nurses, therapists, social workers, clergy, and home health aides can help your family set up a coordinated program of home and/or inpatient care.

The emphasis in hospice care is on palliative, or comfort, care and pain control. Hospice benefits can include physician services, nursing care, terminal care in a skilled nursing facility, respite or rest care for the family, and in-home care. Check your elder's policy for specific information regarding hospice care.

Often, hospice patients have discontinued all medical intervention except for treatments necessary for comfort and reduced pain, including pain medication and oxygen. Feeding tubes, intravenous medications, and other extraordinary measures are usually discontinued.

Hospice care may be provided in your elder's home or in another care setting, such as an adult-care home, a nursing facility, or a hospital. Sometimes an elder is admitted to a hospital for respite care. This means her admission is giving her caregivers a break. Respite care is usually limited to no more than five days in a Medicare-approved hospital or skilled nursing facility.

Or your elder may be admitted to the hospital for terminal care. If he reaches the point where he no longer meets the requirements to stay in the hospital, several options are available:

1. Your elder can stay in the hospital as a private-pay patient.

2. Your elder can be transferred within the hospital to a hospice or comfort-only room, where hospice benefits instead of hospital benefits pay for care.

3. Your elder can be transferred to a skilled or intermediate nursing facility for terminal care. (Although Medicare provides limited coverage for terminal care, some managed-care policies override this benefit, making the nursing-home stay private pay. They may require a need to pay for hospice care.)

4. Your elder can receive terminal care in a qualified adult-care home.

Private Pay

If you do not have insurance or do not meet the eligibility requirement for Medicare or other insurance reimbursements, you may private-pay for home health or hospice services. Private pay means your family is responsible for paying for the home health-care services.

Private pay is an expensive way to receive services. Listed below are approximate rates for home health-care services. These rates can vary depending upon the individual agency. Because of the high cost, some private home health-care agencies have a sliding scale. By having the family complete a financial statement, the agency can determine a reasonable cost and may adjust their rates accordingly. Some agencies may also provide charity care to families with great need.

HOME HEALTH-CARE AGENCY PRIVATE-PAY RATES

registered nurse	$30–$32 per hour for weekday home visits $65 for a two-hour home visit $80 per hour for high-tech or intravenous (IV) care
physical therapist	$110–$125 per home visit
speech therapist	$110–$125 per home visit
occupational therapist	$110–$125 per home visit
medical social worker	$110–$150 per home visit
respiratory therapist	$110–$125 per home visit
licensed practical nurse	$40–$60 per home visit
home-health aide (*may have a higher level of training than CNA*)	$35–$50 per home visit
rehabilitation aide (*may have experience/ competency working with spinal-cord and head injuries*)	$13–$20 per hour, with a two- to three-hour minimum*
certified nurse's aide	$12–$20 per hour, with a two- to three-hour minimum

Minimum hours or the lowest number of hours of care required by the home health-care agency can vary with each agency.

The chart on page 262 will give your family general rate information. These rates can vary by state and agency and can be increased if a high level of care or extended or lengthy visits are required.

Home Health Services Covered Under Medicare

Primary Services

At least one of these primary services must be ordered by your physician to meet Medicare requirements for reimbursement:

part-time or intermittent skilled nursing care by a registered nurse (RN)

physical therapy (PT)

speech-language therapy (ST)

Secondary Services

Secondary services will be covered under Medicare requirements for reimbursement if they are used with at least one primary service. They can include:

licensed practical nurse (LPN)

medical social worker (MSW)

part-time or intermittent certified home health aide (HHA)

occupational therapist (OT)

nutritional therapist

certified nurse's aide (CNA)

respiratory therapist (RT)

rehabilitation aide (RA)

The *licensed practical nurse* (LPN) can provide some of the nursing care under the supervision of a registered nurse.

The *certified home health aide* (HHA) can assist with bathing and personal care under the supervision of an RN. She may also assist with exercises, light housekeeping, meal preparation, and self-administered medications.

A *certified nurse's aide* (CNA) may provide similar care. The main difference between the CNA and the certified HHA is that the HHA has a higher level of training.

Home health-care agencies have many different titles for secondary service providers. They may also be called vocational nurses, registered or nonregistered nursing assistants, or health-care aides. Consider inquiring about required training programs by the home health-care agency at the time of hire.

Other Services

Home health-care staff can assist your elder by:

ordering durable medical equipment. Durable medical equipment and supplies may be covered under Medicare, Medicaid, or private insurance. A physician's prescription stating diagnoses, the reason the equipment is needed, and the length of time it is needed is required by the medical-supply company. Many home health/hospice agencies have a contract with a company and may prefer to place the orders themselves. Check with your elder's home health or hospice nurse before ordering medical equipment.

providing medical supplies, including adult diapers (Depends), tubing, syringes, feeding pumps, dressings, and other items directly from the home health-care agency.

Home Health-Care Services Not Covered by Medicare

Medicare does not pay for:

blood transfusions. *Please note:* The blood is not covered under Medicare. However, the nursing visits for administering the blood transfusions are covered.

some home intravenous therapies. *Please note:* The home health-care agency must check for insurance benefits on home intravenous therapy. While some diagnoses are covered, others are not.

companionship

custodial or personal-care services

full-time or round-the-clock nursing care at home

homemaker or chore services that are unrelated to patient care

live-in care

meals delivered to the home

medication or biologicals (antigens, homeopathic medicines)

Extended or Supportive Services

Extended or supportive services are home health-care agency services that do not fall into either the primary service or secondary service category. These services may not be provided by every home health-care agency and are *not* reimbursable under Medicare, Medicaid, or most private insurance. They can include:

companion, live-in or part-time

gardener

handyman

household service aide

heavy cleaning

house-sitting and pet care

telephone check-in service

The Rights of the Home-Care Patient

Federal law requires that all individuals receiving home-care services be informed of their rights as a patient. Following is a model patient bill of rights the National Association for Home Care (NAHC) has developed, based on the patient rights currently enforced by law. A home-care patients has the right to:

be fully informed of all his rights and responsibilities by the home-care agency

choose care providers

appropriate and professional care in accordance with physician orders

receive a timely response from the agency to his request for service

be admitted for service only if the agency has the ability to provide safe, professional care at the level of intensity needed

receive reasonable continuity of care

receive information necessary to give informed consent prior to the start of any treatment or procedure

be advised of any change in the plan of care before the change is made

refuse treatment within the confines of the law and to be informed of the consequences of his action

be informed of his rights under state law to formulate advanced directives

have health-care providers comply with advance directives in accordance with state law requirements

be informed within reasonable time of anticipated termination of service or plans for transfer to another agency

be fully informed of agency policies and charges for services, including eligibility for third-party reimbursements

be referred elsewhere, if denied service solely on his inability to pay

voice grievances and suggest changes in service or staff without fear of restraint or discrimination

a fair hearing for any individual to whom any service has been denied, reduced, or terminated, or who is otherwise aggrieved by agency action. The fair hearing procedure shall be set forth by each agency as appropriate to the unique patient situation (e.g., funding source, level of care, diagnosis)

be informed of what to do in the event of an emergency

be advised of the telephone number and hours of operation of the state's home-health hot line, which receives questions and complaints about Medicare-certified and state-licensed home-care agencies

QUESTIONS TO ASK A HOME HEALTH-CARE AGENCY

Credentials

1. Is the home health-care agency accredited by the Joint Commission on Accreditation of Health-care Organizations?

2. Is the agency Medicare-certified? (The home health-care agency should be accredited by the JCAHCO and be Medicare-certified.)

Staffing

3. What staff training and instruction are required by the home health-care agency?

4. How much supervision does staff have?

5. What is the average caseload, or number of patients, seen by individual home health-care staff? (An average caseload may vary in each agency. Staff should not visit more than ten patients in one day.)

6. Does the agency seem flexible with its scheduling?

7. Is there a waiting period for any of the services or therapists? (Sometimes a home health-care agency is not able to immediately provide the services of medical social workers or therapists due to a high volume of requests and demands for services. Many agencies try to visit a patient on the day they receive the physician referral. Your elder should not wait more than two days for a visit from a registered nurse and more than five days for a visit from a therapist.)

8. What are the staff's daily working hours? (Most home health-care agencies have standard working hours from 7 A.M. to 6 P.M. Staff should be available during evening hours and on weekends for patients who require skilled nursing care and therapeutic services.)

9. Do they have twenty-four-hour emergency staffing? (Be sure the home health-care agency has emergency staffing twenty-four hours per day.)

Home Health-Care Services

10. What therapists are provided by the home health-care agency?
    registered nurses _____ physical therapists _____
    speech therapists _____ occupational therapists _____
    dietitians _____ certified nurse's aides _____

11. Will it help order or provide necessary medical equipment and sup-plies? (Most home health-care agencies can provide this assistance.)

Billing

12. Does the home health-care agency handle all Medicare billing, as well as other insurance carriers?

13. Does it accept Medicaid payments?

14. Does it have a sliding scale for people with low incomes? (Most home health-care agencies will handle all billing matters, including con-tacting insurance carriers for pre-authorization.)

Communication

15. Will the home health-care agency contact your physician for a refer-ral, medical orders, or prescriptions?

16. Is the home health-care staff easy to talk with?

17. Do staff members patiently answer your questions, explaining medical terms you may not understand?

18. Does the home health-care agency view itself as a liaison between you and your doctor? If not, how do its representatives see their role as health-care professionals?

19. How do you feel when you speak with someone from the agency on the telephone? (The home health-care agency is one of your most important links when your elder needs medical treatment or is recov-ering from illness or injury. It is important to work closely with an agency that makes him feel comfortable.)

Chapter II

Your Guide to Resources

———————— ✿ ————————

How to Use This Chapter

There are many national, state, and local programs and agencies in this country that offer free and easily accessed information to families with aging parents. To help you sift through the vast number of agencies, this chapter lists the most helpful ones, with free, low-cost, or charitable services; toll-free numbers; website and e-mail addresses; and helpful publications, brochures, and videos.

This chapter will offer your family informative resources to supplement the information in this book. These resources are organized by topic. For example, under "Caregiving," you will find The Family Caregiving Alliance; under pharmacy services, you will find MedForum, with a description of its home-delivery prescription drug program. Most listings include the name of the organization, program, or agency, address, telephone number, Internet information, such as the website and e-mail addresses, and a brief descriptive paragraph.

Most of the topics listed are self-explanatory. For example, if you are looking for information on home health care or hospice, look under that specific heading. Other topic headings, such as information and referral and hot lines/help lines, contain information about more general seniors- and health-related subjects.

To help your family utilize as much information as possible, you are sometimes referred to another topic heading that provides additional material on the subject of interest.

For example, under information and referral, you may find the ElderWeb, a website with information on housing alternatives, elder-care organizations, and legal services. You may also find Dr. C. Everett Koop's website with information on family health and wellness, a medical encyclopedia, and news service reports. Under hot lines/help lines you will usually find an 800 or 888 number or a website with informative material on a specific subject. For example, the Medicare hot line discusses Medicare, and the hospice hot line discusses issues related to hospice care.

Some programs or agencies in this section may be found under more than one heading, because they may provide many practical resources in several different areas. For example, the Department of Veterans Affairs may be listed under government agencies and organizations and, more specifically, under funeral and burial services for information about funeral arrangements and burial for veterans.

Internet websites are used extensively, because they provide a wealth of national resources and are free to the Internet user. Most of these sites may also provide links to other helpful websites. When you enter a website by typing the website address into the box at the top of the screen and clicking "enter," you are presented with a menu and/or home page for the organization. The home page is the first page of the website and usually contains the name of the organization, the website address, and a menu that lists the topics and categories found in that website.

Useful key words or phrases to look for on each website include:

about our organization	links
articles	local information
associations	medical
consumer information	newsletters
contact us	news reports
diseases	organizations
general information	post office
government	programs
health	publications
hot links	public information
hot topics	resources
information and referral	sites of interest
information clearinghouse	

These key words, or hypertext, provide a link or pathway to the information within that website or in another one. To access the information, just click on the appropriate key word or phrase.

In this new age of the Internet, it is important to recognize that changes to websites occur on a regular basis. Website addresses, telephone numbers, and content are constantly being updated. If you are unable to find a specific agency by using the given website information, try using a search tool, such as Yahoo® or Alta Vista®. By typing in the name of the organization and clicking search, the computer looks for the resources. Or use the search tool for a specific topic such as caregiving. It will then list any topics with the word *caregiving*. However, you may find yourself with a hundred thousand possible headings to explore. If you find a website you are interested in copying, many websites allow you to print out their content, or you may choose to copy it to a file or disk.

E-mail addresses are also helpful when families need to contact an individual or agency. E-mail enables your family to correspond directly with the person or agency you need by directly sending them a message through the Internet without the charge of a toll call. For example, your family can send a message from Wisconsin to the Family Caregiving Alliance in San Francisco without picking up the telephone. The alliance can respond to you by e-mail. This is an excellent way to request information or to ask specific questions.

For families who have a computer phobia or lack access to or experience with the Internet, check with your local Internet provider regarding businesses or individuals who can help you with a computer search. The local library or a nearby university can often help your family. Or, you can purchase a book such as *The Internet for Dummies* (6th Ed), by John R. Levine, Carol Baroudi, and Margaret Levine Young. (See Helpful Books, Magazines, Newsletters, Catalogs, and Videos in appendix D.)

Following is a summary of resource topic headings. Look for the subject you are most interested in. Also review information and referral, hot lines/help lines, and government agencies. (*Please note:* These listings are not recommendations. They are for information only.)

The topic headings in this chapter contain information on:

adult day care	emergency services
alternative medicine	financial assistance and
assisted living facilities	planning
caregiving	funeral and burial services

geriatric education/research centers

government agencies

health-care organizations

hearing impaired services

home health-care and hospice services

hot lines/help lines

information and referral agencies

insurance benefits and coverage

legal services

long-term-care programs

meal programs

medical equipment and supplies

mental health services

pharmacy services

professional organizations

rehabilitation services

retirement communities

service organizations

transportation

travel opportunities

visually impaired programs and services

Note: (TTY) or (TDD) indicates telephone service for people with hearing and speech impairments. For out-of-area and 800 and 888 telephone calls, please dial a "1" before the number.

National Resources

Adult Day Care

National Adult Day Services Association (NADSA)
The National Council on the Aging, Inc.
409 Third Street S.W., Suite 200
Washington, DC 20024
Telephone: 1-800-424-9046 / (202) 479-1200 / (202) 479-6674 (TDD)
Website: www.ncoa.org/nadsa/
E-mail: info@ncoa.org

National Adult Day Services Association has information on adult day-care services and a checklist for evaluating them. It is an excellent resource for health-care professionals, educators, researchers, and adult day-service administrators. There is a membership fee.

Publications: NADSA and non-NADSA members may order a *Directory of Adult Day Services* with a state-by-state listing of adult day-care centers, manuals, training videos, and other information.

Alternative Medicine

Alternative Health News On-Line
Website: www.altmedicine.com/

Alternative Health News On-Line is an easy-to-use website that contains information on the most recent health news and links.

Alternative Medicine
Integrative Medical Arts Group, Inc.
P.O. Box 308
Beaverton, OR 97075
Telephone: (503) 526-1972
Website: www.healthwwweb.com

Alternative Medicine contains information about alternative medicine, Chinese herbs, acupuncture, nutrition, chiropractic services, and more. It also maintains health links and professional resources.

National Foundation for Alternative Medicine
1155 Connecticut Avenue N.W., Suite 400
Washington, DC 20036
Telephone: (202) 429-6633
Website: www.nfam.org

Founded by Berkley and Elinor Bedell in January 1999, The Foundation for Alternative Medicine serves as a clearinghouse for information on alternative treatments, especially cancer treatments. Here, information in easy-to-understand language is available to the public.

Assisted Living Facilities

Assisted Living Federation of America (ALFA)
10300 Eaton Place, Suite 400
Fairfax, VA 22030
Telephone: (703) 691-8100
Website: www.alfa.org/

The Assisted Living Federation of America provides information about aging and other related topics and has links to helpful organizations. It has a detailed assisted living guide and checklist for evaluating an assisted living/personal-care community. It lists assisted living residences by state.

Publications: *Assisted Living Today*, a magazine that is free for ALFA members or thirty dollars for ten issues. It also has helpful products and videos.

Assisted Living Network
14331 60th Street North
Clearwater, FL 33760
Telephone: 1-888-532-9280 / (727) 532-9280 (in Florida)
Website: www.alfnet.com/
E-mail: admin@alfnet.com

The Assisted Living Network provides information on assisted living facilities with state-by-state listings, as well as other helpful tips and material on independent living and nursing homes.

Assisted Living On-Line (see Retirement Communities)
Website: alol@assistedlivingonline.com

Assisted Living On-Line provides a directory of assisted living and retirement centers for seniors and their families. It also has a list of helpful national resources.

Careguide On-Line Care Resource (see Information and Referral)
1160 Battery, 4th Floor
San Francisco, CA 94111
Telephone: (415) 474-1278
Website: www.careguide.net
E-mail: care@careguide.net

Careguide On-Line is an excellent resource for information on elder care. This website includes information on nursing and assisted living facilities and home health and hospice care. It also has links to resources on caregiving, Alzheimer's disease, and other elder issues.

Publications: A bookstore is maintained on this site, with books on aging issues, elder care, retirement planning, and more.

Consumer Consortium on Assisted Living

P.O. Box 3375
Arlington, VA 22203
Telephone: (703) 841-2333
Website: www.ccal.org
E-mail: membership@CCAL.ORG

The Consumer Consortium on Assisted Living offers lists of questions to ask when choosing an assisted living facility. It also has news and links to other resources.

Marriott Senior Living Services (see Retirement Communities)

One Marriott Drive
Washington, DC 20058
Telephone: 1-800-880-3131
Website: www.marriott.com/senior/

Marriott Senior Living Services provides information about Marriott facilities throughout the United States.

Caregiving

The Caregiver's Handbook

The Caregiver Education and Support Services
Seniors Counseling and Training
Case Management Services of San Diego County Mental Health Services
1250 Moreno Boulevard
San Diego, CA 92110
Telephone: (619) 692-8702
Website: www.biostat.wustl.edu/ALZHEIMER/care.html

The Caregiver's Handbook is an excellent website for obtaining information about many aspects of caregiving. It describes and discusses common problems in caregiving, types of help, caring for the caregiver, personal care, nutrition, medical aspects, emotional and intellectual well-being, legal and financial issues, liability of the caregiver, and choosing a residential facility.

Children of Aging Parents (CAPS)
1609 Woodbourne Road, Suite 302 -A
Levittown, PA 19057
Telephone: (215) 945-6900 / 1-800-227-7294
Website: www.careguide.net

Children of Aging Parents is a nonprofit organization that serves as a national clearinghouse that provides information and emotional support to caregivers of older people. It has links to the National Institute of Aging and the Administration on Aging.

Publications: *Capsule*, a bimonthly newsletter, is published for members.

Family Caregiving Alliance (see Information and Referral)
690 Market Street, Suite 600
San Francisco, CA 94104
Telephone: (415) 434-3388 / 1-800-445-8106 (in California only)
Website: www.caregiver.org
E-mail: info@caregiver.org

The Family Caregiving Alliance offers support services to families and caregivers of brain-impaired adults, including those caring for a stroke victim. It has information and referral services.

National Alliance for Caregiving
4720 Montgomery Lane, Suite 642
Bethesda, MD 20814
Telephone: (301) 718-8444
Website: www.caregiving.org
E-mail: gailhunt.nac@erols.com

The National Alliance for Caregiving maintains a website with tips for caregivers and links to organizations related to caregiving, living arrangements, Medicare and Medicaid, selected federal benefits, selected diseases, and the AARP guide to Internet resources.

National Family Caregivers Association (NFCA)

10605 Concord Street, Suite 501
Kensington, MD 20895-2504
Telephone: 1-800-896-3650 / (301)942-6430
Website: www.nfcacares.org/
E-mail: info@nfcacares.org

The National Family Caregivers Association is a national organization serving all family caregivers. It has many services, including ten tips for caregivers and principles of caregiver empowerment, a support network, and advocacy.

Publications: It publishes a self-help newsletter.

Emergency Services

American Red Cross

Public Inquiry Office
1621 N. Kent Street, 11th Floor
Arlington, VA 22209
Telephone: 1-800-234-5ARC / (703) 248-4222
Website: www.redcross.org

The American Red Cross national office can refer families to local organizations for emergency help and assistance.

Alzheimer's Safe Return Program (see Health Organizations/
Alzheimer's Disease)
Telephone: 1-800-733-0402

The Alzheimer's Safe Return Program is for people with Alzheimer's disease who may wander away from home and become lost. The program includes many benefits, including identification items, listing in a national database, and a twenty-four-hour free crisis line.

Emergency Call Systems

Telephone: 1-800-451-0525

Emergency Call Systems provides Lifeline emergency response services. It can be used by people at risk of falling or with medical problems who live alone and may need emergency medical assistance.

Lifeline Systems, Inc.

640 Memorial Drive
Cambridge, MA 02139-4851
Telephone: 1-800-543-3546

Lifeline Systems, Inc. provides emergency systems for at-risk people, making it easy for them to access immediate assistance in an emergency. Free brochures are available.

MedicAlert Bracelets

Telephone: 1-800-432-5378

MedicAlert bracelets are designed to provide valuable individual medical information for use during a medical emergency. The cost is thirty-five dollars for the basic stainless-steel type. A bracelet can be ordered by telephone.

Salvation Army

National Headquarters
615 Slaters Lane
P.O. Box 269
Alexandria, VA 22313
Telephone: 1-800-SAL-ARMY / (703) 684-5500 / 1-888-321-3433
Website: www.salvationarmy.org/

The Salvation Army provides emergency services, including food boxes, clothing, fuel, and utility and rent assistance.

Financial Assistance and Planning

Consumer Credit Counseling Service

Telephone: 1-800-388-CCCS
Website: cccsedu.org
E-mail: cccinfo@unicom.net

The Consumer Credit Counseling Service is a nonprofit agency that provides information to help you solve debt problems, avoid bankruptcy, and learn to handle money.

Funeral Burial and Services

Cremation Society of Oregon

Administrative Office
11667 S.E. Stevens Road
Portland, OR 97266
Telephone: 1-800-356-4047 / (503) 659-7523

The Cremation Society of Oregon has information and brochures about cremation.

Department of Veterans Affairs (see Government Agencies)

Office of Public Affairs
810 Vermont Avenue N.W.
Washington, DC 20420
Telephone: 1-800-827-1000 / (202) 273-5700

The Department of Veterans Affairs provides burial benefits, including a free burial grave and perpetual care in a national cemetery, reimbursement of burial expenses, free U.S. burial flag, a presidential memorial certificate, and free headstones and markers.

FuneralNet

Telephone: 1-800-721-8166
Website: www.funeralnet.com
E-mail: info@funeralnet.com

FuneralNet is an excellent on-line website for obtaining information about funeral homes throughout the United States. It includes a directory of funeral associations in each state, as well as links to other helpful sites. It also has information on living wills, bereavement, and veterans benefits.

National Funeral Director's Association

13625 Bishop's Drive
Brookfield, WI 53005-6607
Telephone: 1-800-228-6332
Website: www.nfda.org

The National Funeral Director's Association website contains helpful information about funerals and burial and has links to other websites.

SkyMed (see Transportation)
4435 North Saddlebag Trail
Scottsdale, AZ 85251-3418
Telephone: 1-800-475-9633
Website: www.skymed.com
E-mail: info@skymed.com

SkyMed is an emergency air service that provides benefits to members, including the return of physical remains to the member and family.

The Society of Allied and Independent Funeral Directors (SAIF)
1 Ferdinand Place
Camden
London NW1 8EE England
Telephone: 0171-267 6777
Website: www.saif.org.uk/home.html
E-mail: info@saif.org.uk

The Society of Allied and Independent Funeral Directors website has listings with public information and links to other helpful resources.

Geriatric Education/Research Centers

Ethel Percy Andrus Gerontology Center
University of Southern California
Los Angeles, CA 90089-0191
Telephone: (213) 740-5156
Website: www.usc.edu/dept/gero

The Ethel Percy Andrus Gerontology Center at the University of Southern California provides an excellent website for information on aging issues. It includes a gerontology library, search tools for aging issues, material on nutrition and health, and links to other helpful resources.

Publications: *The Caregiver's Resource* may be downloaded from this website.

California Pacific Medical Center (see Vision Services and Programs)
Inpatient Geropsychiatry
P.O. Box 7999
San Francisco, CA 94131
Telephone: (415) 923-3255
Website: www.cpmc.org

The California Pacific Medical Center is a nonprofit health-care organization that provides a wide array of services and programs to people in California and Nevada. It also maintains the Lions Eye Foundation to help elderly people with glaucoma, cataracts, and retinal disease.

Center for Social Services Research
Center for the Advanced Study of Aging Services
School of Social Welfare
University of California
120 Haviland Hall, #7400
Berkeley, CA 94720-7400
Telephone: (510) 642-3285
Website: www.cssr21.socwel.berkeley.edu
E-mail: cssr@uclink.berkeley.edu

The Center for Social Services Research maintains a website with links to government agencies, research centers, caregiving and Alzheimer's disease resources, and associations and sites for seniors.

The Rosalynn Carter Institute of Human Development
Georgia Southwestern College
800 Wheatley Street
Americus, GA 31709
Telephone: (912) 928-1234
Website: rci.gsw.edu
E-mail: ecm@canes.gsw.edu

The Rosalynn Carter Institute of Human Development website contains information helpful to caregivers, including book resources, a caregiver chat room, and a quarterly magazine.

Publications: *American Caregiver*, a quarterly magazine.

Stanford University Geriatric Education and Resource Center (SUGERC)

1000 Welch Road, Suite I
Stanford, CA 94304
Telephone: (650) 723-8559
Website: www.stanford.edu/group/SFDP/sugerc/index.html
E-mail: geri-resources@lists.stanford.edu

The Stanford University Geriatric Education and Resource Center maintains a website with lists of geriatric-research institutions.

Government Agencies

Administration on Aging
U.S. Department of Health and Human Services

400 6th Street, S.W.
Washington, DC 20201
Telephone: (202) 245-0724
Website: www.aoa.dhhs.gov
E-mail: AoAinfo@aoa.gov

The Administration on Aging maintains an excellent website with extensive information on aging and housing. It has an ElderPage, Access America for Seniors, and links to other elder-care sites, such as the Eldercare Locator.

Administration on Aging's Directory of Web Aging Sites

Website: www.aoa.dhhs.gov/aoa/webres/craig.html

The Administration on Aging's Directory of Web Aging Sites lists sites by state, country, organization, subject, or topic. Academic and research sites are also listed. There are links to other aging directories.

Consumer Information Center

Pueblo, CO 81009
Website: www.pueblo.gsa.gov/
E-mail: catalog.pueblo@gsa.gov

The Consumer Information Center has helpful information on health, housing, and federal programs.

Publications: Catalog available.

Department of Health and Human Services

P.O. Box 1133
Washington, DC 20013-1133
Website: www.healthfinder.org
E-mail: healthfinder@health.org

The Department of Health and Human Services is an excellent resource for links to seniors web resources on Medicare, government agencies, health care and diseases, news, on-line journals, and seniors organizations.

Department of Veterans Affairs

Office of Public Affairs
810 Vermont Avenue N.W.
Washington, DC 20420
Telephone: 1-800-827-1000 / (202) 273-5700
Website: www.va.gov
E-mail: Click on "contact us" for a link to many specific e-mail sites, such as medical care, cemeteries, and the Center for Minority Veterans.

The Department of Veterans Affairs provides benefits to eligible veterans of military service and their dependents. It compensates veterans and their families for disabilities or death related to military service. Some services include educational assistance, vocational rehabilitation, home-loan guarantee programs, and comprehensive dental and medical care for eligible veterans in outpatient clinics, medical centers, and nursing homes around the country. Burial benefits include funeral and burial services in national cemeteries; markers and flags are also provided (see Funeral and Burial Services). It helps veterans, their dependents, and beneficiaries to apply for VA benefits.

Publications: "Federal Benefits for Veterans and Dependents." This brochure describes VA medical benefits, compensation, pension, educational, vocational, loan, and other insurance benefits.

Eldercare Locator: U.S. Department of Health and Human Services
National Aging Information Center
Telephone: 1-800-677-1116
Website: www.ageinfo.org/elderloc/elderloc.html

The Eldercare Locator is an excellent resource for information about federally funded assistance programs and services for senior citizens nationwide. Know the county or zip code of a person who needs assistance *before* you call. The Eldercare Locator can give you information about many health-care services, living facilities, and places to get help in your area.

Health Care Financing Administration (HCFA) (see Insurance)
7500 Security Boulevard
Baltimore, Maryland 21244
Telephone: (410) 786-3000
Website: www.hcfa.gov

The Health Care Financing Administration is an excellent website for information on Medicare, Medicaid, managed care, and health insurance. It also includes data, statistics, and an information clearinghouse.

National Institute on Aging Information Center
P.O. Box 8057
Gaithersburg, MD 20898-8057
Telephone: 1-800-222-2225 (Voice) / 1-800-222-4225 (TDD)
Website: www.nih.gov/nia/

The National Institute on Aging Information Center can be contacted for a list of free single copies of publications, fact sheets, and technical reports on health prevention.

National Institutes of Health (NIH)
Division of Public Information
9000 Rockville Pike
Building 31, #2B-10
Bethesda, MD 20892
Telephone: (301) 496-1766
Website: www.nih.gov
Healthfinder: www.healthfinder.gov/

The National Institutes of Health provides information on a wide variety of health topics. Many Internet links are available from these sites. It is an excellent resource for information on specific diseases.

Pension Benefit Guaranty Corporation

1200 K Street N.W.
Washington, DC 20005
Website: www.pbgc.gov

The Pension Benefit Guaranty Corporation can be contacted for assistance in tracking down pension benefits.

Publications: Many reports and publications are available from the Pension and Welfare Benefits Administration Brochure Request Line: 1-800-998-7542.

Social Security Administration

Office of Public Inquiries
6401 Security Boulevard
Baltimore, MD 21235
Telephone: 1-800-772-1213 / (410) 965-7700
Website: www.ssa.gov

The Social Security Administration is the federal governmental agency responsible for the Social Security retirement program, survivors benefits, and the disability insurance program. It pays benefits to retired or disabled workers and their eligible dependents.

Publications: "Understanding Social Security" and many other pamphlets are available free of charge.

Health Organizations

AIDS

American Foundation for AIDS Research (AMFAR)

120 Wall Street, Thirteenth Floor
New York, NY 10005
Telephone: 1-800-392-6327 / (212) 806-1600

The American Foundation for AIDS Research can be contacted for the latest information on treatments and clinical trials.

Publications: These may be ordered from AMFAR or the Centers for Disease Control.

The Community AIDS Treatment Information Exchange

517 College Street, Suite 420
Toronto, Ontario M6G 4A2 Canada
Telephone: 1-800-263-1638 (English/French)
Website: www.catie.ca
E-mail: info@catie.ca

The AIDS Information Network is based in Canada. It has news, quick references, periodicals, treatment resources, forums for discussion, and links to helpful agencies and organizations.

CDC National AIDS Clearinghouse

P.O. Box 6003
Rockville, MD 20849-6003
Telephone: 1-800-458-5231
Website: www.cdcnpin.org

The CDC National AIDS Clearinghouse has educational material, preventions news, a resource and service database, and links to many valuable resources.

Publications: An extensive number of publications are available, ranging from substance abuse, prevention, testing, and counseling to legal resources.

Alcohol-Related Disease

Al-Anon Family Groups

1600 Corporate Landing Parkway
Virginia Beach, VA 23454-5617
Telephone: 1-800-356-9996 / (757) 563-1600
Website: www.alanon.org

Al-Anon Family Groups can be contacted for information about support groups and self-help recovery for families and friends of alcoholics.

Publications: *The Forum* is an international monthly journal of Al-Anon.

Alcoholics Anonymous (AA)

475 Riverside Drive
New York, NY 10115
Telephone: (212) 870-3400 / (212) 870-3400, ext. 4622 (to order publications)
Website: www.aa.org

Alcoholics Anonymous has information, books, and publications for people interested in knowing more about the organization. It also has a directory of AA information centers throughout the United States, listed by state.

Publications: *The Grapevine*, a monthly magazine, includes articles and a list of books and tapes. Subscription cost is nineteen dollars a year. The mailing address is: *The Grapevine*, P.O. Box 1980, Grand Central Station, New York, NY 10163-1980.

National Clearinghouse for Alcohol and Drug Information
P.O. Box 2345
Rockville, MD 20852
Telephone: 1-800-729-6686
Website: www.health.org

The Clearinghouse for Alcohol and Drug Information has an extensive website with alcohol and drug facts, links to resources and referrals, statistics, databases, and more.

Publications: A catalog with listings of publications is available on-line.

Substance Abuse and Mental Health Services Administration (SAMHSA) (see Hot Lines)
Website: www.samhsa.gov/look3.html

The Substance Abuse and Mental Health Services Administration is an excellent website for obtaining information about statistics, programs, and help lines on alcohol and drug abuse and mental health issues.

Alzheimer's Disease

Alzheimer's Association (see Information and Referral)
919 N. Michigan Avenue, #1000
Chicago, IL 60611-1676
Telephone: 1-800-272-3900 / (312) 335-8882 (TDD)
Website: www.alz.org

The Alzheimer's Association is a national nonprofit organization that provides support and assistance to patients and their families and caregivers.

Publications: There are numerous publications and brochures on coping and responding to people with Alzheimer's disease.

Alzheimer's Safe Return

Alzheimer's Safe Return Program is for Alzheimer's disease sufferers who may wander away from home and become lost. The program includes many benefits, such as identification items, listing in a national database, and a twenty-four-hour free crisis line. For information call 1-800-733-0402 (see Emergency Services).

Alzheimers.com

Website: www.alzheimers.com

Alzheimers.com is a website with links to resources. It also has helpful information on patient care, caregivers, treatment, and diagnosis.

Publications: This website has a comprehensive bookstore.

Alzheimer's Disease Education and Referral Center (ADEAR)

P.O. Box 8250

Silver Spring, MD 20907-8250

Telephone: 1-800-438-4380 / (301) 496-1752 (general information)

Website: www.alzheimers.org/

The Alzheimer's Disease Education and Referral Center conducts studies on Alzheimer's, aging, disability and rehabilitation, health, long-term care, and other special problems and needs of older people.

Publications: You can order a variety of books and brochures on Alzheimer's disease, encompassing many issues related to understanding the disease, caregiving, and financial and legal issues.

Alzheimer's Support Network

Website: www.home.sprintmail.com/~alznet/

The Alzheimer's Support Network has links to other websites and a free on-line newsletter and can help you find information on local organizations.

American Health Assistance Foundation (see Information and Referral)

15825 Shady Grove Road, Suite 140

Rockville, MD 20850

Telephone: 1-800-437-2423

Website: www.ahaf.org

The American Health Assistance Foundation is a nonprofit organization that provides funds for several programs, ranging from Alzheimer's disease to glaucoma to heart disease. It supports research, public education, and community outreach, and offers general information.

In addition, it supports the Alzheimer's Family Relief Program, which provides financial assistance to Alzheimer's patients and their caregivers for expenses related to their care. Grants of up to five hundred dollars are awarded to eligible applicants.

For grant guidelines or more information, contact Kelly Kroh-Jones, LSWA, AFRP manager at e-mail: kkroh-jones@ahaf.org; telephone: 1-800-437-AHAF; website: www.ahaf.org/afrpdes.html.

Publications: You can order a variety of books and brochures on Alzheimer's disease, encompassing many issues related to understanding the disease, caregiving, and financial and legal issues.

Dr. Koop's Community–Alzheimer's Resource Center

Website: www.drkoop.com/centers/alzheimers/

Dr. Koop's Community–Alzheimer's Resource Center has links to helpful websites and health topic news on Alzheimer's-related topics.

Amyotrophic Lateral Sclerosis (ALS) or Lou Gehrig's Disease

Amyotrophic Lateral Sclerosis Association National Office

27001 Agoura Road, Suite 150
Calabasas Hills, CA 91301-5104
Telephone: 1-800-782-4747 (information and referral) / (818) 880-9007 (all others)
Website: www.alsa.org

The Amyotrophic Lateral Sclerosis Association funds research and provides information and services to patients and their families and caregivers. It supports public and professional education, the development of ALS chapters, and the establishment of ALS clinical service centers nationwide. It also maintains a computerized database, with medical histories on ALS patients.

Publications: A free copy of *Living with ALS* is available to patients and their families. There is a fee for some of the other publications. An excellent list of helpful books is also available.

National Muscular Dystrophy Association

3300 East Sunrise Drive
Tucson, AZ 85718
Telephone: 1-800-572-1717
Website: www.mdausa.org
E-mail: mda@mdausa.org

The National Muscular Dystrophy Association provides medical services to patients at MDA clinics. It has information on ALS and muscular dystrophy.

Publications: There are many free publications and brochures available.

Arthritis

National Arthritis Foundation

1330 West Peachtree Street
Atlanta, GA 30309
Telephone: (404) 872-7100 / 1-800-283-7800
Website: www.arthritis.org/

The National Arthritis Foundation has educational materials and links to many websites.

Publications: *Arthritis Today,* a newsletter, is published six times a year.

Asthma, Allergies, and Immunology

American Academy of Allergy and Immunology

611 East Well Street
Milwaukee, WI 53202
Telephone: 1-800-822-ASTHMA
Website: www.aaaai.org

The American Academy of Allergy and Immunology website has public and patient information, resources, support services, and organizations.

Allergy, Asthma & Immunology Online

85 West Algonquin Road, Suite 550
Arlington Heights, IL 60005
Website: www.allergy.mcg.edu

The Allergy, Asthma & Immunology Online website can be used for allergist locator services and links to other helpful websites.

Cancer

American Brain Tumor Association

2720 River Road, Suite 146
Des Plaines, IL 60018
Telephone: 1-800-886-2282 (patient line)
Website: www.abta.org
E-mail: info@abta.org

The American Brain Tumor Association provides free information on brain tumors for patients and their families. It has links to helpful resources and support groups, and has personal stories to provide comfort. There is also professional information.

American Cancer Society

1599 Clifton Road, N.E.
Atlanta, GA 30329-4251
Telephone: 1-800-227-2345
Website: www.cancer.org

Contact your local American Cancer Society for information and assistance with medical equipment, supplies, and transportation to medical appointments.

Publications: Many free brochures and booklets on specific types of cancer, living with cancer, nutrition, radiation, and chemotherapy are available.

American Institute for Cancer Research

1759 R Street N.W.
Washington, DC 20009
Telephone: 1-800-843-8114 / (202) 328-7744 (in Washington, DC)
Website: www.aicr.org/
E-mail: aicrweb@aicr.org

The American Institute for Cancer Research has consumer help and information, as well as links to sites with information on cancer and nutrition.

Publications: The "AICR Newsletter" contains information on cancer prevention, diet, and nutrition.

Cancer Care, Inc. (see Pharmacy Services)
1180 Avenue of the Americas, 2nd Floor
New York, NY 10036
Telephone: (212) 221-3300 / 1-800-813-4673 (counseling line)
Website: www.cancercareinc.org

Cancer Care, Inc. provides on-line assistance to patients and their families. It has information on indigent drug programs, financial assistance, transportation, home care, and hospice and support groups.

Publications: *The Helping Hands Resource Guide.*

Medicine On-line
Website: www.meds.com

Medicine On-line has links to information on cancer, search tools for obtaining specific material, articles and news, and a bookstore.

Publications: A bookstore for patients and their families is available.

National Action Plan on Breast Cancer (NAPBC)
Website: www.napbc.org/
E-mail: napbc@imail.napbc.org

The National Action Plan on Breast Cancer provides information on activities and products, web information and links, clinical trials, frequently asked questions, and worldwide events.

National Alliance of Breast Cancer Organizations (NABCO)
Telephone: 1-888-806-2226
Website: www.nabco.org
E-mail: nabcoinfo@aol.com

The National Alliance of Breast Cancer Organizations has material on breast cancer facts, resource lists, helpful links, support groups, and news flashes.

Publications: Check out the breast cancer resource list for books on breast cancer.

National Cancer Institutes' Cancer Information Service

Telephone: 1-800-4-CANCER

Website: www.nci.nih.gov

The National Cancer Institutes' Cancer Information Service has excellent links to cancer resources and information.

OncoLink

A University of Pennsylvania Cancer Center Resource

Website: www.oncolink.upenn.edu/

OncoLink has information about clinical trials, national and worldwide resources, support groups and organizations, and sections on frequently asked questions, medical supportive care, and financial issues.

Publications: Book reviews are available.

The Prostate Cancer InfoLink

CoMed Communications, Inc.

210 West Washington Square

Philadelphia, PA 19106

Telephone: (212) 592-1363

Website: www.comed.com/Prostate/menu/Support.html#Menu

E-mail: peterm@comed.com

The Prostate Cancer InfoLink provides information on U.S. clinics, frequently asked questions, talking with your physician, prostate cancer support organizations, and links to other helpful sites.

Prostate Cancer Research Institute (PCRI)

4676 Admiralty Way, Suite 103

Marina del Rey, CA 90292

Telephone: (310) 827-7707 / (310) 743-2110 (help line)

Website: rattler.cameron.edu/strum/

E-mail: pcri_goyjer@earthlink.net

Publications: This website provides access to *Insights*, the PCRI newsletter.

Prostate Health

Website: www.prostatehealth.com/

Prostate Health is an official website of the Prostate Health Council of American Foundation for Urologic Disease. It contains helpful articles and reports about the prostate, including information about early detection, symptoms, tests, and treatment.

Susan G. Komen Breast Cancer Foundation

5005 LBJ Freeway, Suite 370
Dallas, TX 75244
Telephone: 1-800-462-9273
Website: www.breastcancerinfo.com

The Susan G. Komen Breast Cancer Foundation is a nonprofit organization that supports research, education, and the screening and treatment of breast cancer. It also maintains a help line for questions.

Cerebral Palsy

United Cerebral Palsy Association, Inc.

1660 L Street N.W., Suite 700
Washington, DC 20036
Telephone: 1-800-872-5827
Website: www.ucpa.org
E-mail: ucnatl@ucpa.org

The United Cerebral Palsy Association, Inc. has information on advocacy, projects, and research. It maintains a resource center, with disability-related Internet links.

Diabetes

American Diabetes Association (ADA)

1660 Duke Street
Alexandria, VA 22314
Telephone: (703) 549-1500 / 1-800-342-2383 (general information)
                    1-800-232-6733 (publication information)
Website: www.diabetes.org

The American Diabetes Association is a nationwide voluntary health organization that supports research and education. Its extensive website provides articles, membership information, free helpful information, and links to other Internet sites. Membership is twenty-four dollars per year.

Publications: The monthly *Diabetes Forecast* and a free information packet about diabetes are available.

National Institute of Diabetes and Digestive and Kidney Diseases

National Institutes of Health
Bethesda, MD
Telephone: (301) 496-3583
Website: www.niddk.nih.gov

The National Institute of Diabetes and Digestive and Kidney Diseases has health information and education programs, patient recruitment, research data, and frequently asked questions. It has links to other NIH sites.

Epilepsy

Epilepsy Foundation of America (EFA)

4351 Garden City Drive
Landover, MD 20785-2267
Telephone: (301) 459-3700 (all departments)
            1-800-332-1000 (information and referral only)
            1-800-332-4050 (medical professionals)
Website: www.efa.org

The Epilepsy Foundation of America is a nonprofit organization that provides a wide range of programs, information, education advocacy, research support, and delivery of services to people with epilepsy and their families.

Guillain-Barré Syndrome

Guillain-Barré Foundation International

P.O. Box 262
Wynnewood, PA 19096
Telephone: (610) 667-0131
Website: www.gbs.org
E-mail: gbs.org

The Guillain-Barré Foundation International can be contacted for information about this disease.

The National Organization for Rare Disorders, Inc. (NORD)

P.O. Box 8923

New Fairfield, CT 06812-8923

Telephone: 1-800-999-6673 / (203) 746-6518

Website: www.rarediseases.org

The National Organization for Rare Disorders, Inc. provides information on rare disease and drug databases, used medical equipment, service and products, support groups, and other programs and services.

Publications: *The NORD Orphan Disease Update* and the *NORD ONLine* newsletter.

Heart Disease

American Heart Association

National Center

7272 Greenville Avenue

Dallas, TX 75231-4596

Telephone: 1-800-AHA-USA1 / (214) 373-6300

Website: www.americanheart.org

The American Heart Association provides a nationwide resource for stroke survivors, their families, and professionals. It has information on warning signs, risk assessment, a reference guide, and helpful material on nutrition, exercise programs, and products. For professionals, additional research literature is available.

Publications: *The Stroke Connection* magazine is published six times yearly. Free brochures and information are available.

National Stroke Association

96 Inverness Drive East, Suite 1

Englewood, CO 80112

Telephone: 1-800-STROKES / 1-800-787-6537

Website: www.stroke.org

The National Stroke Association is an excellent resource for helping you adapt to life after a stroke; it offers survivor and caregiver resources, helps locate stroke support groups in your area, and has general information.

Publications: *Adaptive Resources: A Guide to Products and Services.* In addition, the National Stroke Association has many helpful books, brochures, booklets, audiotapes, and videotapes.

Leukemia

Leukemia Society of America

National Headquarters
600 Third Avenue
New York, NY 10016
Telephone: (212) 573-8484
Information Hot line: 1-800-955-4LSA
Website: www.leukemia.org

The Leukemia Society of America is a voluntary health agency that provides financial assistance of up to $750 a year per person to people being treated for lymphomas, multiple myeloma, and specific myelodysplastic syndromes. Services include assistance with drugs, blood screening, transportation, and X-ray therapy. It has links to local chapters.

Publications: Many free brochures and educational material are available.

Liver Disease

American Liver Foundation

1425 Pompton Avenue
Cedar Grove, New Jersey 07009
Telephone: 1-800-465-4837
Website: www.liverfoundation.org

The American Liver Foundation uses research and education for disease prevention, treatment and cure of hepatitis, and liver/gallbladder disease.

Lung and Respiratory Disease

American Lung Association

1740 Broadway
New York, NY 10019
Telephone: 1-800-LUNG-USA / 1-800-586-4872
               1-800-527-3284 (to order publication)
Website: www.lungusa.org

The American Lung Association website can link you to your local chapter for information and brochures.

Publications: *Asthma* magazine is available for $14.95 per year.

National Jewish Medical and Research Center

1400 Jackson Street
Denver, CO 80206
Telephone: 1-800-222-LUNG
Website: www.njc.org

The National Jewish Medical and Research Center maintains a lung line for information and helpful material for health-care consumers and patients.

Lupus

The Lupus Foundation of America, Inc.

11921-A Olive Boulevard
St. Louis, MO 63141
Telephone: 1-800-558-0121 / (301) 670-9292 (24-hour answering machine)
Website: www.lupus.org

The Lupus Foundation of America, Inc. offers information, services, and referral for people with lupus.

Multiple Sclerosis

706 Haddenfield Road

Cherry Hill, NJ 08002
Telephone: 1-800-833-4672
Website: www.msaa.com
E-mail: mail@mssa.com

The Multiple Sclerosis Association of America provides peer counseling, support groups, an equipment-loan program, and educational literature.

National Multiple Sclerosis Society

733 Third Avenue
New York, NY 10017
Telephone: 1-800-FIGHTMS / 1-800-344-4867
Website: www.nmss.org

The National Multiple Sclerosis Society provides referrals to neurologists who treat MS patients. It also provides basic information and educational literature. Some financial and medication assistance may be available. The 800 number will route callers to their local chapter.

Publications: "Inside MS," a quarterly national newsletter, is available. Local chapters also publish a newsletter called "The MS Connection."

Myasthenia Gravis

Myasthenia Gravis Foundation of America, Inc.
123 W. Madison Street, Suite 800
Chicago, IL 60606-9524
Telephone: 1-800-541-5454
Fax: (312) 258-0461
Website: www.myasthenia.org
E-mail: myasthenia@myasthenia.org

The Myasthenia Gravis Foundation of America, Inc. website has links to other organizations and patient services and information. It also has an indigent drug program (see Pharmacy Services).

Parkinson's Disease

American Parkinson's Disease Association, Inc. (ADPDA)
1250 Hylan Boulevard, Suite 4B
Staten Island, NY 10305-1946
Telephone: 1-800-223-2732
Website: www.apdaparkinson.com
E-mail: apda@admin.con2.com

The American Parkinson's Disease Association, Inc. website has information and referral services, a link to chapter locations, links to other related websites and general information about Parkinson's disease.

Publications: The *APDA Newsletter.* The Support Groups Video Library has rentals available.

Parkinson's Disease Foundation

William Black Medical Research Building
710 West 168th Street
New York, N.Y 10032-9982
Telephone: 1-800-457-6676 / (212) 923-4700
Website: www.pdf.org
E-mail: info@pdf.org

The Parkinson's Disease Foundation has information on symptoms, medications, surgical intervention, treatment, daily living, and exercise.

Publications: Publications are free and include: *Progress, Promise and Hope, Parkinson's Patient at Home, Exercises for the Parkinson's Patient with Hints for Daily Living*, and the quarterly *PDF Newsletter*.

National Parkinson's Foundation, Inc.

1501 NW 9th Avenue
Bob Hope Road, Miami, FL
Telephone: 1-800-327-4545
Website: www.parkinson.org
E-mail: mailbox@npf.med.miami.edu

The National Parkinson's Foundation website includes information on patient services, facts about Parkinson's disease, clinical studies, and news. It also has links to other related organizations.

Sickle Cell

Sickle Cell Disease Association of America (SCDAA)

200 Corporate Pointe, #495
Culver City, CA 90230-7633
Telephone: 1-800-421-8453
Website: www.SickleCellDisease.org

The Sickle Cell Disease Association of America is a national organization that provides genetic counseling, vocational rehabilitation, educational materials, and scholarships to people with sickle cell disease.

Publications: Brochures are available.

Urology

American Foundation for Urologic Disease (AFUD)

1126 N. Charles
Baltimore, MD 21201
Telephone: (410) 468-1800
Website: www.afud.org/home.html

The American Foundation for Urologic Disease website contains the latest information on bladder health and a step-by-step guide for people who suffer from incontinence or loss of bladder control.

National Kidney Foundation

30 East 33rd Street
New York, NY 10016
Telephone: 1-800-622-9010 / (212) 889-2210
Website: www.kidney.org
E-mail: info @kidney.org

The National Kidney Foundation website has information on organ and tissue donors and recipients, and information for the health-care professional, patient, and general public.

Hearing Impaired

Deaf & Disabled Telecommunications Program

1939 Harrison Street, Suite #520
Oakland, CA 94612
Telephone: (510) 874-1410 (voice) / (510) 874-1411 (TTY)
1-800-867-4323 (consumer affairs) (voice/TTY)
Website: www.ddtp.org

The Deaf & Disabled Telecommunications Program contains information on equipment and products for people with hearing problems. It includes a consumer purchase program and California telephone-equipment loan program (for residents in California).

Dogs for the Deaf, Inc.

10175 Wheeler Road
Central Point, OR 97502
Telephone: (541) 826-9220 (voice/TDD)
Website: www.dogsforthedeaf.org
E-mail: info@dogsforthedeaf.org

Dogs for the Deaf, Inc. trains dogs for the hearing-impaired. Contact them for information on how to obtain a hearing-ear dog. Call or write for an application. There is no charge to qualified recipients.

Publications: *Canine Listener*, a quarterly newsletter, is available.

National Association of the Deaf (NAD)

814 Thayer Avenue
Silver Spring, MD 20910
Telephone: (301) 587-1788 / (301) 587-1789 (TTY)
Website: www.nad.org
E-mail: NADinfo@nad.org

The National Association of the Deaf website has helpful information and excellent links to deaf-related websites and organizations.

Publications: *The NAD Broadcaster*, published eleven times yearly, is free to members and twenty dollars a year to the general public.

Self-Help for Hard of Hearing People, Inc. (SHHH)

7910 Woodmont Avenue, Suite 1200
Bethesda, MD 20814
Telephone: (301) 657-2248 / (301) 657-2249 (TTY)
Website: www.shhh.org

Self-Help for Hard of Hearing People, Inc. is affiliated with the National Institute on Aging and the Administration on Aging, with links to both websites. It has information on community services and hearing loss.

Publications: *Shhh Journal* is published six times yearly. Other helpful publications are also available.

Home Care and Hospice

American Academy of Hospice and Palliative Medicine (AAHPM)

11250 Roger Bacon Drive, Suite 8
Reston, VA 20190-5202
Telephone: (703) 787-7718
Website: www.aahpm.org
E-mail: aahpm@aahpm.org

The American Academy of Hospice and Palliative Medicine website includes information on hospices, physician and general or public resources, and links to organizations concerned with palliative and hospice care.

Center for Elderly Suicide Prevention and Grief-Related Services

3626 Geary Blvd.
San Francisco, CA 94118
Telephone: (415) 752-3778 (24-hour crisis line) / (415) 752-5355 (grief program)
Website: www.growthhouse.org
E-mail: info@growthhouse.org

Growthhouse is an excellent website for resources related to death, dying, grief, and end-of-life issues. It has many links to health-care organizations, Alzheimer's sites, palliative care, and home health and hospice care.

Publications: Growthhouse maintains a bookstore with many excellent books on death, dying, and caregiving issues. A free newsletter is also available.

Hospice Association of America

228 Seventh Street, S.E.
Washington, DC 20003
Telephone: (202) 546-4759
Website: www.nahc.org/HAA/home.html

The Hospice Association of America website contains consumer information, educational opportunities, legislative news and hospice publications, videos, and products.

Publications: Caring, a monthly magazine, is free to members or forty-five dollars a year for nonmembers. *Hospice: A Consumer's Guide,* which answers basic questions about hospice care, is also available. To order, send a self-addressed fifty-two-cent-stamped envelope to the above address.

Hospice Foundation of America (HFA)

2001 S Street N.W. #300
Washington, DC 20009
Telephone: (202) 638-5419
Website: www.hospicefoundation.org
E-mail: hfa@hospicefoundation.org
or
777 17th Street #401
Miami Beach, FL 33139
Telephone: 1-800-854-3402
Website: www.hospicefoundation.org
E-mail: hfa@hospicefoundation.org

The Hospice Foundation of America has educational aids, hot links to hospice-related sites, hospice stories, and chat rooms.

Publications: *Journeys,* a monthly newsletter, is available for twelve dollars a year. Books, videos, and tapes on "Living with Grief" available for a fee. Free brochures include "Choosing Hospice: A Consumer's Guide," "Hospice Volunteers," and a sample copy of *Journeys*.

Hospice Net

401 Bowling Ave., Suite 51
Nashville, TN 37205-5124
Website: www.hospicenet.org/
E-mail: questions@hospicenet.org (hospice staff)
bereavement@hospicenet.org (grief and bereavement issues)
comments@hospicenet.org (comments)

Hospice Net is an excellent website with information about support services, pain control, insurance benefits, caregiving, and bereavement for people who are facing serious or terminal illnesses.

National Association for Home Care

HomeCare On-Line
228 7th Street S.E.
Washington, DC 20003
Telephone: (202) 547-7424
Website: www.nahc.org

HomeCare On-Line provides information on choosing a home-care provider, types of home-care services, and a home-care and hospice-agency locator. It also provides general information for consumers. Brochures are also available.

Publications: *How to Choose a Home Care Agency* is available.

National Hospice Organization (NHC)

1901 N. Moore St., Suite 901
Arlington, VA 22209
Telephone: 1-800-658-8898 / (703) 243-5900
Website: www.nho.org

The National Hospice Organization website can help you locate a hospice in your area. It also maintains links to other organizations.

Olsten Health Services

Telephone: 1-800-HOMENOW / 1-800-466-3669
Website: www.okqchomehealth.com
E-mail: info@olstenhs.com

Olsten Health Services has helpful information on how to choose a home-care provider, questions and answers about home health care, and links to additional health-care resources.

Visiting Nurse Association of America (VNAA)

11 Beacon Street, Suite 910
Boston, MA 02108
Telephone: 1-800-426-2547 / (617) 523-4042
Website: www.vnaa.org

Visiting Nurse Association of America is a national nonprofit community-based agency that provides information on caregiving and home health-care resources. It has links to the HCFA Oasis website with information on Medicare and more.

Hot Lines

AIDS 24-Hour Hot Line

Telephone: 1-800-342-AIDS / 1-800-344-SIDA (in Spanish)

1-800-AIDS-TTY (for hearing impaired)

Alcohol Abuse Emergency 24-Hour Hot Line

Telephone: 1-800-821-ALCOHOL

Alcohol and Drug Help Line

Telephone: 1-800-821- HELP

American Diabetes Association

Telephone: 1-800-342-2383

Website: www.diabetes.org

American Dietetic Association
National Center for Nutrition and Dietetics
Consumer Nutrition Hot Line

Telephone: 1-800-366-1655 (for referral to a registered dietitian)

Hot line: www.eatright.org/ncnd.html

American Institute for Cancer Research

Telephone: 1-800-8438114

Website: www.aicr.org

The American Institute for Cancer Research Hot Line offers advice on cancer, nutrition, and diet. It does not give medical advice.

Center for Elderly Suicide Prevention and Grief Related Services

Telephone: (415) 752-3778 (24-hour crisis line)

Website: www.growthhouse.org

Cocaine 24-Hour Hot Line

Telephone: 1-800-COCAINE

Consumer Help Line
Telephone: 1-800-942-4242

The Consumer Help Line provides information to consumers about a wide range of health-insurance issues.

Hospice Hot Line
Telephone: 1-800-658-8898

Impotence Information Center
Telephone: 1-800-843-4315

Lung Line Information Service
Telephone: 1-800-222-LUNG

Medicare Hot Line
Telephone: 1-800-638-6833

The Medicare Hot Line coordinates the federal government's participation in Medicare and sponsors health-care quality-assurance programs, such as the Medicare Hot Line.

Medicare Information
Telephone: 1-800-462-9306

National Health Information Hot Line
Telephone: 1-800-336-4797

National Institute on Aging Hot Line
Telephone: 1-800-222-2225

National Insurance Consumer Help Line
Telephone: 1-800-942-4242
Website: www.iii.org

Organ Donor 24-Hour Hot Line
Telephone: 1-800-24-DONOR

Partnership for Long-Term-Care Hot Line
California Department of Aging
Telephone: 1-800-434-0222

Substance Abuse and Mental Health Services Administration (SAMHSA)
Substance Abuse Programs
Telephone: 1-800-662-HELP / 1-800-729-6686 (in Spanish)
          1-800-487-4889 (for hearing impaired)
          1-800-789-2647 (mental health information)
Website: www.samhsa.gov/look3.htm

Information and Referral

American Association of Retired Persons (AARP)
3200 East Carson Street
Lakewood, CA 90712
Telephone: 1-800-424-3410 (membership) / (877) 434-1871 (TTY)
Website: www.aarp.org

The American Association of Retired Persons has excellent health-care information and publications on caregiving, insurance, safety, long-term care, and much more for members only. Membership cost is eight dollars per year or twenty dollars for three years. You must be fifty. Call the membership office to join the AARP and to obtain its free catalog. Publications free for single copies.

Other AARP telephone numbers and websites:

Age Line Research Database
Website: research.aarp.org/ageline/home.html

AARP Health Care Options
Telephone: 1-800-523-5800 (member service) / 1-800-523-7773 (TTY)

AARP Membership and General Inquiries
Telephone: 1-800-424-3410 / 1-800-515-2299

AARP Pharmacy Service (see Pharmacy Services)
Telephone: 1-800-456-2277 (customer service)

Member services include AARP Motoring Plan through the Amoco Motor Club; an AARP Investment Program from Scudder; AARP credit-card services from First

USA Bank; AARP Pharmacy Services; AARP Annuity Program from American Maturity Life; AARP Health Care Options; AARP Life Insurance from New York Life; AARP Automobile Insurance from Hartford; AARP Home owners Insurance from The Hartford; AARP Mobile Home Insurance from Foremost; and an AARP Legal Services Network. Information on these services can be accessed through the AARP website.

Publications/Magazines/Videos: This is a sample of publications listed in the *Consumer Information Catalog* and the *AARP Catalog of Publications: and Audio/Visual Programs.* Allow four to six weeks for delivery. Excellent free publications include:

> *The DO.ABLE Renewable Home: Making Your Home Fit Your Needs* is designed to help aging parents and relatives maintain their independence and live with physical limitations in a safer home environment.

> Free Caregiver Resource Kit (D15267) and the AARP Health Advocacy Services booklet, *Miles Away and Still Caring.*

> *A Consumer Guide to Board and Care Homes and Assisted Living Facilities.*

> *Modern Maturity* magazine is a monthly publication featuring articles of interest to seniors.

> Video: A twenty-five-minute video called "Survival Tips of New Caregivers" is available for four dollars.

American Health Assistance Foundation (see Health
  Organizations/Alzheimer's Disease)
  15825 Shady Grove Road, Suite 140
  Rockville, MD 20850
  Telephone: 1-800-437-2423
  Website: www.ahaf.org

The American Health Assistance Foundation is a nonprofit organization that provides funds for several programs, ranging from Alzheimer's disease to glaucoma to heart disease. It supports research, public education, community outreach, and general information.

Publications: Free newsletters are available.

American Medical Association's Health Insight

Website: www.amaassn.org/home.htm

The American Medical Association's Health Insight website has information on HIV/AIDS, asthma, migraine, and women's health, as well as products, services, and search tools such as an on-line physician finder. It also includes consumer health information and news articles.

Careguide On-Line Care Resource (see Assisted Living Facilities)

1160 Battery, 4th Floor
San Francisco, CA 94111
Telephone: (415) 474-1278
Website: www.careguide.net
E-mail: care@careguide.net

Careguide On-Line is an excellent resource for information on elder care. This website includes information on nursing and assisted living facilities, and home health and hospice care. It also has links to resources on caregiving, Alzheimer's and other elder issues.

Centers for Disease Control (CDC)

1600 Clifton Road N.E.
Atlanta, GA 30333
Telephone: 1-800-311-3435 (public inquiries) / 1-800-344-7432 (in Spanish)
 1-800-243-7889 (for hearing impaired)
Website: www.cdc.gov

The Centers for Disease Control has information on diseases and referrals to helpful agencies.

Center for Elderly Suicide Prevention and
Grief-Related Services (see Hospice Care)

3626 Geary Boulevard
San Francisco, CA 94118
Telephone: (415) 752-3778 (24-hour crisis line) / (415) 752-5355 (grief program)
Website: www.growthhouse.org
E-mail: info@growthhouse.org

Growthhouse is an excellent website for resources related to death, dying, grief, and end-of-life issues. It has many links to health-care organizations, Alzheimer's sites, palliative care, and home health and hospice care.

Publications: Growthhouse maintains a bookstore with many excellent books on death, dying, and caregiving issues. A free newsletter is available.

CenterWatch, Inc.

581 Boylston Street, Suite 200
Boston, MA 02116
Telephone: (617) 247-2327
Website: www.centerwatch.com
E-mail: cntrwatch@aol.com

CenterWatch, Inc. focuses on helping patients access clinical trials for new drugs, therapies, and diseases. It also has news, articles, and additional links and resources.

Council for Jewish Elderly

3003 W. Touhy Avenue
Chicago, IL 60645
Telephone: (773) 508-1000
Website: www.cje.net

The Council for Jewish Elderly is an excellent and extensive website with many links to information on housing options, Alzheimer's care, help in the home, and Jewish and government agencies.

Dr. C. Everett Koop's Website

Website: www.drkoop.com

Dr. C. Everett Koop's Website contains information and links on family health, health and wellness, health search and resources, Reuters news services, and three medical encyclopedias.

ElderWeb

Website: www.elderweb.com

ElderWeb has listings and information about housing alternatives, elder-care organizations, and legal services. Many excellent links to seniors resources and organizations.

Family Caregiving Alliance (see Caregiving)
690 Market Street, Suite 600
San Francisco, CA 94104
Telephone: (415) 434-3388 / 1-800-445-8106 (in California only)
Website: www.caregiver.org/
E-mail: info@careguide.org

The Family Caregiving Alliance offers support services to families and caregivers of brain-impaired adults, including those caring for a stroke victim. It has a clearinghouse, news bureau, notes about Medicare changes, an on-line support group, and a resource center with many links.

Friendly4Seniors
Website: www.friendly4seniors.com

Friendly4Seniors is an excellent website, with links to housing options, associations and organizations, financial and legal services, community resources, social services, government agencies, recreation and leisure, discounts for seniors, and other books and publications.

Publications: A variety of magazines, newsletters, and other publications are listed on this site.

The Hope Heart Institute
International Health Awareness Center, Inc.
350 East Michigan Avenue, Suite 301
Kalamazoo, MI 49007-3851
Telephone: (616) 343-0770
Website: www.hihope.com

The Hope Heart Institute website contains useful health information, including a health-promotion guide, product information, brochures, and a newsletter.

InfoMedical.com
The Medical Business Search Engine
By: C.M.R. Inc. Central Medical Repair
815 East Loula
Olathe, KS 66061
Telephone: (913) 829-4884
Website: www.infomedical.com

InfoMedical.com is an Internet search tool that can be used to find health-care companies, distributors of products, specific products, organizations, services, and worldwide web resources.

iVillage Better Health

Website: www.betterhealth.com/

iVillage Better Health has information about health and diseases, with links to government and health-care organizations.

Joint Commission on Accreditation of Healthcare Organizations

One Renaissance Boulevard
Oakbrook Terrace, IL 60181
Telephone: (630) 792-5000
Internet:www.jcaho.org

The Joint Commission on Accreditation of Healthcare Organizations has excellent links to information on ambulatory care, laboratory services, health-care organizations, health plans, and questions to ask in hospitals and long-term-care facilities.

Mayo Clinic's Health Oasis

Website: www.mayohealth.org

The Mayo Clinic's Health Oasis is an excellent website for obtaining information on diseases. It has links to other helpful sites.

MedForum

Website: www.lifeline.com

MedForum contains information on patient services, including medical equipment (new and previously used), support groups, on-line *Lifeline* medical journal with health-related articles, and a listing of state resources for health-care needs. It also has a home-delivery prescription program (see Pharmacy Services).

Medical Tribune

Website: www.medtrib.com

Medical Tribune contains medical and journal articles, as well as links to other medical sites.

MedicineNet

Website: www.medicinenet.com

MedicineNet maintains a website with topics such as pharmacy, first aid, poison control, diseases and treatment, a medical dictionary, health facts, and news and perspectives.

Medscape

Website: www.medscape.com/

Medscape is a free on-line resource with information on treatment updates, journal articles, patient resources, and health-related issues.

National Aging Information Center

330 Independence Avenue S.W., Room 4656
Washington, DC 20201
Telephone: (202) 619-7501 / (202) 401-7575 (TTY)
Website: www.ageinfo.org/
E-mail: naic@bangate.aoa.dhhs.gov

The National Aging Information Center develops reports for publication on key aging issues and performs analysis of statistical data. Publication list is available.

Publications: *Federal Benefits for Veterans and Dependents* describes VA medical, compensation, pension, educational, vocational, loan, and other insurance benefits.

The National Council on the Aging, Inc (NCOA)

409 Third Street
Washington, DC 20024
Telephone: (202) 479-1200 / (202) 479-6674 (TTD) / 1-800-424-9046
Website: www.ncoa.org
E-mail: info@ncoa.org

The National Council on the Aging provides news, articles, information, and resources on caregiving, aging issues, legal planning, adult day-service centers, and long-term care.

National Library of Medicine, Medline

Website: www.ncbi.nlm.nih.gov/PubMed/

The National Library of Medicine, Medline offers free access to databases with nine million abstracts from four thousand journals.

Shared Housing for Living Opportunities (SHILO)

P.O. Box 60496
Palo Alto, CA 94306
Telephone: (415) 856-8495 / (408) 264-6579
Website: www.shilo.org
E-mail: info@shilo.org

Shared Housing for Living Opportunities program services the greater San Francisco area. However, it has many helpful links to sites with information on disabilities, rehabilitation, health care, government, disabled vets, blindness, deafness, diabetes, spinal injuries, aging, law, computer aids for the disabled, travel, sports, business, and research.

SeniorCom

2023 120th Avenue N.E., Suite 100
Bellevue, WA 98005
Telephone: (425) 452-8439
Website: www.senior.com

SeniorCom has general information of interest to seniors and their families on topics such as housing and health. It also has articles and news.

SeniorNet

121 Second Street, 7th Floor
San Francisco, CA 94105
Telephone: (415) 495-4990
Website: www.seniornet.org

SeniorNet offers computer support and services for people age fifty and older.

SeniorOptions

Website: www.senioroptions.com/

SeniorOptions is an on-line guide to seniors services. It provides free help in evaluating and shopping for seniors insurance and maintains directories on housing options, home care, mental health, insurance, care management, and legal services. It has a community services directory with listings of nonprofit organizations that provide seniors with services. It also has links to other sites.

Seniors-Site

Website: www.seniors-site.com
E-mail: Many e-mail addresses are available depending on your question.
 You will be referred to the professional who can best help you.

Seniors-Site provides excellent information and links to websites of interest to seniors and their caregivers. It covers a wide range of topics, including drugs and prescriptions, health, Medicare and other insurance programs, Alzheimer's disease, computer services, disabilities, legal matters, housing, nursing homes, and Social Security.

Publications: It has lists of books for seniors and bulletins of interest.

United Seniors Health Cooperative

409 Third Street, S.W., 2nd Floor
Washington, DC 20024
Telephone: (202) 479-6973 / (202) 479-6615
Website: www.ushconline.org

The United Seniors Health Cooperative has links to books and other resources, including an elder-care dictionary, elder games, information on long-term-care insurance, consumer information, and elder software programs.

Publications: The United Seniors Health Cooperative has a list of available books and resources.

United Way of America

701 North Fairfax Street
Alexandra, VA 22314-2045
Telephone: (703) 836-7100
Website: www.unitedway.org

United Way is an association of local, independent, and nationwide United Way agencies. It supports social service and public-assistance programs through funding by charitable donations. More than three hundred fifty local agencies are listed with links.

Publications: A list of brochures and videos is available on request.

Insurance

Health Care Financing Administration (HCFA)

Medicare Publications
7500 Security Boulevard
Baltimore, MD 21244-1850
Telephone: (410) 786-3000
Website: www.hcfa.gov

The Health Care Financing Administration provides information on Medicare, Medicaid, and managed care and maintains an information clearinghouse with links to other helpful government and state agencies.

Publications: Pamphlets on Medicare and Medicaid, including "A Guide to Choosing a Nursing Home," are available.

Health Insurance Association of America (HIAA)

555 13th Street N.W., Suite 600 East
Washington, DC 20004
Telephone: 1-888-844-2782 / (202) 824-1600
Website: www.hiaa.org

The Health Insurance Association of America is an advocate for private health care. It sponsors health-care quality-assurance programs such as the Medicare Hot Line and has information on long-term care and other insurance programs.

Publications: Medicare Handbook and Guide to Health Insurance for People on Medicare Financing Review, published annually. There is a fee for publications. A publications listing is available.

Families USA Foundation

1334 G Street N.W.
Washington, DC 20005
Telephone: (202) 628-3030
Website: www.familiesusa.org
E-mail: info@familiesusa.org

Families USA Foundation is an excellent resource for information on Medicaid, health-care research, and research and advocacy groups. It has links to the Medicaid clearinghouse and Managed Care Central.

Publications: Many free publications are available. In addition, the publication list has books and other information for sale.

Medicare and You

Telephone: 1-800-MEDICARE / (877) 486-2048 (TTY)
                    1-800-633-4227 (to order publications)
Website: www.medicare.gov

Medicare and You has easy-to-read on-line Medicare publications and health-plan options, as well as information on nursing homes, wellness, fraud, and abuse.

Publications: *The 1999 Guide to Health Insurance for People with Medicare* and more are available.

National Association of Insurance Commissioners (NAIC)

120 West 12th Street, Suite 1100
Kansas City, MO 64105-1925
Telephone: (816) 842-3600
Website: www.naic.org

The National Association of Insurance Commissioners website has news, help and support services, publications, and consumer information.

Publications: *A Shopper's Guide to Long-Term Care Insurance* and other consumer information guides are available.

National Insurance Consumer Help Line

Insurance Information Institute
Telephone: 1-800-942-4242
Website: www.iii.org

The Consumer Help Line provides information to consumers about a wide range of health-insurance issues, including continuation of group health benefits, major medical, Medicare supplements, and long-term-care insurance. Consumer complaints are referred to appropriate sources.

Publications: *Guide to Medicare Supplement Insurance, Guide to Long-Term-Care Insurance, Guide to Disability Insurance,* and *Consumer's Guide to Health Insurance.* A list of publications is available upon request.

Statewide Health Insurance Benefits Advisors (SHIBA)
Office of Insurance Commisioner Deboran Senn

P.O. Box 40256

Olympia, WA 98504-0256

Telephone: 1-800-397-4422

Website: www.shiba.org

E-mail: info@shiba.org

              pub@shiba.org (for publications)

Statewide Health Insurance Benefits Advisors is funded by the Federal Health Care Financing Administration's Insurance Information, Counseling, and Assistance grant program to help seniors with access to health-insurance information and material. It has excellent links to helpful websites.

Publications: Many free brochures about Medicare and long-term-care insurance are available.

United Seniors Health Cooperative (USHC)

409 Third Street, S.W., Second Floor

Washington, DC 20024

Telephone: (202) 479-6973 / (202) 479-6615 (for list of publications)

Website: www.ushconline.org

The United Seniors Health Cooperative has helpful seniors links, health-insurance counseling, seniors tips, and information on long-term-care insurance.

Publications: Many books and resources are available on long-term care, health-care finances, Medicare, Medigap, and managed care.

Legal

Choice in Dying (see Hospice)

National Office

1035 30th Street, N.W.

Washington, DC 20007

Telephone: 1-800-989-WILL (9455) / (202) 338-9790

Website: www.choices.org

E-mail: info@choices.org

Choice in Dying has information on living wills, advanced directives and death, dying, and bereavement questions, as well as other educational resources. This nonprofit organization advocates better communication and discussion for end-of-life issues.

Publications: A free sample copy of the "Choice in Dying" newsletter is available. Legal forms may be downloaded or ordered on advanced directives for all fifty states. In addition, it has publications available on end-of-life issues and physician-assisted suicide.

Center for Ethics in Health Care

Oregon Health Sciences University
3181 S.W. Sam Jackson Park Road, Mail Code UHN-85
Portland, OR 97201-3098
Telephone: (503) 494-4466
Website: www.ohsu.edu/ethics

The Center for Ethics in Health Care has material available on the care of the terminally ill and links to national health organizations and resources. (The POLST, or Physician Orders for Life Sustaining Treatment form, may also be acquired by having your physician contact the center.)

ElderCare Advocates, Inc.

5810 Southwyck Boulevard, Suite 100
Toledo, OH 43614
Telephone: (419) 865-5700
Website: www.eldercareadvocates.com/
E-mail: info@eldercareadvocates.com

ElderCare Advocates is a private geriatric-care management service. Its website includes helpful information on elder-care topics such as financial planning, grief, and moving, and ways to improve communication. It also has links to other seniors sites.

Equal Justice On-line Directory for Legal Services

Website: www.equaljustice.org/hotline/index.html

Equal Justice On-line Directory for Legal Services has nationwide listings, information, and referral for legal services for the elderly. It has links to national support centers. Clients must be sixty years or older and have an income of less than or equal to $1,350 per individual per month for free services (or age fifty-five and older, if the case is a disability case). Hot line fees are $20 per call for clients with an individual income that exceeds $1,350 per month.

Fleming and Curti, P.L.C.
Elder Law, Bankruptcy, and Personal Injury
330 North Granada Avenue
Tucson, AZ 85701
Telephone: 1-800-395-3714
Website: www.desert.net/elder/index.html

Fleming and Curti, P.L.C., a private law firm, provides a website with helpful legal information and articles on guardianship, conservatorship, long-term-care planning, and more. It also provides links to other legal-related sites.

Publication: "Elder Law Issue," a monthly newsletter.

National Academy of Elder Law Attorneys
1604 North Country Club Road
Tucson, AZ 85716
Telephone: (520) 881-4005
Website: www.naela.org

The National Academy of Elder Law Attorneys lists specialists nationwide. Sometimes the lawyers can also recommend qualified financial planners. It also has hot links to helpful associations and organizations and elder law resources.

National Senior Citizens Law Center
2025 M Street N.W., Suite 400
Washington, DC 20036
Telephone: (202) 887-5280
Website: www.nsclc.org/

The National Senior Citizens Law Center is an advocate for low-income elderly and people with disabilities. It can assist with litigation, research and consulting, and support manuals. It provides information on Medicare, Social Security, and nursing homes.

SeniorScape
Website: www.seniorscape.com

SeniorScape provides free lists of elder-care resources to the public, as well as elder-care links and a resource directory. It is written for case managers, elder-law attorneys, guardians, and elder-care professionals, facilities, and providers.

Long-Term Care

AgeNet

Telephone: (202) 898-4794 / 1-888-405-4242 (membership)
Website: www.agenet.com

AgeNet has information on resources for older adults and caregivers. It includes information on housing and living alternatives, caregiver support, legal services, insurance issues, and financial planning.

Publications: It provides information on long-term care and community health services. A list of materials is available upon request.

American Association of Homes and Services for the Aging (AAHSA)

901 E Street N.W., Suite 500
Washington, DC 20004-2037
Telephone: (202) 783-2242 / 1-800-508-9442 (publications)
Website: www.aahsa.org
E-mail: info@aahsa.org (other e-mail addresses available)

The American Association of Homes and Services for the Aging can be contacted for information on long-term care and housing for older people, requirements for receiving accreditation, a guidebook for consumers, and a list of currently accredited facilities.

Publications: The American Association of Homes and Services for the Aging publishes a monthly magazine, *Currents,* for AAHSA members, and lists groups that provide services to older people.

American Health Care Association

1201 L Street N.W.
Washington, DC 20005
Telephone: (202) 842-4444
Website: www.ahca.org

The American Health Care Association is a national trade association representing U.S. long-term-care facilities. Its sites of interest include health and medicine, aging and resources, health-related publications, associations, financial links, and more.

Publications: It includes links to the *The New England Journal of Medicine* and *Modern Healthcare,* a weekly business newsmagazine.

CareGuide (see Information and Referral)
1160 Battery, 4th Floor
San Francisco, CA 94111
Telephone: (415) 474-1278
Website: www.careguide.com
E-mail: care@careguide.net

CareGuide provides information and listings on home health care, assisted living, independent living, congregate care, and continuing care. It also has many links and helpful information and articles on health care for seniors, caregiving, and Alzheimer's disease.

National Citizen's Coalition for Nursing Home Reform
1424 16th Street N.W., Suite 202
Washington, DC 20036
Telephone: (202) 332-2275
Website: www.nccnhr.org

The National Citizen's Coalition for Nursing Home Reform supports the ongoing development and operation of the fifty-two stateside long-term-care ombudsmen programs that function under a federal mandate to investigate and try to resolve problems experienced by residents of long-term-care facilities.

Publications: "InfoBulletin," a newsletter published five times a year for the network, is available on request.

National Eldercare Referral Systems, LLC (NERS)
21 Grantland Road
Wellesley, MA 02481
Telephone: 1-800-571-1918
Website: www.NursingHomeReports.com

The National Eldercare Referral Systems is a consumer-oriented site for obtaining information about nursing homes. It includes a listing of state ombudsmen programs and helpful ratings on nursing facilities nationwide.

Publications: Excellent book resources are listed.

SeniorSites

Website: www.seniorsites.com

SeniorSites has listings of nonprofit housing and services, including a state-by-state listing of seniors housing associations.

Medical Equipment and Supplies

AlumiRamp, Inc.

90 Taylor Street
Quincy, MI 49082
Telephone: 1-800-800- 3864
Website: www.alumiramp.com

AlumiRamp, Inc. specializes in ramping products and offers simple, modular, mini, and quick ramp systems and kits. It also provides ramp accessories, such as handrails, support assemblies, and platforms.

Auto Mobility Program (see Transportation Services)
DaimlerChrysler Motors Corporation

P.O. Box 3124
Bloomfield Hills, MI 48302-3124
Telephone: 1-800-255-9877 / 1-800-922-3826 (TTY)
Website: www.automobility.daimlerchrysler.com

The Auto Mobility Program provides assistance to people who have disabilities and who require adaptive equipment to drive, enter, exit, or be safely transported in a car or van. It provides financial assistance and reimbursements and lease-incentive programs. For eligibility information and an application for this service, call the above number or review the website.

Chrysler Corporation (see Transportation Services)
Physically-Challenged Assistance Program

1220 Rankin Street
Troy, MI 48083-6004
Telephone: 1-800-255-9877
Website: www.automobility.chrysler.com

Chrysler Corporation provides cash reimbursement to assist in reducing the cost of adaptive driving or passenger aids on new-model Chrysler cars, trucks, or vans. A resource center for information on adaptive products is available to the physically challenged. Free brochures are also available.

Ford Mobility Motoring Program (see Transportation Services)
Program Headquarters
P.O. Box 529
Bloomfield Hills, MI 48303-9857
Telephone: 1-800-952-2248 / 1-800-833-0312 (for hearing impaired)
Website: www.ford.com/showrooms/mobility

The Ford Mobility Motoring Program reimburses up to one thousand dollars for the cost of placing adaptive equipment in 1998 or 1999 Ford, Mercury, or Lincoln vehicles. For program details, call the above number or review the website.

General Motors Mobility Program (see Transportation Services)
For Persons with Disabilities
P.O. Box 9011
Detroit, MI 48202
Telephone: 1-800-323-9935 / 1-800-833-9935 (TTY)
Website: www.gm.com/vehicles/us/mobility.html

The General Motors Mobility Program for Persons with Disabilities can provide up to a one thousand dollar reimbursement toward the cost of aftermarket driving equipment, passenger aids, or reinstalled equipment on purchased or leased eligible new GM vehicles.

Publications: Free resource information. A free video, "On the Move Again," is available.

Guy & O'Neill, Inc.
617 Tower Drive
Fredonia, WI 53024
Telephone: (414) 692-2469 / 1-800-325-5358
Website: www.guyandoneill.com

Guy & O'Neill, Inc. has free samples of Joey wet-wipes complete bath system available by calling its 800 number.

Handi-Ramp, Inc.
1414 Armour Boulevard
Mundelein, IL 60060
Telephone: 1-800-876-RAMP
Website: www.marketzone.com/handi-ramp/
E-mail: HandiRamp@aol.com

Handi-Ramp, Inc. offers many different types of ramps for vans or homes: in-stock, custom, portable, permanent, or semipermanent.

Homecare Products, Inc.
15824 S.E. 296th Street
Kent, WA 98042
Telephone: 1-800-451-1903
Website: www.coastresources.com/homecareproducts/
E-mail: EZAccess@homecareproducts.com

Homecare Products, Inc. manufactures EZ-ACCESS portable wheelchair ramps. Free brochures are available.

Mental Health Services

Center for Mental Health Services (CMHS)
KEN-Knowledge Exchange Network
P.O. Box 42490
Washington, DC 20015
Telephone: 1-800-789-2647 / (301) 443-9006 (TDD)
Website: www.mentalhealth.org
E-mail: ken@mentalhealth.org

The Center for Mental Health Services provides information, statistics, and news releases on substance abuse and mental-health issues.

Publications: Has more than two hundred publications available to elders and their families.

Mental Health Association of Southeastern Pennsylvania
Mental Health and Aging

1211 Chestnut Street
Philadelphia, PA 19107
Telephone: 1-800-688-4246 / (215) 751-9655 (TDD)
Website: www.mhaging.org/index.html

The Mental Health and Aging website is designed to help elders and their families find mental-health services and information. It is part of the Mental Health Association of Southeastern Pennsylvania.

National Institutes of Mental Health (NIMH)
NIMH Public Inquiries

6001 Executive Boulevard, Room MSC 9663
Bethesda, MD 20892-9663
Website: www.nimh.nih.gov/
E-mail: nimhinfo@nih.gov

The National Institutes of Mental Health website is an excellent way to access public information, news, and events information, as well as grant information for professionals.

Publications: Brochures and videos are available.

Widownet

Website: www.fortnet.org/WidowNet/index.html
E-mail: widownet@fortnet.org

Widownet has information for people who have experienced the loss of a spouse or loved one. It has listing of books and publications on grief and bereavement, support groups, chat rooms, and other helpful links.

Nutrition and Meal Programs

American Dietetic Association

216 West Jackson Boulevard

Chicago, IL 60606-6995

Telephone: 1-800-366-1655 / 1-900-225-5267 (This is a charge call of $1.95 for the
first minute and .95 for each additional minute. It provides customized answers
to questions about food and nutrition.)

Website: www.eatright.org

Infocenter Website: www.eatright.org/nuresources.html

This is a quick-reference nutrition-information network that can refer you to a local registered dietitian in your area for individual nutritional advice.

Publications: Use the website to link to many websites with fact sheets, Internet links, and catalogs of publications.

Meals-on-Wheels Association of America

1414 Prince Street, Suite 202

Alexandria, VA 22314

Telephone: (703) 548-5558

Website: www.mealsonwheelsassn.org

The Meals-on-Wheels Association of America is the oldest organization in the United States that represents those who provide meal services to people in need.

Publications: *NAMP News* magazine and *NAMP Notice* newsletter are published quarterly.

Nutrition Action
Center for Science in the Public Interest

1875 Connecticut Avenue, N.W., Suite 300

Washington, DC 20009

Telephone: (202) 332-9110

Website: www.cspinet.org

The Center for Science in the Public Interest is a nonprofit education and advocacy organization that focuses on improving the safety and nutritional quality of our food supply, as well as promoting health through public education.

Publication: *Nutrition Action Healthletter.*

Tuft's University Nutrition Navigator

Website: www.navigator.tufts.edu

E-mail: navigator@tufts.edu

Tuft's University Nutrition Navigator has information on seniors health, nutrition sites for health professionals, special dietary needs, and general nutrition.

Pharmacy Services

American Association of Retired Persons (AARP) (see Information
and Referral)

Telephone: 1-800-456-2277 (customer service)

1-800-456-2226 (price quote or catalog)

1-800-456-2277 (to talk to a pharmacist) / 1-800-933-4327 (TTY)

Website: www.rpspharmacy.com

Cancer Care, Inc
Central Office

1180 Avenue of the Americas, 2nd Floor

New York, NY 10036

Telephone: (212) 221-3300 / 1-800-813-4673 (counseling line)

Website: www.cancercareinc.org/services/drug_companies.html

Cancer Care, Inc. has an excellent resource list of Medication Manufacturers' Indigent Drug Programs, which can help provide medication to patients unable to afford them.

Compumed, Inc.

1 Pitchfork Road

Meeteetse, WY 82433

Telephone: 1-800-722-4417

Website: www.compumed.net

Compumed, Inc. can assist with ensuring that elders take medications at the right time and dosage. It can be linked to an emergency response system to automatically telephone a caregiver if medication is not taken within a preprogrammed time.

Drugstore.com
Telephone: 1-800-DRUGSTORE / 1-800-378-4786
Website: www.drugstore.com
E-mail: customercare@drugstore.com

Drugstore.com maintains a resource center with health-care and wellness information and prices of new and current prescription drugs. These may be ordered online. Prescriptions are delivered to your door.

Health Insurance Association of America (HIAA)
555 13th Street N.W., Suite 600 E
Washington, DC 20004
Telephone: (202) 824-1600
Website: www.hiaa.org

The Health Insurance Association of America has consumer information on disability, health and general insurance, medical savings accounts, and long-term care.

MedForum
Website: www.lifeline.com/prescptn.html

MedForum has a home-delivery prescription-drug program with discounts of up to 50 percent wholesale by mail. The site includes detailed information about using the program and a comprehensive listing of participating pharmacies across the nation.

Myasthenia Gravis Foundation of America (see Health Care
   Organizations/Myasthenia Gravis)
Indigent Drug Program
123 W. Madison Street, Suite 800
Chicago, IL 60602
Telephone: 1-800-541-5454
Website: www.myasthenia
E-mail: myasthenia@myasthenia.org

The Myasthenia Gravis Indigent Drug Program is for people who have been diagnosed with myasthenia gravis and need financial assistance to obtain their medication.

Pharmaceutical Research and Manufacturers of America

1100 Fifteenth Street, N.W.
Washington, DC 20005
Telephone: 1-800-862-5110
Website: www.phrma.org

Pharmaceutical Research and Manufacturers of America has free health guides on cancer, medication, Alzheimer's disease, HIV/AIDS, mental health, and prostate disease. For people who have difficulty buying medications or lack insurance coverage, contact this program for a list of all drug-manufacturer programs. It maintains the *1998 Directory of Prescription Drug Patient Assistance Programs*, which can be downloaded.

SOMA Pharmacy

Website: www.soma.com

SOMA is one of many pharmaceutical sites where a person can order prescription and nonprescription medications on-line twenty-four hours a day, seven days a week, with door-to-door delivery. It also has prescription information about specific drugs, which includes uses, how to take the medication, side effects, precautions, interactions with other drugs, storage, and other helpful material.

Professional Organizations

American Association for Geriatric Psychiatry

7910 Woodmont Avenue, Suite 1050
Bethesda, MD 20814
Telephone: (301) 654-7850
Website: www.aagpgpa.org (general information)
       www.aagpgpa.org/bookstore.html (publications)

The American Association for Geriatric Psychiatry website provides information on mental-health issues and concerns.

Publications: Free brochures are available to the general public and health professionals. There are charges for other publications and products.

American Medical Association (AMA) (see Information and Referral)

Website: www.ama-assn.org

The American Medical Association website contains information and journal articles on health-related issues such as HIV/AIDS, asthma, migraines, women's health, and more.

National Association of Professional Geriatric-Care Managers

1604 North Country Club Road
Tucson, AZ 85716
Telephone: (520) 881-8008
Website: www.caremanager.org

The National Association of Professional Geriatric-Care Managers is an organization of professional care managers trained to help seniors and their families.

Publications: For nationwide listings, state by state, of geriatric-care managers and their qualifications, the association publishes *The GCM Consumer Directory.*

National Association of Social Workers (NASW)

750 First Street NE, Suite 700
Washington, DC 20002-4241
Telephone: 1-800-638-8799 / (202) 408-8600
Website: www.socialworkers.org

The National Association of Social Workers can be contacted for information and assistance in locating qualified social workers in your area.

Rehabilitation Services

American Occupational Therapy Association (AOTA)

4720 Montgomery Lane
Bethesda, MD 20814-3425
Telephone: (301) 652-2682
Website: www.aota.org

The American Occupational Therapy Association provides information for professionals and the public on occupational therapy. It has an excellent link to other helpful resources.

American Physical Therapy Association (APTA)

1111 North Fairfax Street
Alexandria, VA 22314
Telephone: (703) 684-APTA
Website: www.apta.org

The American Physical Therapy Association is primarily designed for professional physical therapists. It has helpful links to health-related sites.

Amputee Coalition of America (ACA)
900 East Hill Avenue, Suite 285
Knoxsville, TN 37915-2568
Telephone: 1-888-267-5669 / (423) 524-8772
Website: www.amputee-coalition.org

The Amputee Coalition of America supports the National Limb Loss Information Center, a clearinghouse for information on limb loss. It also has technical assistance and education for consumers and professional and peer-support groups.

Publications: InMotion magazine and many pamphlets and brochures are available.

American Speech-Language-Hearing Association
10801 Rockville Pike
Rockville, MD 20852
Telephone: 1-800-638-8255 (V/TTY)
Website: www.asha.org/
E-mail: irc@asha.org

The American Speech-Language-Hearing Association has information on aphasia and swallowing disorders. It has referral services to speech-language therapists in your area.

Canine Companions for Independence
National Headquarters
P.O. Box 446
Santa Rosa, CA 95402-0446
Telephone: 1-800-572-2275 (V/TDD)
Website: www.caninecompanions.org

Canine Companions for Independence is a nonprofit organizations that trains dogs to assist people with disabilities. For more information and eligibility requirements, call the above number or review the website.

Commission on Accreditation of Rehabilitation Facilities (CARF)

4891 E. Grant Road
Tucson, AZ 85712
Telephone: (520) 325-1044 (Voice/TDD)
Website: www.carf.org

The Commission on Accreditation of Rehabilitation Facilities can be contacted for a list of accredited organizations, a copy of CARF standards, or other information.

Crestwood Company

Communication Aids for Children and Adults
6625 N. Sidney Place
Milwaukee, WI 53209-5678
Telephone: (414) 352-5678
Website: www.communicationaids.com
E-mail: crestcomm@aol.com

Crestwood Company has a free product catalog available with communication aids for children and adults.

National Aphasia Association (NAA)

Murray Hill Station
P.O. Box 1887
New York, NY 10156-0611
Telephone: 1-800-922-4NAA (4622)
Website: www.aphasia.org

The National Aphasia Association has information about aphasia. It includes a reading list, fact sheets, newsletter, community groups, volunteer regional representatives, and information on starting your own resources group.

National Easter Seal Society

230 W. Monroe, #1800
Chicago, IL 60606-4802
Telephone: 1-800-727-8785 / (312) 726-6200 / (312) 726-4258 (TDD)
Website: www.seals.com

The National Easter Seal Society maintains an enabling fund for direct assistance, equipment services, information and referral, public education, respite care, and support groups for people with disabilities.

National Rehabilitation Information Center (NARIC)

8455 Colesville Road, Suite 935

Silver Spring, MD 20910-3319

Telephone: (301) 588-9284 / 1-800-346-2742 (information service)

1-800-227-0216 (information service) (voice and TTY)

Website: www.naric.com

The National Rehabilitation Information Center provides information to the public, professionals, and others involved in the rehabilitation of people with physical or mental disabilities.

Publications: *NARIC Quarterly: A Newsletter of Disability and Rehabilitation Research and Resources*, the NARIC resource guides, and the *NIDRR (National Institute on Disability and Rehabilitation Research) Program Directory* are available at no charge. A list of additional publications is available.

National Subacute Resource Center

7315 Wisconsin Boulevard, Suite 424 East

Bethesda, MD 20814

Telephone: 1-800-IHS-CARE / 1-800-447-2273

Website: www.nsca.net/

The National Subacute Resource Center can help with the referral process, consultation, and nationwide accessibility. This line is open twenty-four hours, seven days a week.

Retirement Communities

American Association of Homes and Services for the Aging
(AAHSA) (see Long-Term Care)

901 E. Street N.W., Suite 500

Washington, DC 20004-2837

Telephone: 1-800-508-9442 / (202) 783-2242

Website: www.aahsa.com

Publications: *The Continuing Care Retirement Community: A Guidebook for Consumers* (32 pages, $5) and *The Consumers' Continuing Care Retirement Directory*, which contains complete profiles on three hundred CCRC, listed by state (610 pages).

Assisted Living On-Line (see Assisted Living Facilities)
Website: alol@assistedlivingonline.com

Assisted Living On-Line provides a directory of assisted living and retirement centers for seniors and their families. It also has a list of helpful national resources.

The Guide to Retirement Living
Telephone: 1-800-394-9990
Website: www.retirement-living.com

The Guide to Retirement Living has free listings of facilities including retirement communities, assisted living and group homes, and nursing facilities in metropolitan Washington, D.C., Virginia, Maryland, and Philadelphia. Information for other states is listed as well. It also has helpful information on remodeling for easier access, home health care, medical equipment, supplies, and more.

Marriott Senior Living Services (see Assisted Living Facilities)
One Marriott Drive
Washington, DC 20058
Telephone: 1-800-880-3131 / 1-800-447-4792
Website: www.marriott.com/senior/

Marriott Senior Living Services contains information about Marriott facilities throughout the United States. Call the above number to request a general information packet.

Service Organizations

Elks National Foundation
2750 N. Lakeview Avenue
Chicago, IL 60614
Telephone: (773) 755-4728
Website: www.elks.org
E-mail: enf@elks.org

The Elks National Foundation provides charitable assistance to veterans and in-home treatment for people with disabilities.

Lions Clubs International Activities (see Vision Services and Programs)
Telephone: 1-800-747-4440 / (630) 571-5466, ext. 328
Website: www.lionsclubs.org
E-mail: lionlcif@worldnet.att.net

The Lions Clubs International Activities program sponsors the Sightfirst program, which provides 600,000 free, professional glaucoma screenings and assists with 20,000 corneal transplants. It provides free eye care, eyeglasses, Braille-writers, large-print texts, white canes, and guide dogs.

Rotary International
One Rotary Center
1560 Sherman Avenue
Evanston, IL 60201
Telephone: (847) 866-3000
Website: www.rotary.org

Rotary International members visit nursing homes, support meal programs, hold nutrition classes, sponsor retirement-planning workshops and organize transportation for shopping, medical appointments, and other activities.

Transportation

American Association of Motor Vehicle Administrators (AAMVA)
4301 Wilson Boulevard, Suite 400
Arlington, VA 22203
Telephone: (703) 522-4200
Website: www.aamva.org
Email: webmail@amva.org

The American Association of Motor Vehicle Administrators maintains a helpful website with links to transportation-related services and organizations.

Publications: A free Aging Drivers Information Kit can be ordered through the website or by writing to: Publications Order, P.O. Box 79702, Baltimore, MD 21279-0702.

Angel Flight West
Telephone: 1-888-426-2643 / 1-888-4-AN-ANGEL
Website: www.angelflight.org/

Angel Flight West is a nonprofit volunteer organization based in Santa Monica, California, which transports people for chemotherapy, dialysis, surgery, and other non-emergency needs. Although this organization serves the West, the Volunteer Pilots Association of Hickory, Pennsylvania, and others are available in other parts of the country. Call for additional information.

Auto Mobility Program (see Medical Equipment and Supplies)
DaimlerChrysler Motors Corporation
P.O. Box 3124
Bloomfield Hills, MI 48302-3124
Telephone: 1-800-255-9877 / 1-800-922-3826 (TTY)
Website: www.automobility.daimlerchrysler.com

The Auto Mobility Program provides assistance to people with disabilities who require adaptive equipment to drive, enter, exit, or be safely transported in a car or van. It provides financial assistance and reimbursements and lease-incentive programs. For eligibility information and an application for this service, call the above number or review the website.

Chrysler Corporation (see Medical Equipment and Supplies)
Physically Challenged Assistance Program
1220 Rankin Street
Troy, MI 48083-6004
Telephone: 1-800-255-9877
Website: www.automobility.chrysler.com/

Chrysler Corporation provides cash reimbursement to assist in reducing the cost of adaptive driving or passenger aids on new-model Chrysler cars, trucks, or vans. A resource center for information on adaptive products is available to the physically challenged.

Publications: Free brochures are available.

Ford Mobility Motoring Program (see Medical Equipment and Supplies)
Program Headquarters
P.O. Box 529
Bloomfield Hills, MI 48303-9857
Telephone: 1-800-952-2248 / 1-800-833-0312 (for hearing impaired)
Website: www.ford.com/showrooms/mobility

The Ford Mobility Motoring Program reimburses up to one thousand dollars for the cost of placing adaptive equipment in 1998 or 1999 Ford, Mercury, or Lincoln vehicles. For program details, call the above number or review the website.

General Motors Mobility Program (see Medical Equipment and Supplies)
For Persons with Disabilities
P.O. Box 9011
Detroit, MI 48202
Telephone: 1-800-323-9935 / 1-800-833-9935 (TTY)
Website: www.gm.com/vehicles/us/mobility.html

The General Motors Mobility Program for Persons with Disabilities can provide up to one thousand dollars reimbursement toward the cost of aftermarket driving equipment, passenger aids, or reinstalled equipment on purchased or leased eligible new GM vehicles. Free resource information. Free video, "On the Move Again."

SkyMed (see Funeral Services)
4435 North Saddlebag Trail
Scotsdale, AZ 85251-3418
Telephone: 1-800-475-9633
Website: www.skymed.com
E-mail: info@skymed.com

SkyMed is an emergency air-ambulance service available for people traveling in the United States, Canada, Mexico, the Caribbean, and the Bahamas. This service provides hospital-to-hospital emergency air transportation, escort transportation for spouses or significant others, vehicle return for people who need to leave their initial method of transportation due to an emergency, organ retrieval and transportation, and the returning of physical remains.

Membership for this service can be for family or an individual. A one-year family membership is $300. A one-year individual membership is $168.

Travel Opportunities

Access Tours

P.O. Box 2985
Jackson, WY 83001
Telephone: 1-800-929-4811

Access Tours is a nonprofit organization with package travel programs in the West for people with mobility impairments. Vehicles are wheelchair-lift-equipped, and all trips are accessible. Call for information.

International Association for Medical Assistance (IAMAT)

1287 St. Clair Avenue West
Toronto, M6E 1B8 Canada
Telephone: (416) 652-0137
Website: www.sentex.net/~iamat
E-mail: iamat@sentex.net

The International Association for Medical Assistance is an essential resource for people of all ages who travel to other countries. It provides, in a small, easily carried blue book, 500 listings of North American– and European-trained physicians who speak English and French. It also offers information regarding unusual diseases and required and recommended immunizations.

Travelin' Talk

P.O. Box 3534
Clarksville, TN 37043-3334
Telephone: (615) 552-6670

Travelin' Talk is a membership network of people who assist travelers with disabilities.

Publications: It has a quarterly newsletter with tips and resources and a 500-page directory of resources.

Wheelers Accessible Van Rentals, Inc.

7101 North 55th Avenue
Department NSA
Glendale, AZ 85304
Telephone: 1-800-456-1371
           1-800-313-5678 (for information on vehicles available for purchase)

Wheelers Accessible Van Rentals, Inc. rents wheelchairs and scooter-accessible minivans by the day, week, or long-term, nationwide.

Vision Services and Programs

American Foundation for the Blind

11 Penn Plaza, Suite 300
New York, NY 10011
Telephone: 1-800-232-5463 / (212) 502-7661
Website: www.afb.org
E- mail: afbinfo@afb.net

The American Foundation for the Blind provides resources for visually impaired people and their families, rehabilitation professionals, and educators. It also has information on talking books and audiovisual materials.

American Council for the Blind

1155 15th Street, NW, Suite 720
Washington, DC 20005
Telephone: 1-800-424-8666
Website: www.acb.org

The American Council for the Blind provides general information about its services and other helpful resources.

Publications: The Braille Forum, a monthly publication. Back issues are available in large print, audio, and Braille.

American Printing House for the Blind, Inc.

1839 Frankfort Avenue
P.O. Box 6085
Louisville, KY 40206-0085
Telephone: 1-800-223-1839
Website: www.aph.org
E-mail: Check the e-mail directory for the appropriate department.

The American Printing House for the Blind, Inc. is a nonprofit organization that offers educational and daily living aids, and publications.

Publications: APH Catalog of Accessible Books for People Who Are Visually Impaired and The APH Products Catalog for People Who Are Visually Impaired or Blind.

California Pacific Medical Center (see Geriatric Education/
Research Centers)
P.O. Box 7999
San Francisco, CA 94131
Telephone: (415) 923-3255
Website: www.cpmc.org

The California Pacific Medical Center is a nonprofit health-care organization that provides a wide array of services and programs to people in California and Nevada. It also maintains the Lions Eye Foundation to help elders with glaucoma, cataracts, and retinal disease.

Eyenet
American Academy of Opthamology
P.O. Box 7424
San Francisco, CA 94120-8500
Telephone: (415) 561-8500
Website: www.eyenet.org/

Eyenet is a website with an on-line education center, products, and publications and many eye-care Internet links throughout the world.

Library of Congress for the Blind and Physically Handicapped
101 Independence Avenue S.E.
Washington, DC 20540
Telephone: 1-800-424-8567 / (202) 707-5000
Website: www.loc.gov/nls
Email: nls@loc.gov

The Library of Congress National Library for the Blind and Physically Handicapped is a free national library that lends Braille and cassette tapes of up to 59,000 books and magazines.

It provides talking-book players and accessories without cost. The Library of Congress has general information on services available for people with disabilities. This includes assistive listening devices, Braille displays, a close-circuit magnification system, and interpreting services, including American Sign Language and oral and/or tactile contact signing.

Publications: Large-print on-line catalog access is available.

The Lighthouse Inc.
III East 59th Street
New York, NY 10022
Telephone: 1-800-334-5497 (Tuesday through Friday) / (212) 821-9713
Website: www.lighthouse.org

The Lighthouse Inc. has national programs for the vision-impaired in research, education, and rehabilitation services.

Lions Clubs International Activities
Telephone: (630) 571-5466, ext. 328
Website: www.lionsclubs.org
E-mail: lionlcif@worldnet.att.net

Lions Clubs International Activities sponsors the Sightfirst program, which provides 600,000 free, professional glaucoma screenings and assists with 20,000 corneal transplants. It provides free eye care, eyeglasses, Braille-writers, large-print texts, white canes, and guide dogs.

Lions Eye Foundation of California-Nevada, Inc.
2340 Clay Street
San Francisco, CA 94115
Telephone: (415) 923-3937
Website: www.cpmc.org

The Lions Eye Foundation provides eye care services for the elderly with glaucoma, cataracts, and retinal disease.

National Association for the Visually Handicapped
22 West 21st Street, 6th Floor
New York, NY 10010
Telephone: (212) 889-3141
Website: www.navh.org
E-mail: staff@navh.org
or
3201 Balboa Street
San Francisco, CA 94121
Telephone: (415) 221-3201
E-mail: staffca@navh.org

The National Association for the Visually Handicapped is a nonprofit national organization that offers youth services, adult services, large-print publications, library services, visual aids, and public and professional education, and has a low-vision-aids store. It maintains a large-print website.

National Federation of the Blind

1800 Johnson Street
Baltimore, MD 21230
Telephone: 1-800-422-7093
Website: www.nfb.org

The National Federation of the Blind has many helpful links to blind and impaired-vision services and programs.

Glossary

Accreditation. Desirable standards for health care and administration, approved by the Joint Commission on Accreditation of Healthcare Organizations (JCAHO).

Activities of daily living. The routine activities of everyday living, such as bed mobility, walking, eating, dressing, grooming, bathing, toileting, and personal care.

Adult-care homes. Also called adult foster-care, group, or domiciliary homes, these provide basic personal care and limited medical care to seniors and the disabled. The amount of medical care may depend on the level of care provided in the home and the adult-home providers' skills and training.

Adult day care. A structured program for seniors or disabled people that provides activities, meals, health care, therapies, and supportive services.

Advanced directive. A legal form that allows a person to express her wishes and desires for medical treatment, care, and intervention in advance. A living will and a health-care power of attorney are two types of advanced directives.

Alzheimer's disease. A disease of the brain in aging people characterized by progressive dementia and a loss over time of intellectual functioning.

Assisted living. A residence, usually for seniors, that provides for independent living and helpful services, such as meals, transportation, laundry and housekeeping services, medication management, and general health and personal care.

At risk. When an elderly person places himself in danger of personal injury or harm.

Base rate. An established charge.

Burnout. Strong feelings of physical and emotional exhaustion experienced by caregivers.

Caregiver. A person responsible for providing care and assistance to another person.

Care plan. An organized approach to medical treatment devised by health-care professionals.

Caseworker. A professional social services worker, registered nurse, or health-care professional who reviews, evaluates, coordinates, and directs services for seniors and others with health-care issues.

Competent. Being qualified to understand information and make decisions on your own behalf. Legally qualified to perform an act.

Conservatorship. A form of guardianship in which a court-appointed person is given legal right to manage specific or general authority for a person no longer able to manage his own affairs.

Continuing-care retirement community. A seniors housing community that provides a wide range of residences, from independent homes and assisted living to skilled-care health facilities.

Custodial care. General care and assistance with the activities of daily living, as well as supervision to prevent personal harm. This care can be provided by an unskilled person and is not considered medically necessary. It is not covered by Medicare or private-insurance companies.

Deductible. A dollar amount paid by an individual before an insurance company will pay for benefits.

Depression. A decrease in physical and emotional energy, which can interfere with a person's normal daily functioning.

Discharge planners. Health-care professionals responsible for organizing and arranging follow-up services for patients released from the hospital.

Disorientation. Inability to recognize and accurately relate to the time of day or familiar surroundings and people.

Durable medical equipment (DME). Medical equipment and supplies used during the treatment of an illness, injury, or disability necessary for a safe home environment.

Durable power of attorney. A legal document in which a person can appoint a legal representative to manage his affairs if he is no longer able to do so.

Elderproof. To make an area safe for an elderly person who might injure himself.

Electrotherapy. Electrical stimulation usually performed by a physical therapist.

Enteral nutrition. An essential source of nutrition that passes through a tube placed in the nose or stomach wall to be disintegrated in the intestines or stomach.

Guardianship. A person appointed by the court to make decisions on another person's behalf.

Health-care power of attorney. A legal document in which a person appoints a family member, attorney, or other health-care agent to make health-care decisions for him when he is no longer capable of making his own medical decisions.

Hidden charges. Fees that are not obvious.

Homebound. To be confined to the home and unable to leave without difficulty. A homebound person leaves the home only for a short time, infrequently, and primarily for medical reasons.

Home-care worker. A hired person who provides care and assistance in the home.

Home health-care agency. A health-oriented nonprofit or private business—often affiliated with a medical facility—that provides health-care professionals to visit people in their homes.

Homemaker services. Homemaker services include the general maintenance and cleaning of a home, chore services, meal preparation, and grocery shopping.

Incontinence. Involuntary discharge of urine or stool.

Incompetent. Not legally qualified to handle specific legal rights.

Information and referral. To contact, send, or direct information to a person or place an order to receive aid, material, or treatment.

Levels of care. Different degrees of care designated by a health-care or residential facility.

Living will. A type of advanced directive in which a person places in writing her wishes for medical treatment should she not be able to communicate this during a life-threatening situation. State law may limit the medical treatments stated in the living will.

Long-term care. Homes or institutions that provide nursing and personal care to people who are unable to care for themselves due to age, health, or disabilities.

Long-term-care insurance. A supplemental health-care insurance plan that provides benefits for some non–Medicare covered care in a nursing home, an assisted living facility, adult day care, and more.

Medicaid. (Also known as medical assistance, welfare, public aid, or, in California, Medi-cal.) The national insurance program administered by the states for low-income and disabled people, which provides health and long-term care. Eligibility and benefits vary widely in each state.

Medically necessary. Medical care, services, and supplies essential to the treatment and diagnosis of an illness or injury. (*Please note:* Insurance companies often review the prescribed treatment, services, and recommendations of a physician and can determine that the medical treatment could have been provided in a different way and/or at lower cost.)

Medically stable. To be in a state of unchanging health, which does not need immediate medical attention.

Medicare. The national health-insurance program available to most people older than age sixty-five and the disabled, which covers hospital care, physician bills, and other medical expenses.

Medicare-certified. A certified or approved provider of care that meets federal regulations to provide Medicare services.

Medicare HMO. (Also known as Medicare managed care.) An option to the national Medicare health program in which health-care benefits are provided by an individual health-care organization that has agreed to provide care to Medicare beneficiaries in exchange for a fixed amount of payment.

Medication box. A small box designed to help people easily keep track of their medication schedule.

Medication management. The administration and supervision of medication by a qualified health professional.

Medigap insurance. (Also known as Medicare supplemental insurance.) Private-pay insurance that supplements some of the "gaps" in Medicare insurance benefits, including deductibles and coinsurance.

Ombudsman. A person who investigates complaints and mediates disagreements and grievances. Ombudsmen play an integral role in overseeing patient care in nursing facilities.

Parenteral nutrition. A fluid medicinal preparation administered through the vein.

Personal care. Basic care given to an individual, which includes bathing, dressing, grooming, toileting, and eating.

Physiatrist. A physician who specializes in physical medicine and rehabilitation.

Physical restoration. Skilled care and therapies provided to a patient after a lengthy or debilitating illness with a goal of improving a person's level of functioning.

Pre-authorization. Approval needed from the insurance company before medical treatment can be administered. It may be necessary to receive permission and guarantee of payment before specific medical treatment can be initiated.

Primary-care physician. The doctor responsible for coordinating an individual's medical care with other physicians, hospitals, and health-care agencies.

Ramp. A walkway without steps that is easily accessible to people using walkers and wheelchairs.

Reasonable and necessary care. The physical care and medical treatment deemed essential for management of a medical condition.

Referral. To contact, send, or direct information to a person or place in order to receive aid, material, or treatment.

Respite care. Break or rest time for a caregiver.

Service-connected disability. To receive money or services for an injury received while in military service.

Skilled nursing care. This is reasonable and necessary medical care provided by a skilled health professional working under the orders of a physician. This care is required to assure the safety or to achieve the desired medical result requested by a physician.

Sliding fee. A flexible charge dependent on income.

Stairglide. Durable medical equipment used to enable disabled or elderly people to ride up a stairway.

Supervision. Management by an individual who provides charge and direction to another person to ensure her safety.

Supportive services. Assistance from family, friends, and community that helps a person remain in their home.

Transfer training. To move from one place to another. For example, to move from a bed to a chair or from a chair to a toilet or commode.

Usual, customary, and reasonable costs. This refers to the standard payment for charges or the fixed rates of reimbursement set by the insurance carrier.

Appendix A

Using the Yellow Pages in Your Telephone Book

Under "A," you can find information on attorneys and associations, such as health and social service associations.

Under "C," you can locate information on chambers of commerce, church organizations, and crisis intervention services, as well as city and county offices.
County listings can include:

- department of health and human services
- mental health services
- seniors programs
- veterans services

City listings can include:

- community service volunteers
- fire and police departments
- public library
- seniors program

Under "D," look for day-care centers—adult, deaf services, disabled person's assistance, products and services, and domestic help.

Under "E," you can find information on elder care.

Under "H," you can easily find home-care equipment and supplies, home-health services, hot lines, help lines, and human-service organizations.

Under "L," you can find legal services and libraries—public.

Look under "M" for information on medical billing services, medical insurance plans, and mental health services.

Under "P," look for information on pharmacies, physical therapists, and physicians.

Under "S," you can locate state offices as well as social service agencies, senior citizen's services, social workers, and synagogues. Listings under state agencies can include:

- adult and family services (eligibility and information)
- disabilities commission (client assistance program)
- employment department (veterans assistance and job information)
- senior and disabled services division
- Veterans Affairs department

Under "U," you can locate United States Government Offices in the white or blue pages of the telephone book. This listing can include information on:

- senate and congressional offices
- Veterans Affairs department (benefits and information: 1-800-829-4833)
- health and human services (Medicare and Social Security, general information and services: 1-800-772-1213)

Appendix B

State Agencies on Aging

ALABAMA
Region IV

Melissa M. Galvin, Executive Director
Alabama Commission on Aging
RSA Plaza, Suite 470
770 Washington Avenue
Montgomery, AL 36130-1851
(334) 242-5743
Fax: (334) 242-5594

ALASKA
Region X

Jane Demmert, Director
Alaska Commission on Aging
Division of Senior Services
Department of Administration
Juneau, AK 99811-0209
(907) 465-3250
Fax: (907) 465-4716

ARIZONA
Region IX

Henry Blanco, Program Director
Aging and Adult Administration
Department of Economic Security
1789 West Jefferson Street, #950A
Phoenix, AZ 85007
(602) 542-4446
Fax: (602) 542-6575

ARKANSAS
Region VI

Herb Sanderson, Director
Division on Aging and Adult Services
Arkansas Department of Human Services
P.O. Box 1437, Slot 1412
1417 Donaghey Plaza South
Little Rock, AR 72203-1437
(501) 682-2441
Fax: (501) 682-8155

CALIFORNIA
Region I

Gary Kuwabara, Acting Director
California Department of Aging
1600 K Street
Sacramento, CA 95814
(916) 322-5290
Fax: (916) 324-1903

COLORADO
Region VIII

Rita Barreras, Director
Aging and Adult Services
Department of Social Services
110 16th Street, Suite 200
Denver, CO 80202-4147
(303) 620-4147
Fax: (303) 620-4191

CONNECTICUT
Region I

Christine M. Lewis, Director of
    Community Services
Division of Elderly Services
25 Sigourney Street, 10th Floor
Hartford, CT 06106-5033
(860) 424-5277
Fax: (860) 424-4966

DELAWARE
Region III

Eleanor Cain, Director
Delaware Division of Services for Aging
    and Adults with Physical Disabilities
    Department of Health and Social
    Services
1901 North DuPont Highway
New Castle, DE 19720
(302) 577-4791
Fax: (302) 577-4793

DISTRICT OF COLUMBIA
Region III

E. Veronica Pace, Director
District of Columbia Office on Aging
One Judiciary Square, 9th Floor
441 4th Street, N.W.
Washington, DC 20001
(202) 724-5622
Fax: (202) 724-4979

FLORIDA
Region IV

Gema G. Hernandez, Secretary
Department of Elder Affairs
Building B, Suite 152
4040 Esplanade Way
Tallahassee, FL 32399-7000
(904) 414-2000
Fax: (904) 414-2004

GEORGIA
Region IV

Jeff Minor, Acting Director
Division of Aging Services
Department of Human Resources
2 Peachtree Street N.E., 36th Floor
Atlanta, GA 30303-3176
(404) 657-5258
Fax: (404) 657-5285

GUAM
Region IX

Arthur U. San Augstin, Administrator
Division of Senior Citizens
Department of Public Health and
    Social Services
P.O. Box 2816
Agana, Guam 96910
011-671-475-0263
Fax: 671-477-2930

HAWAII
Region IX

Marilyn Seely, Director
Hawaii Executive Office on Aging
250 South Hotel Street, Suite 109
Honolulu, HI 96813-2831
(808) 586-0100
Fax: (808) 586-0185

IDAHO
Region X

Marie Guadelupe, Director
Idaho Commission on Aging
P.O. Box 83720
Boise, ID 83706
(208) 334-3833
Fax: (208) 334-3033

ILLINOIS
Region V

Margo E. Schreiber, Director
Illinois Department on Aging
421 East Capitol Avenue, Suite 100
Springfield, IL 62701-1789
(217) 785-2870
Chicago office: (312) 814-2916
Fax: (217) 785-4477

INDIANA
Region V

Geneva Shedd, Director
Bureau of Aging and In-Home Services
Division of Disability, Aging, and
    Rehabilitative Services
Family and Social Services
    Administration
402 W. Washington Street, #W454
P.O. Box 7083
Indianapolis, IN 46207-7083
(317) 232-7020
Fax: (317) 232-7867

IOWA
Region VII

Dr. Judy Conlint, Executive Director
Iowa Department of Elder Affairs
Clemens Building, 3rd Floor
200 Tenth Street
Des Moines, IA 50309-3609
(515) 281-4646
Fax: (515) 281-4036

KANSAS
Region VII

Thelma Hunter Gordon, Secretary
Department on Aging
New England Building
503 S. Kansas Avenue
Topeka, KS 66603-3404
(785) 296-4986
Fax: (785) 296-0256

KENTUCKY
Region IV

Jerry Whitley, Director
Office of Aging Services
Cabinet for Families and Children
Commonwealth of Kentucky
275 East Main Street
Frankfort, KY 40621
(502) 564-6930
Fax: (502) 564-4595

LOUISIANA
Region VI

Paul "Pete" F. Arcineaux, Jr., Director
Governor's Office of Elderly Affairs
P.O. Box 80374
Baton Rouge, LA 70898-0374
(504) 342-7100
Fax: (504) 342-7133

MAINE
Region I

Christine Gianopoulos, Director
Bureau of Elder and Adult Services
Department of Human Services
35 Anthony Avenue
State House, Station #11
Augusta, ME 04333
(207) 624-5335
Fax: (207) 624-5361

MARYLAND
Region III

Sue Fryer Ward, Secretary
Maryland Department of Aging
State Office Building, Room 1007
301 West Preston Street
Baltimore, MD 21201-2374
(410) 767-1100
Fax: (410) 333-7943
E-mail: sfw@mail.ooa.state.md.us

MASSACHUSETTS
Region I

Lillian Glickman, Acting Secretary
Massachusetts Executive Office of
    Elder Affairs
One Ashburton Place, 5th Floor
Boston, MA 02108
(617) 727-7750
Fax: (617) 727-9368

MICHIGAN
Region V

Lynn Alexander, Director
Michigan Office of Services to the Aging
611 W. Ottawa, N. Ottawa Tower,
    3rd Floor
P.O. Box 30676
Lansing, MI 48909
(517) 373-8230
Fax: (517) 373-4092

MINNESOTA
Region V

James G. Varpness, Executive Secretary
Minnesota Board on Aging
444 Lafayette Road
St. Paul, MN 55155-3843
(612) 297-7855
Fax: (612) 296-7855

MISSISSIPPI
Region IV

Eddie Anderson, Director
Division of Aging and Adult Services
750 N. State Street
Jackson, MS 39202
(601) 359-4925
Fax: (601) 359-4370
E-mail: ELANDERSON@
    msdh.state.ms.us

MISSOURI
Region VII

Andrea Routh, Director
Division on Aging
Department of Social Services
P.O. Box 1337
615 Howerton Court
Jefferson City, MO 65102-1337
(573) 751-3082
Fax: (573) 751-8687

MONTANA
Region VIII

Charles Rehbein, State Aging
    Coordinator
Senior and Long-Term Care Division
Department of Public Health and
    Human Services
P.O. Box 4210
111 Sanders, Room 211
Helena, MT 59620
(406) 444-7788
Fax: (406) 444-7743

NEBRASKA
Region VII

Mark Intermill, Administrator
Department of Health and Human
    Services
Division on Aging
P.O. Box 95044
1343 M Street
Lincoln, NE 68509-5044
(402) 471-2307
Fax: (402) 471-4619

NEVADA
Region IX

Carla Sloane, Administrator
Nevada Division for Aging Services
Department of Human Resources
State Mail Room Complex
340 North 11th Street, Suite 203
Las Vegas, NV 89101
(702) 486-3545
Fax: (702) 486-3572

NEW HAMPSHIRE
Region I

Catherine A. Keane, Director
Division of Elderly and Adult Services
State Office Park South
129 Pleasant Street, Brown Bldg. #1
Concord, NH 03301
(603) 271-4680
Fax: (603) 271-4643

NEW JERSEY
Region II

Ruth Reader, Assistant Commissioner
Department of Health and Senior
    Services
New Jersey Division of Senior Affairs
P.O. Box 807
Trenton, NJ 08625-0807
(609) 588-3141
1-800-792-8820
Fax: (609) 588-3601

NEW MEXICO
Region VI

Michelle Lujan Grisham, Director
State Agency on Aging
La Villa Rivera Building
228 East Palace Avenue, Ground Floor
Santa Fe, NM 87501
(505) 827-7640
Fax: (505) 827-7649

NEW YORK
Region II

Walter G. Hoefer, Executive Director
New York State Office for the Aging
2 Empire State Plaza
Albany, NY 12223-1251
1-800-342-9871
(518) 474-5731
Fax: (518) 474-0608

NORTH CAROLINA
Region IV

Karen E. Gottovi, Director
Department of Health and Human
  Services
Division of Aging
2101 Mail Service Center
Raleigh, NC 27699-2101
(919) 733-3983
Fax: (919) 733-0443

NORTH DAKOTA
Region VIII

Linda Wright, Director
Department of Human Services
Aging Services Division
600 South 2nd Street, Suite 1C
Bismarck, ND 58504
(701) 328-8910
Fax: (701) 328-8989

NORTH MARIANA ISLANDS
Region IX

Ana Flores, Administrator and Director
CNMI Office on Aging
P.O. Box 2178
Commonwealth of the Northern
  Mariana Islands
Saipan, MP 96950
(670) 233-1320/1321
Fax: (670) 233-1327/0369

OHIO
Region V

Joan W. Lawrence, Director
Ohio Department of Aging
50 West Broad Street, 9th Floor
Columbus, OH 43215-5928
(614) 466-5500
Fax: (614) 466-5741

OKLAHOMA
Region VI

Roy R. Keen, Division Administrator
Aging Services Division
Department of Human Services
P.O. Box 25352
312 N.E. 28th Street
Oklahoma City, OK 73125
(405) 521-2281 or 521-2327
Fax: (405) 521-2086

OREGON
Region X

Roger Auerbach, Administrator
Senior and Disabled Services Division
500 Summer Street, N.E., 2nd Floor
Salem, OR 97310-1015
(503) 945-5811
Fax: (503) 373-7823

PALAU
Region X

Lillian Nakamura, Director
State Agency on Aging
Republic of Palau
Koror, PW 96940
9-10-288-011-680-488-2736
Fax: 9-10-288-680-488-1662 or 1597

PENNSYLVANIA
Region III

Richard Browdie, Secretary
Pennsylvania Department of Aging
Commonwealth of Pennsylvania
555 Walnut Street, 5th Floor
Harrisburg, PA 17101-1919
(717) 783-1550
Fax: (717) 772-3382

PUERTO RICO
Region II

Ruby Rodriguez Ramirez, M.H.S.A.,
    Executive Director
Commonwealth of Puerto Rico
Governor's Office of Elderly Affairs
Call Box 50063
Old San Juan Station, PR 00902
(787) 721-5710, 721-4560, 721-6121
Fax: (787) 721-6510
E-mail: rubyrodz@prtc.net

RHODE ISLAND
Region I

Barbara A. Raynor, Director
Department of Elderly Affairs
160 Pine Street
Providence, RI 02903-3708
(401) 277-2858
Fax: (401) 277-2130

AMERICAN SAMOA
Region IX

Lualemaga E. Faoa, Director
Territorial Administration on Aging
Government of American Samoa
Pago Pago, American Samoa 96799
011-684-633-2207
Fax: 011-864-633-2533 or 633-7723

SOUTH CAROLINA
Region IV

Elizabeth Fuller, Deputy Director
Office of Senior and Long Term Care
    Services
Department of Health and Human
    Services
P.O. Box 8206
Columbia, SC 29202-8206
(803) 898-2501
Fax: (803) 898-4515
E-mail: FullerB@DHHS.State.sc.us

SOUTH DAKOTA
Region VIII

Gail Ferris, Administrator
Office of Adult Services and Aging
Richard F. Kneip Building
700 Governors Drive
Pierre, SD 57501-2291
(605) 773-3656
Fax: (605) 773-6834

TENNESSEE
Region IV

James S. Whaley, Executive Director
Commission on Aging
Andrew Jackson Building, 9th Floor
500 Deaderick Street
Nashville, TN 37243-0860
(615) 741-2056
Fax: (615) 741-3309

TEXAS
Region VI

Mary Sapp, Executive Director
Texas Department on Aging
4900 North Lamar, 4th Floor
Austin, TX 78751-2316
(512) 424-6840
Fax: (512) 424-6890

UTAH
Region VIII

Helen Goddard, Director
Division of Aging and Adult Services
Box 45500
120 North 200 West
Salt Lake City, UT 84145-0500
(801) 538-3910
Fax: (801) 538-4395

VERMONT
Region I

David Yavocone, Commissioner
Vermont Department of Aging and
    Disabilities
Waterbury Complex
103 South Main Street
Waterbury, VT 05671-2301
(802) 241-2400
Fax: (802) 241-2325
E-mail: dyaco@dad.state.vt.us

VIRGINIA
Region II

Dr. Ann Magee, Commissioner
Virginia Department for the Aging
1600 Forest Avenue, Suite 102
Richmond, VA 23229
(804) 662-9333
Fax: (804) 662-9354

VIRGIN ISLANDS
Region II

Sedonie Halbert, Commissioner
Senior Citizen Affairs
Virgin Islands Department of Human
  Services
Knud Hansen Complex, Building A
1303 Hospital Ground
Charlotte Amalie, Virgin Islands 00802
(340) 774-0930
Fax: (340) 774-3466

WASHINGTON
Region X

Ralph W. Smith, Assistant Secretary
Aging and Adult Services
  Administration
Department of Social and Health
  Services
P.O. Box 45050
Olympia, WA 98504-5050
(360) 493-2500
Fax: (360) 438-8633

WEST VIRGINIA
Region III

Gaylene A. Miller, Commissioner
West Virginia Bureau of Senior Services
Holly Grove, Building 10
1900 Kanawha Boulevard East
Charleston, WV 25305
(304) 558-3317
Fax: (304) 558-0004

WISCONSIN
Region V

Donna McDowell, Director
Bureau of Aging and Long Term
  Care Resources
Department of Health and Family
  Services
P.O. Box 7851
Madison, WI 53707
(608) 266-2536
Fax: (608) 267-3203

WYOMING
Region VIII

Wayne Milton, Administrator
Office on Aging
Department of Health
117 Hathaway Building, Room 139
Cheyenne, WY 82002-0710
(307) 777-7986
Fax: (307) 777-5340

Appendix C

State Long-Term-Care Omsbudmen Programs*

ALABAMA
State LTC Ombudsman
Commission on Aging
770 Washington Avenue
RSA Plaza, Suite 470
Montgomery, AL 36130
(334) 242-5743
Fax: (334) 242-5594

ALASKA
Office of the LTC Ombudsman
Alaska Commission on Aging
State LTC Ombudsman Office
3601 C Street, Suite 260
Anchorage, AK 99503-5209
(907) 563-6393
Fax: (907) 561-3862

ARIZONA
State LTC Ombudsman
Aging and Adult Administration
1789 West Jefferson
Site Code 950A
Phoenix, AZ 85007
(602) 542-4446
Fax: (602) 542-6575

ARKANSAS
State LTC Ombudsman
Department of Human Services
State LTC Ombudsman Office
P.O. Box 1437, Slot 1412
Little Rock, AR 72203-1437
(501) 682-8952
Fax: (501) 682-8155

CALIFORNIA
State LTC Ombudsman
California Department of Aging
1600 K Street
Sacramento, CA 95814
(916) 323-6681
Fax: (916) 323-7299

COLORADO
State LTC Ombudsman
The Legal Center
455 Sherman Street, Suite 130
Denver, CO 80203
(303) 722-0300
Fax: (303) 722-0720

Permission to reprint this list granted by the National Citizens' Coalition for Nursing Home Reform, 1424 16th Street N.W., Washington, DC 20036.

CONNECTICUT

State LTC Ombudsman
Elder Services Division
25 Sigourney Street, 10th Floor
Hartford, CT 06106
(203) 424-5200
Fax: (203) 424-4966

DELAWARE

State LTC Ombudsman
DH&SS Division
Services for the Aging and Disabled
New Castle County
256 Chapman Road, Oxford
  Building, Suite 200
Newark, DE 19702
(302) 453-3820
Fax: (302) 453-3836

DISTRICT OF COLUMBIA

State LTC Ombudsman
AARP Legal Counsel for the Elderly
State LTC Ombudsman Office
601 E Street N.W., 4th Floor, Building A
Washington, DC 20049
(202) 662-4933
Fax: (202) 434-6464

FLORIDA

State LTC Ombudsman
State LTC Ombudsman Council
Carlton Building, Office of the Governor
501 South Calhoun Street
Tallahassee, FL 32399-0001
(904) 488-6190
Fax: (904) 488-5657

GEORGIA

LTC State Ombudsman
Division of Aging Services
2 Peachtree Street N.W., 18th Floor
Atlanta, GA 30303
(404) 657-5319
Fax: (404) 657-5285

HAWAII

State LTC Ombudsman
Office of the Governor
Executive Office on Aging
250 South Hotel Street, Suite 107
Honolulu, HI 96813
(808) 586-0100
Fax: (808) 586-0185

IDAHO

State LTC Ombudsman
Idaho Commission on Aging
P.O. Box 83720
Statehouse, Room 108
Boise, ID 83720-0007
(208) 334-2220
Fax: (208) 334-3033

ILLINOIS

State LTC Ombudsman
Illinois Department on Aging
421 East Capitol Avenue
Springfield, IL 62701
(217) 785-3143
Fax: (217) 785-4477

INDIANA

State LTC Ombudsman
Division of Aging and
   Rehabilitation Services
P.O. Box 708 3-W454
402 West Washington Street, #W-454
Indianapolis, IN 46207-7083
(317) 232-7134
Fax: (317) 232-7867

IOWA

State LTC Ombudsman
Iowa Department of Elder Affairs
Clemens Building
200 10th Street, 3rd Floor
Des Moines, IA 50309-3609
(515) 281-5187
Fax: (515) 281-4036

KANSAS

State LTC Ombudsman
Kansas Department on Aging
State Office Building
915 S.W. Harrison, Docking, #150
Topeka, KS 66612-1500
(913) 296-6539
Fax: (913) 296-0256

KENTUCKY

State LTC Ombudsman
Division of Aging Services
State LTC Ombudsman Office
275 East Main Street, 5th Floor West
Frankfort, KY 40621
(502) 564-6930
Fax: (502) 564-4595

LOUISIANA

State LTC Ombudsman
Governor's Office of Elderly Affairs
State LTC Ombudsman Office
4550 North Boulevard, 2nd Floor
Baton Rouge, LA 70806
(504) 925-1700
Fax: (504) 925-1749

MAINE

State LTC Ombudsman
State LTC Ombudsman Program
21 Bangor Street
P.O. Box 126
Augusta, ME 04332
(207) 621-1079
Fax: (207) 621-0742

MARYLAND

Maryland Office on Aging
301 West Preston Street, Room 1007
Baltimore, MD 21201
(410) 225-1100
Fax: (410) 333-7943

MASSACHUSETTS

State LTC Ombudsman
Executive Office of Elder Affairs
1 Ashburton Place, 5th Floor
Boston, MA 02108-1518
(617) 727-7750
Fax: (617) 727-9368

MICHIGAN
State LTC Ombudsman
Citizens for Better Care
State LTC Ombudsman Office
416 North Homer Street, Suite 101
Lansing, MI 48912-4700
(517) 336-6753
Fax: (517) 336-7718

MINNESOTA
State LTC Ombudsman
Office of Ombudsman
444 Lafayette Road, 4th Floor
St. Paul, MN 55155-3843
(612) 296-0382
Fax: (612) 297-7855

MISSISSIPPI
State LTC Ombudsman
Division of Aging and Adult Services
750 North State Street
Jackson, MS 39202
(601) 359-4929
Fax: (601) 359-4970

MISSOURI
State LTC Ombudsman
Missouri Division of Aging
Department of Social Services
P.O. Box 1337
Jefferson City, MO 65102
(314) 751-3082
Fax: (314) 751-8687

MONTANA
State LTC Ombudsman
Office on Aging
Department of Family Services
P.O. Box 8005
Helena, MT 59604-8005
(406) 444-5900
Fax: (406) 444-7743

NEBRASKA
State LTC Ombudsman
Nebraska Department on Aging
301 Centennial Mall South
P.O. Box 95044
Lincoln, NE 68509-5044
(402) 471-2306
Fax: (402) 471-4619

NEVADA
State LTC Ombudsman
Compliance Investigator
340 North 11th Street, Suite 114
Las Vegas, NV 89101
(702) 486-3545
Fax: (702) 486-3572

NEW HAMPSHIRE
State LTC Ombudsman
Division of Elderly and Adult Services
115 Pleasant Street, Annex 1
Concord, NH 03301-3843
(603) 271-4375
Fax: (603) 271-4643

NEW JERSEY

State LTC Ombudsman
Ombudsman Office for the
  Institutionalized Elderly
101 South Broad Street, 7th Floor,
  CN 807
Trenton, NJ 08625-0808
(609) 984-7831
Fax: (609) 984-1810

NEW MEXICO

State LTC Ombudsman
State Agency on Aging
State LTC Ombudsman Office
228 East Palace Avenue
Santa Fe, NM 87501
(505) 827-7663
Fax: (505) 827-7649

NEW YORK

State LTC Ombudsman
New York State Office for the Aging
2 Empire State Plaza
Albany, NY 12223-0001
(518) 474-0108
Fax: (518) 474-0608

NORTH CAROLINA

State LTC Ombudsman
Division of Aging
693 Palmer Drive
Caller Box Number 29531
Raleigh, NC 27626-0531
(919) 733-3983
Fax: (919) 733-0443

NORTH DAKOTA

State LTC Ombudsman
Department of Human Services
Aging Services Division
1929 North Washington
P.O. Box 7070
Bismarck, ND 58507-7070
(701) 328-2577
Fax: (701) 221-5466

OHIO

State LTC Ombudsman
Ohio Department of Aging
50 West Broad Street, 9th Floor
Columbus, OH 43215-5928
(614) 466-7922
Fax: (614) 466-5741

OKLAHOMA

State LTC Ombudsman
Aging Services Division
Oklahoma Department of Human
  Services
312 N.E. 28th Street
Oklahoma City, OK 73105
(405) 521-6734
Fax: (405) 521-2086

OREGON

State LTC Ombudsman
Office of the LTC Ombudsman
2475 Lancaster Drive N.E., #B-9
Salem, OR 97310
(503) 378-6533
Fax: (503) 373-0852

PENNSYLVANIA

State LTC Ombudsman
Pennsylvania Department of Aging
LTC Ombudsman Program
400 Market Street, 6th Floor
Harrisburg, PA 17101-2301
(717) 783-7247
Fax: (717) 783-6842

PUERTO RICO

State LTC Ombudsman
Governor's Office of Elderly Affairs
P.O. Box 50063
Old San Juan Station
San Juan, PR 00902
(809) 721-8225
Fax: (809) 721-6510

RHODE ISLAND

State LTC Ombudsman
Department of Elderly Affairs
160 Pine Street
Providence, RI 02903-3708
(401) 277-2858
Fax: (401) 277-2130

SOUTH CAROLINA

State LTC Ombudsman
Division on Aging
202 Arbor Lake Drive, Suite 301
Columbia, SC 29223-4535
(803) 737-7500
Fax: (803) 737-7501

SOUTH DAKOTA

State LTC Ombudsman
Office of Adult Services and Aging
Department of Social Services
700 Governors Drive
Pierre, SD 57501-2291
(605) 773-3656
Fax: (605) 773-6834

TENNESSEE

Acting State LTC Ombudsman
Tennessee Commission on Aging
Andrew Jackson Building, 9th Floor
500 Deaderick Street
Nashville, TN 37243-0860
(615) 741-2056
Fax: (615) 741-3309

TEXAS

State LTC Ombudsman
Texas Department on Aging
State LTC Ombudsman Office
P.O. Box 12786
Austin, TX 78711
(512) 444-2727
Fax: (512) 440-5252

UTAH

State LTC Ombudsman
Department of Human Services
Division of Aging and Adult Services
120 North 200 West, Room 401
Salt Lake City, UT 84145
(801) 538-3924
Fax: (801) 538-4395

VERMONT

State LTC Ombudsman
Vermont Senior Citizen Law Project
18 Main Street
St. Johnsbury, VT 05819
(802) 748-8721
Fax: (802) 748-4610

VIRGINIA

State LTC Ombudsman Program
Virginia Department for the Aging
530 East Main Street, #428
Richmond, VA 23219-2327
1-800-664-2933
Fax: (804) 644-5640

WASHINGTON

State LTC Ombudsman
South King County Multiservice Center
State LTC Ombudsman Office
1200 South 336th Street
Federal Way, WA 98003-7452
(206) 838-6810
Fax: (206) 874-7831

WEST VIRGINIA

DHHR Specialist
West Virginia Commission on Aging
State LTC Ombudsman Office
1900 Kanawha Boulevard East
Charleston, WV 25305-0160
(304) 558-3317
Fax: (304) 558-0004

WISCONSIN

State LTC Ombudsman
Board on Aging and Long-Term Care
214 North Hamilton Street
Madison, WI 53703-2118
(608) 266-8944
Fax: (608) 261-6570

WYOMING

State LTC Ombudsman
Wyoming Senior Citizens Inc.
756 Gilchrist
P.O. Box 94
Wheatland, WY 82201
(307) 322-5553
Fax: (307) 322-2890

Appendix D

Helpful Books, Magazines, Newsletters, Catalogs, and Videos

Helpful Books

The Aging Parent Handbook, by Virginia Schomp, Harper Collins, 1997, 432 pages.

The Aging Parent Handbook offers practical advice to adult children regarding aging. It helps them focus on specific aging issues, determine the appropriate level of care, and decide when family intervention is needed.

The Baby Boomer's Guide to Caring for Aging Parents, by Bart Astor, MacMillan General Reference, 1997, 282 pages.

The Baby Boomer's Guide to Caring for Aging Parents contains practical information about legal issues, long-term care, and medical conditions facing the elderly, such as dementia and Alzheimer's disease. It was written after the author experienced seven years of caring for the physical, emotional, and financial needs of his dying mother-in-law.

Beat the Nursing Home Trap: A Consumer's Guide to Choosing and Financing Long-Term Care, by Joseph Matthews, Nolo Press Self-Help Law, 1995.

Beat the Nursing Home Trap provides detailed legal information regarding making decisions about long-term care. It contains chapters on home care, organizing elder residences, nursing home facilities, Medicare and veterans benefits, medical assistance for long-term care, protecting your assets, estate planning, and long-term-care insurance. The book's emphasis is on legal and financial aspects of elder care. Readers are adult children, aging parents, and health-care professionals.

The Caregiver's Guide: Helping Elderly Relatives Cope with Health & Safety Issues, by Caroline Rob, R.N., with Janet Reynolds, G.N.P., Houghton Mifflin Company, 1991, 458 pages.

The Caregiver's Guide focuses on medical issues that occur in the elderly. The content is geared toward caregivers, providing practical information and showing them how to recognize and understand medical issues. It includes a brief section on places to find help in the home, arranging alternative housing, and legal issues. Although the reader is primarily the caregiver, it would also be helpful for aging relatives and health professionals.

The Caregivers Manual: A Guide to Helping the Elderly and Infirm, by Gene B. Williams and Pattie Kay, Citadel Press Book, Carol Publishing Group, 1995, 336 pages.

The Caregivers Manual was written after the author had a personal experience with an aging parent. It tends to be wordy but contains practical information about the legal and financial aspects of caregiving. It also addresses communication with medical staff. Emphasis is placed on the emotional needs of the elderly. It contains a section on community resources and information about setting up a safe home.

Caring for Elderly Parents, by Ruth Whybrow, Crossroad Publishing Company, 1996, 177 pages.

Caring for Elderly Parents focuses on the emotional issues that many adult children and families face with aging parents. The audience is adult children and their aging parents.

Caring for the Parents Who Cared for You: What to Do When an Aging Parent Needs You, by Kenneth P. Scileppi, Citadel Press, 1998, 256 pages.

Caring for the Parents Who Cared for You focuses on the health problems facing our aging parents, including falling, nutrition, and incontinence. It provides tips for caregivers on providing care to their elder parents. The chapters include sections on why parents fail, mental deterioration, physical ailments, and coping with health changes. It includes a glossary, drug reference list, and listing of Alzheimer's disease centers. The tone is geared toward the caregiver.

Caring for Your Aging Parents: A Source Book of Timesaving Techniques and Tips, **by Kerri S. Smith, Amer Source Books, 1994, 100 pages.**

Caring for Your Aging Parents is a small-print book with information for adult children on how to make the home safer, how to restructure the workday, and how to organize caregiver responsibilities. It includes material on potential medical problems, legal and financial issues, and where to find free and low-cost help.

Caring for Yourself While Caring for Your Aging Parents: How to Help, How to Survive, **by Claire Berman, An Owl Book, Henry Holt and Company, 1997, 272 pages.**

Caring for Yourself While Caring for Your Aging Parents uses personal experience, case studies, and interviews with geriatric professionals to provide information to caregivers. It discusses caregiver burnout, and practical advice on adult day care, in-home care support, support groups, working with other family members, finances, and making hard decisions regarding nursing-home care.

Children of a Certain Age: Adults and Their Aging Parents, **by Vivian E. Greenberg, Lexington Books, an imprint of Macmillan, Inc., 1994, 177 pages.**

Children of a Certain Age examines the relationship between adult children and their aging parents. It uses short anecdotes and professional terms, such as separation/individuation, displacement, codependency, and interdependence, to explore the complexities of caregiving. The tone is geared toward professionals and universities.

The Comfort of Home: An Illustrated Step-by-Step Guide for Caregivers, **by Maria M. Meyer, with Paula, Derr, R.N., CareTrust Publications LLC, 1998.**

The Comfort of Home addresses practical concerns and issues faced by many caregivers. Divided into three parts, it offers advice on communicating with health-care providers and daily-care needs for people with Alzheimer's disease and simplifies the medical terminology used in health care. The chapters include helpful illustrations and information on using home-health care, medical equipment and supplies, care plans, caregiver burnout, activities of daily living, nutrition, body mechanics, and death and dying.

The Complete Eldercare Planner: Where to Start, Questions to Ask, and How to Find Help, by Joy Loverde, Revised and Updated Edition, Hyperion, 1997.

The Complete Eldercare Planner is a comprehensive, well-organized resource for adult children for families beginning to think about what to do with their aging parents.

Elder Care: What to Look For, What to Look Out For!, by Thomas M. Cassidy, New Horizon Press, 1997, 211 pages.

Elder Care: What to Look For, What to Look Out For! focuses on the abuses that occur in unlicensed or unsupervised facilities providing care to the elderly. It uses extensive case studies to demonstrate abusive situations. The readers are adult children and social services professionals.

The Helpers' Journey: Working with People Facing Grief, Loss, and Life-Threatening Illness, by Dale Larson, Ph.D., Research Press, 1993, 292 pages.

The Helpers' Journey is written for hospice staff and volunteers but contains helpful information for family members and caregivers.

The Hospice Handbook: A Complete Guide, by Larry Beresford, Little, Brown and Company, 1993 165 pages.

The Hospice Handbook is written by a hospice volunteer and administrator and covers all aspects of hospice care.

How to Care for Aging Parents : A Complete Guide, by Virginia Morris, Workman Publishing Company, 1996, 460 pages.

How to Care for Aging Parents addresses the medical and emotional needs of elders and their caregivers. The chapters include information on gathering data, the relationship between the adult child and elder, emotional and medical issues, questions to ask in the hospital, getting help, tips for daily living, legal and financial issues, dementia, and end-of-life issues. The readers include elders and their caregivers or adult children.

How to Care for Your Parents: A Practical Guide to Eldercare, by Nora Jean Levin, W. W. Norton & Company, 1997, 271 pages.

How to Care for Your Parents focuses on understanding managed care, medical assistance, and long-term care. It includes information on home safety, housing options, using the Internet, and community resources. Readers include adult children, caregivers, and aging parents.

The Internet for Dummies (6th Ed), by John R. Levine, Carol Baroudi, and Margaret Levine Young, IDG Books Worldwide, February 1999.

The Internet for Dummies is a hands-on book that introduces families to the Internet. It takes the novice step-by-step through the process of learning how to access information on the Internet. It is an excellent book for beginners who are interested in learning how to use the worldwide web.

The Joslin Guide to Diabetes: A Program to Managing Your Treatment, by Richard S. Beaser, M.D., with Joan V.C. Hill, R.D.,C.D.E., Simon & Schuster, 1995, 351 pages.

The Joslin Guide to Diabetes offers practical advice for families caring for family or friends with diabetes at home.

The Medicaid Planning Handbook: A Guide to Protecting Your Family's Assets from Catastrophic Nursing Home Costs, by Alexander A. Bove, Jr., Little, Brown and Company, 1996, 188 pages.

The Medicaid Planning Handbook is an excellent resource for adult children or aging parents who have limited financial resources and who anticipate they'll need nursing-home care. This book discusses living trusts, protecting your home, durable power of attorney, avoiding probate, and Medicaid appeals.

Parentcare Survival Guide: Helping Your Folks Through the Not-So-Golden Years, by Enid Pritikin, M.S.W., L.C.S.W., and Trudy Reece, M.S.O.T., Barron's Educational Series, 1993, 212 pages.

Parentcare Survival Guide focuses on talking with your aging parents by using a down-to-earth approach, practical tips, and real-life situations. It discusses the emotions of caregiving and the other changes that occur in aging. Readers are adult children, caregivers, and aging parents.

***Retiring Right,* by Lawrence J. Kaplan, Avery Publishing Group, 1996, 377 pages.**

Retiring Right focuses on the retirement aspects of aging and includes information on budgeting, investments, Social Security, housing, health coverage, Medicare, estate planning, insurance, legal affairs, and more.

***When Parents Age What Children Can Do: A Practical and Loving Guide to Giving Them the Help, Support, and Independence They Need,* by Tom Adams and Kathryn Armstrong, The Berkeley Publishing Group, 1993, 192 pages.**

When Parents Age What Children Can Do contains lengthy anecdotes about independent living, living with paid caregivers, and living in retirement and residential-care communities and in nursing homes. It provides general medical information and helpful hints about health-care issues and preparation for the future. Readers include adult children, caregivers, and aging individuals.

Other Book Resources

Growth House, Inc., Bookstore

Website: www.growthhouse.org/books/books.html

Growth House, Inc., Bookstore has lists of books on hospice care, death and dying, living with grief, pain management, and palliative care.

Pathway Books

700 Parkview Terrace
Golden Valley, MN 55416
Telephone: 1-800-958-3375
Website: www.caregiver911.com/html/caregiver_books.html

Pathway Books publishes the *Caregiver Survival Series,* self-help books that are written for caregivers and the professionals who serve them. Current titles include: *Preventing Caregiver Burnout, Creative Caregiving, Positive Caregiving Attitudes, Coping with Caregiver Worries,* and *The Magic of Humor in Caregiving.* Additional titles and book resources are available. Call Pathway Books or visit the Internet to order.

The University of Georgia Press

330 Research Drive
Athens, GA 30602-4901
Telephone: 1-800-266-5842
E-mail: books@ugapress.uga.edu

The University of Georgia Press publishes several books on caregiving that were developed by the Rosalynn Carter Institute. A listing of books may be obtained by contacting the above number or e-mail address.

Helpful Magazines and Newsletters

Assisted Living Today

10300 Eaton Place, Suite 400
Fairfax, VA 22030
Telephone: (703) 691-8100
Website: www.alfa.org
E-mail: info@alfa.org

Assisted Living Today is a magazine for seniors interested in learning more about assisted living facilities. A sample issue may be requested. For subscription information, call, e-mail, or check out the website.

Consumer Reports
CR Reprints, October 1997

P.O. Box 53016
Boulder, CO 80322
Website: www.consumerreports.org

Consumer Reports has informative reprints available for five dollars each, which include: Managed-care plans, 8/96; Medical information on the Net, 2/97; Viagra, 7/98; Medicare, 9/98; HMOs, 10/98; and Medicare HMOs, getting dumped, 12/98.

Continuing Care
Stevens Publishing Corporation
5151 Beltline Road, 10th Floor
Dallas, TX 75240
Telephone: (972) 687-6700
Website: www.ccareonline.com

Continuing Care is a free national magazine for health-care case managers, discharge planners, and professionals to help them keep up with changes in health care.

Dr. Andrew Weil's Self-Healing
Creating Natural Health for Your Body and Mind
Telephone: 1-800-523-3296

Dr. Andrew Weil's Self-Healing is a newsletter with information on alternative medicine.

Elder Law Issues
Website: http://www.desert.net/elder/1999/issue630.html

Elder Law Issues is a weekly newsletter with easy-to-read articles on legal issues important to seniors.

Living Well
Live Well Publications
4039 Lakefront
Waterford, MI 48328
Telephone: 1-888-777-1003
Website: www.living-well.net
E-mail: info@aaaai.org

Living Well is a free magazine published by Live Well Publications. It features reader-friendly information and resources on medical issues, such as diabetes, asthma, allergies, Medicare, and more.

Nutrition Action
Center for Science in the Public Interest
1875 Connecticut Avenue, N.W., Suite 300
Washington, DC 20009
Telephone: (202) 332-9110
Fax: (202) 265-4954
Website: www.cspinet.org

Nutrition Action is the newsletter published by the Center for Science in the Public Interest, a nonprofit education and advocacy organization that focuses on improving the safety and nutritional quality of our food supply and promoting health through public education.

Seniority Magazine and Pension Plus Newsletter
National Council of Senior Citizens
8403 Colesville Road, Suite 1200
Silver Spring, MD 20910-3314
Telephone: 1-888-3-SENIOR (373-6467)
Website: www.ncscinc.org

The National Council of Senior Citizens publishes *Seniority*, a bimonthly magazine, and *Pension Plus*, a monthly newsletter. *Seniority* includes information on national legislation that may affect older Americans, health information, and more. The *Pension Plus* newsletter includes money-saving news and tips for retirees. Contact the National Council of Senior Citizens for membership and subscription information.

Time Magazine On-Line Archives
Website:
http://www.pathfinder.com/time/magazine/archive/text/0,2647,0,00.html

Many issues with articles related to elder care and caregiving are easy to access from this website. Several to note in the August 30, 1999 issue (vol. 154, no. 9) are: "Elder Care: Making the Right Choice" by John Greenwald and "Taking Care of Our Aging Parents" by Cathy Booth.

Today's Caregiver

P.O. Box 21646
Ft. Lauderdale, FL 33335
Telephone: 1-800-829-2734 / (954) 462-7511 (outside Florida)
Website: www.caregiver.com
E-mail: editor@caregiver.com

Today's Caregiver, a quarterly magazine, is written for caregivers and contains information about many aspects of caregiving. E-mail or write for subscription information.

Catalogs

Channing L. Bete Co., Inc.

200 State Road
South Deerfield, MA 01373-0200
Telephone: 1-800-628-7733
Website: www.channing-bete.com
E-mail: custsvcs@channing-bete.com

Channing L. Bete Co. prints a catalog of easy-to-read and easily understandable health-education materials—booklets, videos, handbooks, and full-color booklets on patient education, mental health issues, health promotion, and staff training. There is a charge for materials. Free samples may also be available.

Disability Specialties

802 South Drew Street
Saint Albans, WV 25177
Telephone: 1-888-892-7878
Website: www.disabilityspecialties.com/health.html

Disability Specialties offers products for people with disabilities. These include a four-alarm pillbox and alarm clock, a clock/alarm with personalized messages, pill holders, and organizers with tactual markers.

Dr. Leonard's Healthcare Products

P.O. Box 7821
Edison, NJ 08818-7821
Telephone: 1-800-785-0880
Website: http://www.drleonards.com/index.html

Dr. Leonard's Healthcare Products catalog includes health and personal-care items, posture aids and supports, foot-care products and walking aids, and comfort items for easy living.

The Lighthouse Catalog

111 East 59th Street, 12th Floor
New York, NY 10022-1202
Telephone: 1-800-829-0500

The Lighthouse Catalog, developed by Lighthouse International, contains resources and products for people with vision impairment or who need vision rehabilitation.

Maxi Aids

42 Executive Boulevard
Farmingdale, NY 11735
Telephone: 1-800-522-6294
Website: www.maxiaids.com

The *Maxi Aids* catalog has independent living products for people with disabilities, including the visually impaired and physically challenged.

NurseWeek/HealthWeek

Website: http://www.nurseweek.com/

The NurseWeek/HealthWeek website contains helpful information for nurses and health professionals on health-related issues. New articles appear every Monday and Thursday with subjects ranging from managed care and HMOs to communicating with patients and current legislation.

Sight Connection
Community Services for the Blind and Partially Sighted
9709 Third Avenue N.E., #100
Seattle, WA 98115-2027
Telephone: (206) 525-5556 / 1-800-458-4888 (Washington only)
Website: www.sightconnection.com
E-mail: csbstore@csbps.com

Sight Connection has products, such as magnifiers, telephones, books, clocks, and watches, available for visually impaired people.

Videos

The Home Care Companion Video Series
Healing Arts Communications
33 N. Central, Suite 211
Medford, OR 97501
Telephone: 1-888-846-7008
Website: www.homecarecompanion.com
E-mail: info@homecarecompanion.com

The Home Care Companion Video Series is an excellent, easy-to-view and -understand series of videos for caregivers and health-care professionals. The series has six volumes, including: "How to Care for Someone on Bedrest," "How to Help Someone Who Uses a Wheelchair Without Hurting Yourself," "Creating Healthy Home Care Conditions: Infection Control," "How to Manage Medications," "Fall Prevention," and "Fire Safety." A new series includes communiction and hearing loss. Each video comes with a complete training packet. Pricing is based on public performance rights for institutions and agencies. They are also available for individual families. Discounts are available.

Appendix E

Helpful Forms

SCHEDULE GUIDE

	Names of Agencies	Telephone Numbers of Agencies	Names of People Providing Care	Hours (split shift?)	Services Provided
Mon.					
Tues.					
Wed.					
Thurs.					
Fri.					
Sat.					
Sun.					

KEEPING TRACK OF YOUR SERVICES

Date _____

Name and address of agency

_____

_____

Contact person _____

Telephone # _____   **Fax #** _____

Best time to call is _____   **Date to call agency back** _____

Available Services

_____ evaluation of care needs

_____ chore services

_____ counseling services

_____ assistance with filing applications

_____ financial assistance

_____ grocery shopping

_____ home health aides

_____ home safety evaluations

_____ homemaker assistance

_____ information and referral services

_____ insurance billing

_____ legal services

_____ live-in care

_____ meal preparation and assistance

_____ medical equipment and supplies

_____ nursing care

_____ personal care

_____ placement services

_____ social activities

_____ telephone check-in services

_____ transportation services

_____ yard services

_____ other _____

Starting date for services _____   **Cost of services** _____

Are insurance benefits available? Yes _____   **No** _____

Is a doctor's order or prescription needed? Yes _____   **No** _____

Does an application need to be completed? Yes _____   **No** _____

HIRING HELP IN YOUR HOME

Name of applicant _____

Social Security # _____ - _____ - _____   **Age** _____

Address _____

Telephone # _____

References: Name _____ **Telephone #** _____

          Name _____ **Telephone #** _____

          Name _____ **Telephone #** _____

Remarks _____

_____

_____

Job Requirements

Days: Monday _____ Tuesday _____ Wednesday _____ Thursday _____

       Friday _____ Saturday _____ Sunday _____

Hours: _____ Live-in needed? Yes _____ No _____

Responsibilities and Care

Personal Care

_____ bathing

_____ grooming

_____ dressing

_____ toileting

_____ feeding

_____ lifting

_____ other _____

Household

_____ laundry

_____ light housework

_____ grocery shopping

_____ meal preparation

_____ other _____

Social

_____ activities

_____ companion

_____ outings

_____ other _____

Supervision

_____ safety

_____ walking

_____ getting in and out of bed

_____ wandering

_____ other _____

Medical care

_____ injections

_____ gressing changes

_____ give medications

_____ incontinence care

_____ other _____

Questions to Ask the Applicant

1. Have you cared for an elderly person before? Yes _____ No _____

2. When? _____ For how long? _____

3. What were your responsibilities? _____

4. What did you like most about the work? _____

5. What did you like least about the work? _____

6. Are you currently employed? Yes _____ No _____

7. What kind of work are you looking for? _____

8. For how long? _____

9. What days and hours are you available? _____

10. Are you available in the evening? Yes _____ No _____

11. On weekends? Yes _____ No _____

12. Are your hours flexible? Yes _____ No _____

13. What is your usual fee? _____

14. Do you smoke? Yes _____ No _____

15. Are you comfortable with me calling your references?
    Yes _____ No _____

Questions to Ask the References

16. How would you describe the applicant?

_____ calm		_____ inattentive	
_____ dependable		_____ patient	
_____ easy to talk to		_____ punctual	
_____ enjoyable		_____ talkative	
_____ flexible		_____ trustworthy	
_____ hard-working		_____ unclean	
_____ helpful		_____ other _____	
_____ impatient			

17. What were the applicant's strong points? _____

18. What were the applicant's weak points? _____

19. Did you have any difficulties with the applicant?
    Yes _____ No _____
    If yes, please describe. _____

20. How did the applicant handle difficult situations? _____

21. Did you feel comfortable leaving the applicant alone with your elder family member? Yes _____ No _____

22. How would you rate the applicant?
    Excellent _____ Good _____ Fair _____ Unsatisfactory _____

23. On a scale of 1 to 10, with 1 being poor and 10 being outstanding, how would you rate the applicant? _____

    _____

Comparing Average Private-Pay Rates

The following chart shows the average daily private-pay rates for care in an adult day-care center, hired in-home help, home health care, and care in a nursing facility.

PRIVATE-PAY RATES

Type of Care	Average Daily Rates
Adult day-care agency	$40/day (This may include meals, therapies, social activities, supervision, assistance with ADLs.)
Hired in-home help	
private agency	$40–$120/day (Rates may depend on the skill level of the person hired. For example, a companion will cost less than a licensed practical nurse. A minimum number of hours, usually 2–4, may be required with each visit.)
individual	$8–$15/hour
Home health-care agency	$30–$35/hour for a registered nurse $110–$125/home visit for a medical social worker, or physical or occupational therapist Home health staff work on an hourly basis. (Medicare, Medicaid, and private insurance will usually cover intermittent skilled care, home health-aide services, durable medical equipment and supplies, and other services. Visits must be ordered by the primary-care physician.)
Nusring home	$100/day plus extras (This rate may vary depending on the level of nursing care: custodial, intermediate, or skilled. Extras include therapies, supplies, and more.)

Note: *Medicaid benefits will vary from state to state.*

Index

DISCARDED
from
New Hanover County Public Library

NEW HANOVER COUNTY PUBLIC LIBRARY
201 CHESTNUT STREET
WILMINGTON, NC 28401

GAYLORD S